Women in Contemporary Britain

This book draws together a wide range of theoretical and empirical material on women in contemporary Britain, and emphasises the continuing significance of gender as a key social division.

Comprehensive and accessible, *Women in Contemporary Britain* presents the latest data on important aspects of women's experiences, including:

- Education and training
- Paid work
- Household work and caring
- Love and sexuality
- Crime and punishment
- Politics and participation

Also included are overviews of ongoing debates on women's bodies and the cultural representation of femininities. A key consideration is the emphasis on the interrelations between these various aspects of women's experiences, and the ways they are shaped by class, ethnicity, age and sexuality.

Women in Contemporary Britain clearly shows that, at the beginning of the twenty-first century, women remain a disadvantaged grouping within society compared to men.

Jane Pilcher is Lecturer in Sociology at the University of Leicester.

Women in Contemporary Britain

An introduction

Jane Pilcher

London and New York

First published in 1999
by Routledge
11 New Fetter Lane, London EC4P 4EE

Simultaneously published in the USA and Canada
by Routledge
29 West 35th Street, New York, NY 10001

Routledge is an imprint of the Taylor & Francis Group

© 1999 Jane Pilcher

Typeset in Sabon by J&L Composition Ltd, Filey, North Yorkshire
Printed and bound in Great Britain by
T.J. International Ltd, Padstow, UK

British Library Cataloguing in Publication Data
A catalogue record for this book is available
from the British Library

Library of Congress Cataloging in Publication Data
Pilcher, Jane.
    Women in contemporary Britain : an introduction/Jane
Pilcher.
          p.   cm.
    Includes bibliographical references (p.   ) and index.
    ISBN 0-415-18273-5 (hbk).—ISBN 0-415-18274-3 (pbk)
    1. Women—Great Britain—Social conditions.   I. Title.
HQ1593.P55   1999
305.42'0941—dc21   99-11392
                                                    CIP

ISBN 0-415-18273-5 (hbk)
ISBN 0-415-18274-3 (pbk)

To my sister, Claire Pilcher

Contents

List of illustrations

Figures

Tables

Boxes

Acknowledgements

Colleagues past and present commented upon drafts of various chapters or otherwise helped to clarify my thoughts (any remaining inadequacies are fully my own responsibility, rather than theirs): Sara Delamont, Amanda Coffey, Rosemary Crompton, James Fulcher, Julia O'Connell Davidson, Helen Peace, Cathy Pope, Stephen Wagg. Thanks also to Roger Dickinson, Stevi Jackson and Marsha Jones. Skilled and lightning-quick word processing of the manuscript was provided by Pat Mumby, Dianne Orme and especially, Barbara Freer (all at the Department of Sociology, University of Leicester). I am happy to acknowledge the help given to me by the Library staff of the University of Leicester, especially those in the Official Publications section. Throughout, the encouragement and support given to me by my editor, Mari Shullaw, made the experience of writing this book all the more pleasant.

The Audit Bureau of Circulation Limited generously provided circulation statistics. Staff at the Research and Statistics Directorate of the Home Office helpfully dealt with my queries. The offices of the Equal Opportunities Commission in Manchester, Cardiff and Glasgow provided me with some of their publications. Thanks also to Neil Kerber for permission to reproduce his cartoon, and to Jo Brand and Dawn French for permission to use their photographs. The Office of National Statistics and the Home Office granted permission to reproduce various figures and tables used in this book. Part of Chapter 1 was previously published as 'Hormones or Hegemonic Masculinity? Explaining Gender Inequalities', *Sociology Review* 7 (3), February 1998 © Philip Allan Publishers Ltd. Parts of Chapter 9 draw on material which previously appeared in my book, *Women of Their Time*, published by Ashgate (1998).

Finally, special love and thanks to Eddie May and Jack Pilcher May for just being who you are and for putting up with me when writing this book.

Chapter 1

Women and gender: sociological perspectives

This book draws together the latest evidence on women in Britain, and reviews recent sociological interpretations and debates, in order to re-emphasise the fundamental importance of gender as a social division. It shows that despite a degree of change, at the close of the twentieth century, women continue to be disadvantaged relative to men. In this introductory chapter, I set out the reasons for focusing on women in contemporary Britain, identifying key aspects of current debates about late twentieth-century gender relations. These include debates about post-feminism, post-modernism, and plurality and difference (arising from class, ethnicity, racism, age and sexuality, for example). In developing this argument, I also summarise sociological and feminist theoretical perspectives on gender and gender relations, with an especial focus on the work of Walby (1990, 1997) and Connell (1987, 1995).

Women and the sociological gaze

As a discipline, sociology has progressed through a number of stages in terms of the attention it has paid to gender issues (see Maynard 1990; Charles 1993 for review). This progression has closely mirrored the increased recognition given to inequalities between women and men generally in society, which, in turn, is a result of feminist critiques. Before the 1970s or there-abouts, sociology largely concentrated on men as 'people'. Women were largely invisible, other than as wives and mothers within families. On the whole, differences between women and men tended not to be regarded as problematic, nor as something sociology should concern itself with. After the 1970s, or thereabouts, sociologists (or at least, some, mainly women, sociologists) began to criticise the discipline's neglect of women. Increasingly, sociologists began to make a distinction between *sex* (as the bodily, biologically based differences between women and men) and *gender* (the socially constructed differences between women and men). More recently, the idea that there are 'natural', biological sexes (male and female) has been challenged. Writers such as Butler (1990) argue that the practice of classifying bodies as either female or male is, in fact, a social construction rather than the value-free labelling of a pre-existing 'natural' reality. For example, some babies are born with indeterminate genitalia, but are then sexed either as female or male. Adult transsexuals also challenge the dichotomy between 'naturally' male and 'naturally' female bodies. More generally, people routinely transform their 'natural' bodies, in order to make them become more, or less, 'male' or 'female' (Connell 1987; Haraway 1991. See also Chapter 6). Following on from this understanding of sex and gender, and in the light of historical and cross-cultural evidence, which shows much variation in men's and women's roles and status, sociologists argue that gender differences and inequalities are not determined by 'natural biology' but instead are the outcome of a complex range of social practices. Consequently, gender differences can be altered through changed social practices and, ultimately, inequalities can be eradicated. Clearly, this is a perspective on differences between women and men that is shared by feminism; if women's inequality were biologically determined, there would be little point in struggling to improve women's status and position in society.

'Gender-blind' sociology tended to concentrate on aspects of the social world which were important to men, especially in the 'public sphere'. As gender difference was increasingly regarded as a sociological problem to be explored and explained, many studies were undertaken in order to 'fill in the gaps' in knowledge about women in society in these areas. Later, new aspects of the social world began to come under sociological scrutiny, especially those important to the 'private world' of the domestic sphere: housework, childcare and motherhood, childbirth, male violence, food, and so on. Often in the early stages of study, 'gender' was used to mean 'women', whilst men continued to be studied as if they were 'genderless' (see Morgan 1992 for an extended discussion of this tendency). Gradually, however, gender came to be understood as involving the study of women *and* men, and the relationships between them. Consequently, texts on men and masculinity have proliferated in recent years.

Postmodernist and poststructuralist analyses, drawing on the work of Foucault, Derrida and Lacan, for example, have had an important influence on the sociology of gender, through challenging whether it is possible any longer to speak of 'women' or 'men' as unitary categories. In postmodernist analyses, the relative status and position of 'women' and 'men' is said to vary historically and cross-culturally so greatly, that there is little basis for grouping them together in this way (see, for example, Butler and Scott 1992; Nicholson 1990). Similarly, poststructuralists deny the unitary categories of 'women' and 'men' (for example, Butler 1990). Femininities and masculinities are argued to be the outcome of ongoing processes of symbolic construction, achieved through language (or discourse), performance and repetition, which consequently come to take on the appearance of existing in reality (see Marshall 1994 for review and critique). As noted later, not all sociologists of gender agree with postmodernist and poststructuralist arguments. However, one general consequence of the postmodernist and poststructuralist emphasis on plurality, diversity and difference, has been that inequalities *within* genders, based on class, ethnicity, sexuality and age (for example), as well as *between* genders, are now increasingly recognised.

Sociology has come a long way in a relatively short period of time in terms of the attention paid to women, and to gender as an important social division. From being gender-blind, sociology now recognises gender as a complex source of inequality, interacting with class, 'race' and age, for example. Developments around diversity and difference are progressive and have extended sociological understandings of gender relations through encouraging a greater recognition of the complexity of gender as a social division. However, a consequence of the emphasis on difference and diversity within gender relations is a tendency to underplay the enduring inequalities between women as a grouping and men as a grouping within contemporary society (Oakley 1998). Moreover, the recent growth of interest in men and masculinity has arguably deflected attention away from women and femininity. Developments outside of sociological theorising have exacerbated the tendency to 'decentre' women's experiences. Following legislation which formally gave women equality with men (see Box 1.1 on p. 14), Britain in the 1980s and 1990s has been described by some commentators as a 'post-feminist' society. The precise meaning of the term 'post-feminism' is hard to establish (Coppock, Haydon and Richter 1995). However, in the context in which it is most often used, it seems to suggest that women have now achieved the equality with men that feminists had long been fighting for. One aspect of the post-feminist society is the idea of the 'New Man' who, being non-sexist, caring and in touch with his feminine side, contributes equally to housework and childcare. 'Post-feminist society' and the 'New Man' arguably originated in journalists' reflections on the real changes that have taken place in the position and status of women in British society in the second half of the twentieth century. These reflections may also incorporate the idea that any remaining inequalities are suffered by *men*, who are beginning to be disadvantaged in a variety of arenas compared to women. Although, as shown in this book, sociological evidence for the widespread existence of such phenomena is thin on the ground, notions of post-feminism, the New Man and inequalities faced by men have shaped popular understandings of the condition of gender relations at the close of the twentieth century.

The reconceptualisation of gender, the theoretical developments around postmodernism and poststructuralism and the popular currency of 'post-feminism' have, then, had a combined effect of downplaying the enduring inequalities between women and men in British society and deflecting attention away from women toward men. In contrast, this book focuses on women and their disadvantaged position relative to men across a wide range of societal institutions within contemporary Britain (defined as England, Wales and, to a lesser extent, Scotland). Throughout, where evidence permits, attention is paid to the ways in which women's experiences are shaped by their class, their ethnicity, their age and their sexuality. Each chapter is concerned with an important aspect of women's experiences and provides both factual information and overviews of the debates which evidence on these experiences has generated amongst sociologists and feminists. The chapters are carefully positioned so the reader is gradually encouraged to recognise the interrelations between the various aspects of women's experiences. On first reading therefore, it is probably better to read the whole book from beginning to end, and then return to individual chapters of particular interest. So much has sociology been transformed from a pre-feminist, gender-blind discipline that a short introductory text such as this one cannot hope to be entirely comprehensive in its coverage of evidence and debate about women in contemporary Britain. In selecting the topics, I chose those which lent themselves to an approach which emphasises the interrelated processes which in combination structure women's position in society. The content of the book, while covering the 'standard' areas of education, paid work and housework, for example, also aims to reflect the increased attention paid within sociology to issues now recognised as highly relevant to the analysis of women's status, including the body, science and technology and popular media culture.

The empirical study of women has undeniably expanded greatly since the 1970s. The progression of sociology through a number of stages in terms of the attention paid to women and gender, outlined earlier, is also reflected in the development of theory which seeks to explain the origin and persistence of inequalities between women and men, as we shall see next.

Theorising gender inequalities

Why are there gender inequalities? How are they sustained? Can gender inequality be eradicated? There are a number of theories (sociological and otherwise) which claim to answer these questions. In the rest of this chapter, I briefly summarise some of the main theories of gender inequality, pointing out their strengths and weaknesses (for more detailed reviews and critiques, see Abbott and Wallace 1996; Charles 1993; Marshall 1994; Walby 1990). Then, I focus on the arguments of two sociologists, Sylvia Walby and Bob Connell, each of whom has proposed a broad-ranging explanation of gender inequality which attempts to overcome the weaknesses of earlier theories.

Biological theories

'Common-sense' explanations of gender inequalities centre around biology as a cause of inequalities between women and men. Such 'everyday' theories of gender inequalities have their 'scientific' equivalent in explanations put forward by natural scientists and by socio-biologists. These scientists vary as to which aspect of human biology (for example, hormones, genetics, chromosomes, size and/or 'wiring' of the brain) 'naturally' determines gender inequality. Goldberg (1979), for example, argues that the 'neuro-endocrine system' (the interaction of the nervous system with the hormone system) is the biological basis of male dominance (see Charles 1993 for critique; see also Hakim 1996). Biologically based theories suggest that it is physiological, natural factors which cause and sustain universal inequalities between women and men, making it practically impossible to achieve a fully equal society. One of the main criticisms of biologically based theories is that they often use data on animal behaviour, which are then applied to human behaviour. Moreover, such theories often ignore historical, anthropological and sociological evidence on human behaviour, in particular evidence which points to variability in women and men's behaviour, status and roles over time and place. A related weakness is a tendency toward ethnocentrism. In other words, a tendency to assume that the gender relations of the white, middle class in western industrialised society are normal and typical of human behaviour. Despite such weaknesses, versions of biological theory continue to have huge popular currency. Connell (1987) argues that this is because biological theories are mirrors: they reflect back what is familiar, call it 'science', and thereby justify what many people already believe. Although, biologically based theories offer unsatisfactory explanations of gender inequality, their concern with the physicality of human life is increasingly accepted as valid (see Shilling 1993). Sociologists like Connell (1987, 1995) have started to re-evaluate the role of the body in gender relations, although as shown in Chapter 6, 'body matters' have often featured in feminist analyses (see also Davis 1997a).

Socialisation theories

Functionalist-influenced socialisation theories stress social factors, rather than biological factors, in the explanation of gender inequalities. In this perspective, there are two sex roles, the female and the male, each with different 'scripts' attached to them. Females and males learn the appropriate scripts via socialisation, particularly in infancy and early childhood. Children are taught to conform to their feminine or masculine role as appropriate, through meeting the expectations or norms attached to that role, and are encouraged to do so via the application of positive ('What a big, strong boy you are!') and negative ('Little girls shouldn't play football') sanctions.

In this theory, there are gender inequalities because women and men are socialised into different roles. Some versions of this perspective suggest that gender inequality can be reduced or even eradicated if the social scripts learnt via socialisation are changed, through mechanisms like non-sexist child rearing. Socialisation theories offer a plausible explanation of how individuals learn to be masculine or feminine. However, such theories neglect important issues including, where do the norms and values attached to masculine and feminine scripts come from and whose interests do they represent? Socialisation theories overemphasise voluntary conformity to the 'norm' at the expense of structural and institutional factors which constrain masculine and feminine behaviour. Moreover, the two sex roles identified by this perspective are based on biological differences between males and females, which are regarded as unproblematic. Connell (1987) argues that because socialisation theory implicitly depends upon biology for its starting point, it is a theoretical approach which has a non-social conception of the basic cause of inequality between women and men.

Feminist theories

In comparison to socialisation theories, feminist theories of gender relations can offer a more sociological conception of the differences between women and men and often place greater stress on structural and institutional factors. There are a number of feminist theories, drawing on a range of intellectual traditions and focusing on different aspects of gender relations in their explanation of gender inequality (for overview, see Abbott and Wallace 1996; Walby 1990). Since the 1970s, it has become common practice to divide feminist theories into categories ('marxist feminism' and 'radical feminism', for example), in order to highlight the contrasts between them. However, during the 1990s, several feminist writers argued that such categories are no longer useful (for example, Maynard 1995; Stacey 1997). Such rigid demarcations are said to be artificial and to fail to do justice to the sophistication, scope and complexity of contemporary feminist theories, which are often multiple and overlapping in both their approaches and in their substantive focus. Clearly, the 'labelling approach' is problematic, not least because a label may be inconsistently applied to a theorist, or may not match an author's own preferred description of her work. However, both historically and currently within feminist theorising, individual authors have either labelled themselves or, at the least, have aligned themselves with a particular feminist perspective, rather than with others. For this reason, I believe it necessary to review the main feminist perspectives, using the labels commonly applied, and to convey a sense of what makes each a relatively distinctive grouping. Nevertheless, the reader needs to recognise that, in addition to the problems noted above, the application of labels can operate to *falsely unify* (for example, not all 'radical feminist' analyses are identical in method or focus) and to *falsely dichotomise* (those writing from a 'black feminist' perspective can simultaneously be 'radical feminist' in their analyses) what is in reality a complex, intertwined and continuously developing body of feminist theory.

In some analyses (often labelled as 'marxist feminism'), gender inequalities are argued to arise from the workings of the capitalist economic system: it requires, and benefits from, women's unpaid labour in the home. The subordination of women to men in society (or patriarchy), therefore, tends to be regarded as a by-product of capital's subordination of labour. Class inequality is the central feature of society and it is this which determines gender inequality. It is implicit in this perspective that gender inequality will only be eradicated once class has ceased to be a fundamental social division. Some examples of feminist analyses influenced by marxist class theory can be found in Chapter 3, in explanations of women's experiences of paid work. As one author often identified as a 'marxist feminist' herself notes (Barrett 1988), one weakness of this perspective is that it inadequately accounts for the subordination of women in pre-capitalist and in socialist societies. In general, marxist-influenced accounts of gender relations have been criticised for overemphasising class relations and capitalism and for downplaying gender as an independent social division (for example, Bottero 1998).

In another grouping of feminist theoretical perspectives, the importance of gender is very much emphasised. Maynard suggests that 'radical feminist' analyses are so called because of a shared concern 'to formulate new ways of theorising women's relationship to men' (1995: 259). In such perspectives, the subordination of women by men (patriarchy) is regarded as the primary and fundamental social division. A key theme in radical feminist accounts of gender inequality is the control of women's bodies by men, for example through sexuality, reproduction, motherhood and male violence in the form of rape. Examples of radical feminist perspectives can be found in Chapter 6, in the context of reproductive technologies. Arising from their concern with the role of the body in gender relations, some versions of radical feminist theories have been criticised for implying that there are essential and unchanging, biological differences between all women and all men. However, this criticism is not valid for radical feminist analyses as a whole.

A further grouping of feminist perspectives gives theoretical priority to two systems – capitalism and patriarchy – in explanation of the subordination of women. Often referred to as 'dual systems theory', this perspective in many ways represents a synthesis of marxist and radical feminist accounts of gender relations. The work of Delphy and Leonard serves as an example of this approach. They write, 'Radical feminism and marxism have often been presented as antithetical to one another, but we believe not only that men are the primary beneficiaries of the subordination of women in western societies, but also that a marxist approach is the one which best helps us to understand why and how men oppress women' (1992: 2). Indeed, the dual systems approach can be seen to have emerged out of the critiques levelled at Marxist theories, which may overemphasise class and capitalism, and the critiques levelled at radical feminist theories, which may over-emphasise biological sex and/or patriarchy. In some versions of dual systems theory, capitalism and patriarchy are understood as interdependent, mutually accommodating systems of oppression, whereby both systems structure and benefit from women's subordination (for example, Hartmann 1979). In dual systems theories, it is implied that both systems of oppression would have to be challenged if gender inequality is to be eradicated. Although avoiding some of the disadvantages of Marxist feminist and radical feminist theories, critics of dual systems theory point to, amongst other weaknesses, a lack of clarity about the precise nature of the relationship between patriarchy and capitalism, or gender and class (see, for example, Gottfried 1998).

Another grouping of feminist perspectives are less concerned with how to adequately theorise the connections between capitalism and patriarchy than with addressing the implicit ethnocentrism and racism of all the theories examined so far. In Black feminist critiques (sometimes also labelled black or 'black' depending on an individual author's preferences – see Mirza 1997), it is argued that analyses of gender which fail to fully examine and theorise racism are flawed and incomplete (for example, hooks 1984). The main argument is that most theories of gender implicitly use the experiences of white, middle-class housewives to develop their explanation of gender inequality. Black feminist critiques have been at the forefront of questioning the category 'women', through emphasising the diversity in experiences that this concept serves to conceal. For critics of 'white feminism', women's subordination can only be eliminated if the system of racism is challenged, alongside patriarchy and capitalism. Early black feminist critiques were criticised for using 'black' and 'white' as unifying categories and thereby revealing their own universalist tendencies. However, this is not a valid criticism of more recent analyses, as the use of the label 'black' by authors in the latest collection of writings by black British feminists shows (Mirza 1997).

The critique put forward by black feminists can be linked to a broader set of concerns about a tendency toward universalism in theories of gender relations, concerns which have been voiced most strongly by postmodernists. Postmodernists focus on complexity, fragmentation and disorganisation as the condition of society in the late twentieth century. They argue that this condition of society means that it is no longer possible – if it ever was – to speak of categories such as 'women' or 'men' or to use large-scale theories (or 'grand narratives') such as patriarchy and class theory. As noted earlier, postmodernists also contend that women and men are too divided (by age, class, ethnicity and racism, for example) for the concepts of 'women' and of 'men' to be useful. Postmodernist analyses rightly emphasise diversity and difference within gender relations, and their questioning of the plausibility of 'grand narratives' has some value. However, critics suggest that the perspective goes too far in denying that there is shared gender oppression, systematically structured, that exists across time and space (Maynard 1995; Walby 1994).

In the light of such criticisms, proposals have been made to analyse gender relations from a 'postmodernist feminist' perspective. Fraser and Nicholson (1989) argue that postmodern feminists must not abandon large theories like patriarchy or large concepts like 'women', because the problems they are attempting to grapple with are large problems, with a long history. However, a postmodern feminist analysis of gender relations must have a number of features. It must be explicitly historical, it must be non-universalist and sensitive to cultural contexts, and it must replace singular notions of feminine and masculine identity with plural notions – of femininities and masculinities made up of complexities of class, sexuality, ethnicity and age. The idea that there can be such a thing as 'postmodern feminism' is contested by some writers, with Evans (1995) arguing that it represents a contradiction in terms. In other words, feminism is an example of a 'grand narrative', the relevance of which postmodernism fundamentally questions (see also Whelehan 1995). Whether or not a 'postmodern feminism' is possible, the approach to gender theorising outlined by Fraser and Nicholson has found increasing support, albeit in a variety of different formulations. Maynard is not alone in advocating what might be called 'post-postmodernist' gender theory, which 'encourages a focus on the specifics of social relations, rather than on homogeneous social systems' (1995: 276. See also Bottero 1998; Gottfried 1998; Marshall 1994; Pollert 1996).

Areas of weakness

Having outlined some of the main theories of gender inequality, we can now identify several problematical issues or areas of weakness within gender theorising which have become the focus of much debate. The first issue is the relationship between gender and other social inequalities, particularly class and 'race'. As we have seen, most attempts to theorise gender have either completely neglected class and/or racism, or have inadequately theorised the precise nature of the relationships between the two/three systems of oppression. A second problematical issue concerns structure and agency. Most of the theories stress the role of structured, systemic gender oppression, based either on biology, or capitalism and/or patriarchy/racism. However, this stress on structure means that the individual women and men necessarily involved in gender relations are invisible. Their agency, as oppressors and oppressed, their resistance, struggle and defiance, is often lost. Furthermore, because of the concern to theorise the structural and sys-temic qualities of gender relations, it becomes difficult to explain how change occurs over time. A third problematical issue is the relationship between the body and gender. In most of the theories we have reviewed so far, the bodies of women and men do not even feature. Where they do, in biological theories and in some versions of radical feminist theories, there is a tendency towards determinism. The fourth issue I want to identify arises from postmodernist-influenced critiques, which have led to calls for theories to be explicitly historical, sensitive to cultural contexts, and to analyse femininities and masculinities as made up of class, sexuality, eth-nicity and age. As we have seen, most of the theories are insensitive to his-torical change, to cultural variation and to the diversity of 'women' and 'men'. With these four issues in mind, we can now turn to the theories pro-posed by Sylvia Walby (1990, 1997) and R.W. Connell (1987, 1995), since in many respects, their work attempts to overcome the weaknesses of earlier gender theorising.

Walby's theory of patriarchy

Building on the work of Hartmann (1979) and Delphy (1984), Walby's ex-planation of why gender inequalities exist and how they are sustained centres around the concept of patriarchy. For Walby, patriarchy is a system of social structures and practices in which men dominate, oppress and exploit women. Walby identifies six structures of patriarchy (household production, paid work, the state, male violence, sexuality, culture) which together are argued to capture the depth, pervasiveness and interconnect-edness of women's subordination. Her theory of patriarchy also allows for change over historical time. Walby argues that, in Britain during the twen-tieth century, patriarchy changed from the 'private' form to the 'public' form. Private patriarchy is based around the family and the household and involves individual men exploiting the labour of individual women. Women are largely confined to the household sphere and have limited participa-tion in public life. In public patriarchy, women are not excluded from pub-lic life but face inequality and discrimination within it, for example, in paid work. For Walby, the feminist movement was a key factor in bringing about the change from private to public patriarchy, via the struggle for the vote, for access to education and to the professions, to have legal rights of property ownership, rights in marriage and divorce, and so on. However, patriarchy itself was and is not defeated. Walby says that it has merely changed its form so that now, as she puts it, rather than being restricted to the household, women have 'the whole of society in which to roam and be exploited' (1990: 201).

Does Walby's theory successfully address the four issues in gender theo-rising identified earlier? First, the issue of the relationship between gender and other forms of inequalities. Walby's work is claimed by herself and others to belong to the dual systems branch of explanations of gender relations. In other words, she argues that to understand gender inequalities it is necessary to recognise patriarchy and capitalism. Unlike earlier dual systems theorists (for example, Hartmann 1979) though, Walby thinks the relationship between the two systems is often one of tension and conflict, with capitalism and patriarchy competing with each other to exploit women. Walby does recognise racism as a third system of oppression, saying that it 'intersects' with the other systems, but it does not feature prominently in her analysis. Walby has been criticised for her treatment of the relationship between gender and other forms of social inequality. Anthias and Yuval-Davies (1992), for example, argue that Walby's theory portrays the three systems as, to a large extent, separate and independent of one another. The implication is that class and race are merely extra layers of oppression faced by some women. For Anthias and Yuval-Davies (1992), this does not adequately account for the fully fused nature of the relationships between patriarchy, capitalism and racism, nor for the way that class and 'race' make for a qualitatively different kind of gender inequality.

Walby's theory can also be assessed in terms of whether it gives proper recognition to human agency. Walby claims to be working with a Giddens-type understanding of the relationship between structure and agency, where each are mutually constitutive of the other. Her definition of patriarchy specifies systems, structures and practices (or agency). She also cites practice or agency as a key factor in bringing about the change from private to public patriarchy, when she emphasises the important role played by feminists in securing the advancement of women into the public world. Despite these strengths, however, Walby has been criticised for her overarching tendencies towards structural analysis and for neglecting real people. For example, Anna Pollert (1996) says that Walby has a tendency to speak of 'patriarchal interests' and 'capitalist interests' as if these were real entities which existed independently of actual people. Therefore, although Walby claims to work with an integrated conception of structure and agency in her theory of patriarchy, critics suggest that in fact, structures are emphasised more than agency.

One major area of weakness in Walby's theory is that it underemphasises the importance of the body in gender relations. Moreover, because of weaknesses in her theory around the relationship between gender and other forms of social inequality and the relationship between structure and agency, Walby also largely fails to meet the criteria of 'post-postmodernist' theories of gender. Although her theory is sensitive to historical contexts, it is less successful in exploring cultural variation and the diversity of experiences between women (and men). Although Walby's theory improves on earlier theories, these criticisms suggest that her work is not without its own weaknesses.

Connell's social theory of gender

Rather than explaining why there are gender inequalities, Connell's main concern is to explain how they are sustained. For Connell, the relationship between the body and gender is a crucial issue for any theory of gender. He argues that gender is the end-product of ongoing interpretations of and definitions placed upon the reproductive and sexual capacities of the human body. Masculinities and femininities can be understood as the effects of these interpretations and definitions: on bodies, on personalities and on a society's culture and institutions. Gender is therefore an ongoing creation of human agency, which at an institutional and structural level also acts to constrain individual agency.

For Connell, empirical research has revealed labour, power and cathexis (concerned with emotional relationships, including sexuality) to be the major structures of gender relations, or the major ways in which the agency or practice of women and men is constrained. The three structures constantly interweave with each other creating the 'gender order', or the structure of gender relations in a particular society (see also Matthews 1984). Whether at the individual, institutional or 'gender order' level, masculinities and femininities are organised around a single fact: the dominance of men over women. The justifying ideology for this organisation of gender relations is the 'gender hierarchy', involving the ranking of masculinities and femininities. At the top of this hierarchy is 'hegemonic masculinity', the culturally dominant ideal of masculinity centred around authority, physical toughness and strength, heterosexuality and paid work. This is an ideal of masculinity that few actual men live up to, but from which most gain advantage: Connell calls this next level 'complicit masculinity'. Next in the hierarchy are 'subordinated masculinites', the most important of which is homosexual masculinity. More generally, this form of masculinity includes a range of masculine behaviour which does not fully match up to the macho ideals of hegemonic masculinity. At the bottom of the gender hierarchy are femininities. Although these may take a variety of forms, for example 'emphasised' (or compliant) femininity and 'resistant' (for example, feminist) femininity, femininity is always subordinated to masculinity.

In Connell's theory, gender relations are far from being a fixed or a 'sure thing'. They are an ongoing process, the outcome of human practice or agency, and they are subject to resistance as well as conformity, contestation as well as acceptance. All this means that gender relations are open to disruption and change, and hegemonic masculinity is subject to challenge. Connell argues that, in the contemporary industrialised world, hegemonic masculinity is indeed becoming less hegemonic and that, consequently, there are 'crisis tendencies' in the gender order. For example, in family relationships, Connell says that state policies have inevitably disrupted the legitimacy of men's domination over women (via laws on divorce, domestic violence and rape within marriage, independent pensions and taxation for married women, for example). Connell also identifies a tendency towards a crisis of sexuality, where under pressure from women's more assertive sexuality and from gay sexuality, hegemonic masculine heterosexuality becomes less hegemonic. A further example of a tendency toward crisis is the joining together of women and men in groupings which challenge the current gender order, including women's liberation movements, gay liberation, working-class feminism and anti-sexist politics amongst heterosexual men. Connell concludes that it is through individuals and groups, collectively and on a mass scale, 'prising open' the crisis tendencies in the gender order that gender inequality, along with other forms of inequality, can be eradicated.

Does Connell's theory successfully address the four issues in gender theorising identified earlier? First, the issue of the relationship between gender and other social inequalities. When describing the gender structure of labour, Connell does say that gender divisions are a fundamental and essential feature of capitalism, but in general his theory has been criticised for not paying full attention to 'race' or ethnicity (West 1989). However, in Connell's more recent book, he does address this weakness. In *Masculinities* (1995), he says that gender is 'unavoidably involved' with 'race' and class, as well as with nationality or position in the world order and that to fully understand gender, we must constantly go beyond gender. Second, the issue of structure and agency. This is an area of strength within Connell's theory. He is very much concerned to show the ways in which people constitute social institutions and structures and the ways in which social institutions and structures constitute people. Issues of power, conflict, resistance and change are central to his theory, as is a concern with identifying the constraints of gender as a structure and recognising that this is an ongoing creation of human practice or agency. Another area of strength within Connell's theory is the centrality of the body to his arguments about what gender is and how gender inequalities are sustained. Finally, Connell's theory does meet some criteria of 'post-postmodernist' theories of gender because it is historical, sensitive to cultural difference and to variations in masculinities and femininities. However, Connell's tendency to under-explain the precise relationship between gender and other forms of social inequality, especially 'race', remains a weakness here.

Clearly, theorising gender relations is a very difficult task. Each of the theoretical approaches reviewed here has some value, but none represents a completely comprehensive theory. Arguably, though, the theory proposed by Connell, with its emphasis on the body, agency and structure, the diversity of gender and the possibility of change, represents the most developed general sociological explanation of why there are gender inequalities, how they are sustained and how they might be eradicated. More so than Walby, who stresses the partial nature of 'gender transformations' (1997), Connell seems cautiously optimistic about the potential for further change in the gender order and the ways it can be brought about. Having read the chapters that follow, I leave it to the reader to decide whether they find the evidence and debates more supportive of Walby's ambivalence or Connell's optimism as to the prospects for achieving gender equality in the twenty-first century.

Box 1.1 Some important milestones for British women

1907	Women win right to be elected as county or borough councillors
1908	First woman mayor, Elizabeth Garrett Anderson
1913	First woman professor, Caroline Spurgeon
1918	Women over 30 given the vote in general elections Women win right to be elected as Members of the House of Commons
1919	*Sex Disqualification (Removal) Act*, opened most professions to women First woman Member of Parliament to take her seat in the House of Commons, Lady Astor
1921	First woman to be called to the English Bar, Dr Ivy Williams First birth control clinic opened, in London
1923	Women able to obtain a divorce on the same terms as men
1928	Women over 21 given the vote
1929	First woman Cabinet minister, Margaret Bondfield
1943	First woman president of the Trades Union Congress, Dame Anne Loughlin
1945	*Family Allowance Act*, child benefits paid directly to mothers
1958	First women to be created life peers
1961	First birth control pill goes on sale
1964	First woman Nobel Prize winner, Dorothy Hodgkin for Chemistry
1965	First woman High Court Judge, Judge Elizabeth Lane
1967	*Abortion Act*, allowing abortion on medical or psychological grounds
1969	Wives can enter into financial and legal contracts in their own right
1970	First female ministers ordained in the Methodist Church
1973	Equal right of guardianship of children

1975   International Women's Year
First woman to lead a major British political party, Margaret Thatcher
Sex Discrimination Act makes sex discrimination unlawful in employment, training and related matters and in the supply of goods, facilities and services
Equal Pay Act 1970 comes into force, providing for equal pay for men and women
Rights to paid maternity leave and other rights for working women

1978   World's first test tube baby (a girl) born in Oldham

1979   First woman Prime Minister, Margaret Thatcher

1980   Equality of entitlement to most social security benefits

1981   First woman Leader of the House of Lords, Baroness Young

1984   First woman general secretary of a major union, Brenda Dean
Equal pay for work of equal value

1987   First woman editor of a major national newspaper, Wendy Henry
First woman Court of Appeal Judge, Dame Elizabeth Butler-Sloss

1990   Independent taxation of husband and wife

1991   First British woman in space, Helen Sharman

1992   First woman Speaker of the House of Commons, Betty Boothroyd

1993   First woman Civil Service Commissioner, Ann Bowtell
Maternity rights extended and enhanced

1994   First women priests ordained in the Anglican Church

1995   First woman fighter pilot, Flt Lieutenant Jo Salter
First woman Chief Constable, Pauline Clare
UN Fourth World Conference on Women, Beijing
Arrangements for future equalisation of state pension age and equal treatment for occupational pensions

1997   Women double their representation in the House of Commons, to 120 seats or 18% of MPs

Sources: Holdsworth (1988), Central Office of Information (1996), Central Statistical Office (1995)

Chapter 2

Learning for life: education and training

Most pupils, students or other learners within the education system are young: infants in nurseries and primary schools, children in secondary schools, young adults in colleges and universities. Even those who receive vocational or job-related training tend to be individuals in the early rather than the later part of their working lives. This association between education and young people suggests that education plays a crucial role in preparing individuals, not yet regarded as fully 'mature' or 'developed', for their future lives as adult citizens. Particularly in the context of a modern, industrial society, with specialised occupations, the education system is important in generating an educated and qualified workforce.

The experiences of children and young people in education and training, culminating in the range and level of qualifications they gain, have a crucial effect on their chances and prospects throughout their subsequent lives. Because of its importance in preparing young people for their future, sociologists have examined the education system in terms of the role it plays in reproducing social inequalities. The introduction of compulsory free elementary education after 1870 and of secondary education in 1944 largely removed barriers to participating in education on the grounds of social class. However, sociologists have argued that experiences of education remained differentiated according to social class, 'race' and gender. These social characteristics of pupils and students have been shown crucially to influence educational outcomes, particularly in terms of types and levels of qualifications gained.

This chapter examines research evidence on the ways in which the education system acts to (re)produce gender inequalities. It details the findings of a number of studies which have examined the experiences of girls and women across the different levels of education and training. Taken together, this body of research evidence suggests that, whether in primary schools, secondary schools or higher levels of education and training, there exist a number of common processes which in combination lead to the disadvantage of girls and women. The chapter also provides an account of the various legislative changes and policy initiatives developed wholly or partly in response to concerns over the disadvantage experienced by girls and women within the education system. The impact of these interventions is then assessed in the light of recent arguments that girls are now outperforming boys in examinations. Given that Scotland has a different education system from England and Wales, the chapter mainly focuses on English and Welsh evidence (for Scotland, see Darling and Glendinning 1996; Turner, Riddell and Brown 1995).

In focusing on the ways the education system contributes to the persistence of gender inequality, researchers fully recognise the role played by other institutions in society, including family life, the media, paid employment and social policy. The education system is not argued single-handedly to create gender inequality, but it is identified as a key institution which simultaneously produces and reinforces gender distinctions to the particular detriment of girls and women. Research in a range of educational settings has identified a number of common processes which, taken together, mean that girls' and women's experiences of education and training are quite different to those of boys and mens, ultimately affecting their access to forms and types of paid work. Processes through which an educational institution may act to differentiate on the basis of gender include its bureaucratic and spatial organisation, its teachers' attitudes and actions, its curriculum and teaching materials and the cultures of children and young people themselves.

Primary education

By the time they enter the formal education system, around the age of four, the home-based experiences of boys and girls, gained through interaction with parents and other adults, and through toys, books, clothing and television, mean that they are highly skilled in 'doing gender'. In other words, girls and boys enter the formal education system looking and behaving in 'gender-appropriate' ways and with their own firmly held expectations and understandings about the differences between girls and women on the one hand and boys and men on the other. Once children begin their formal educational careers, the primary school environment often acts to replicate, emphasise and elaborate pre-existing gendered behaviour and expectations, rather than downplaying or challenging them.

An important way gender differences are emphasised is through a school's bureaucratic and spatial organisation. Pupils are often divided into gender groups, for purposes where gender has no effective relevance. For example, class registers may be arranged by gender (with boys' names listed first) rather than alphabetically. Similarly, when returning from the playground, pupils may be asked to line themselves up by gender. Primary schools may operate gendered dress codes, where girls may be discouraged from wearing trousers in the winter and shorts in the summer. Areas of space within the school building may be formally allocated according to gender. For example, coat pegs may be ranged by gender and toilet facilities may be separate. This demarcation of gender through the bureaucratic and spatial organisation of the school emphasises to pupils that they are either girls or boys, and that this difference is a fundamentally relevant and significant one (Delamont 1990).

Apart from parents and near relatives, teachers are probably the most significant adults in a young child's social world. For this reason, researchers have been interested in studying the ways gender is present within teacher-pupil interactions. Studies have shown that many teachers convey stereo-typical messages about gender to pupils, through their teaching methods, their behaviour, and through what they say. Clarricoates' (1987a) study of primary schools illustrates the range of ways gender is present within teacher-pupil interactions, and the ways that girl pupils are disadvantaged as a result. Clarricoates found that teachers held gendered expectations about their pupils' aptitudes and abilities. In particular, boys were said to be more interesting and rewarding to teach than girls. Clarricoates argued that teachers related to pupils on the basis of their gender in these ways because of their primary concern to maintain order and discipline within the classroom. Other studies, and Clarricoates' own evidence, shows that boys are often more disruptive and require more disciplinary attention from teachers than girls. As a strategy of controlling boys therefore, teachers may gear the content of lessons to 'boys' topics', so that they remain interested and better behaved. Because boys were seen to be in need of more control, teachers also spent more time talking, listening to and assisting boys during lessons. The greater conformity and passivity of the girls compared to the demanding and disruptive behaviour of the boys also explained why teachers found boys more interesting and rewarding to teach than girls. 'The girls' conscientiousness and diligence makes them "less bothersome" and "less interesting" to the teachers who consequently turn all their energies and skills to the boys' (Clarricoates 1987a: 160). Even though evidence suggests that girls outperform boys in most subjects at primary school level (see below), Clarricoates' research suggests that many teachers attribute their achievements to stereotypically feminine characteristics of conformity and acquiescence rather than real intellectual ability.

Evidence such as that provided by Clarricoates highlights the ways teachers, through their actions and attitudes, unconsciously replicate and elaborate gender distinctions, prioritising boys and marginalising girls in the process. (Of course, some teachers actively and consciously practice anti-sexist education, as documented by Lloyd and Duveen (1992), for example.) Studies of gender in primary education have also pointed to the importance of the formal curriculum and the books, toys, games, activities and projects used to teach it. The introduction of a core set of subjects under the National Curriculum (from 1988 in all English and Welsh state schools) is likely to have reduced the opportunity for primary schools to offer boys and girls separate subjects. Nevertheless, Clarricoates' (1987a) research reminds us that, even where girls and boys are together taught the same subjects in the same classroom, the lesson content may be presented and received in a gendered way. Clarricoates reports the following incident which occurred during her observation of a primary school class. The class teacher asked the pupils to get out their books on dinosaurs. This request was met with objections from the girls, to the effect that they were 'always doing boys' topics'. The teacher acknowledged this, through her suggestion that they would study 'houses and flowers' later on in the term, a promise which led to disgruntled murmurs from the boys (Clarricoates 1987a: 157). Topics of prehistory such as dinosaurs may be gendered, but evidence suggests that contemporary topics such as computing are gendered too. Bradshaw, Clegg and Trayhum (1995) argue that there are gendered inequalities in computing, indicated by, for example, boys gaining greater access to classroom computers and dominating their use, and the extent to which teachers spend more time with boys than girls when computers are being used.

Research by Glenys Lobban (1974) indicated that reading material used in primary schools was heavily stereotyped according to gender. First, twice as many male as female characters were depicted in the reading materials. Second, the materials depicted female characters only in domestic settings and activities, while the male characters had proactive roles and engaged in a wider range of contexts and activities. More recent research indicates that, twenty years after Lobban's famous study, things have not changed a great deal. Evidence suggests that masculine characters still predominate in children's literature, numerically and qualitatively. Cairns and Inglis (1989) examined history textbooks and found that only 14.8 per cent of the material dealt with women (see also Richardson 1986). One small-scale study aimed to assess the continuing relevance of Lobban's findings, through examining books aimed at pre-school children (Best 1993). The researchers found that the books depicted twice as many male characters as female ones. Feminine characters were largely shown in domestic situations (75 per cent), whereas 81 per cent of masculine characters were shown outside the home doing paid work. Despite the popularity of the Teletubbies, it seems that Postman Pat, Fireman Sam and the various characters associated with Thomas the Tank Engine are more representative of the continuing dominance of masculine characters and contexts within pre-school and primary school reading materials.

Researchers presenting their findings on gender stereotyping within reading materials and textbooks suggest that, in addition to academic knowledge about, say, history, maths or science, these texts implicitly convey another sort of knowledge. They give out 'lessons' on what is normal, natural, good and proper in terms of gender and thereby promote traditional gender stereotypes which prioritise boys and men over girls and women. The implicit messages about gender contained within reading materials are part of what is called 'the hidden curriculum'. The hidden curriculum is present in all of the aspects of primary education already discussed, including the bureaucratic and spatial organisation of the school and the actions and attitudes of teachers. As Clarricoates explains, 'The "hidden curriculum" does what the official curriculum is presumably not supposed to do; it differentiates on the basis of sex' (1987a: 155).

So far in this review of evidence on gender in primary school settings, little has been said about children themselves. Recent work in the sociology of childhood has emphasised that children are not passive recipients of socialisation directed at them by parents and teachers. Instead, children must be recognised as active, reactive and creative in the establishment of their own social worlds (James and Prout 1997; Prout and James 1990). This new view of children means that, when assessing evidence about the gendered hidden curriculum, we must be careful not to make blanket assumptions about how the messages it conveys or the lessons it teaches are received by pupils.

Evidence on cultures of school children certainly suggests they are active in the construction of their gendered schooling experience (Lloyd and Duveen 1992; Walkerdine 1990). As we have seen in the 'dinosaur' incident reported by Clarricoates (1987a), children themselves hold deeply stereo-typed views about gender-appropriate behaviour and activities. Consequently, children who display gender-atypical behaviour, interests or preferences may be censured by other children. Research also indicates that children segregate themselves by gender (and to a lesser extent, ethnicity – see Connolly 1995, 1998). For example, when playing in the playground, certain types of games and/or areas of play may effectively be girls or boys 'only'. Delamont (1990) notes that pupils in primary schools also set each gender against the other, competing so that the girls are first to complete a task or the boys are the ones to get more correct answers.

Clarricoates (1987b) says that children's cultures are so gendered that, within primary schools, there exists a girls' world and a boys' world. In her study, she found that boys actively differentiated themselves from girls and constructed a 'status hierarchy' from which girls were excluded. Girls also created their own 'world' but this had lesser value since, unlike that constructed by boys, it did not receive validation through the 'hidden curriculum' of the school environment, nor was it given credence by the wider culture which children experienced. Importantly, Clarricoates emphasises that the girls' culture was not wholly subservient to that of the boys, even though this was heavily dominant. In part, girls actively segregated themselves off from boys as a form of resistance to their dominance, as a strategy for dealing with the confrontation, ridicule and sexual harassment they faced.

The strength of children's own gendered cultures may mean that, amongst other things, they are resistant to teaching materials which aim to avoid gender stereotyping. Bradshaw, Clegg and Trayhum (1995) studied computer software used in English primary schools. They found that manufacturers had attempted to exclude obvious gender bias and some androgynous characters were featured in software. However, even when characters were neither obviously masculine or feminine, children tended to identify the characters as masculine. Bradshaw *et al.* concluded that the apparently androgynous characters still had a gendered meaning to children. This is because the broader cultural context of children's lives is one where people and animals are always either male or female. Moreover, in the absence of evidence to the contrary, it is the 'norm' to assume that people and animals are male, rather than female. This explanation serves to remind us that, although children's own culture is an important process through which gender inequality gets reproduced, it does not exist in a vacuum. Children do actively construct their own gendered social worlds but they do not do so with material of their own choosing or with complete freedom and control. The evidence reviewed in this section suggests that primary schools are settings where, all too often, traditional gender stereotypes are replicated and elaborated, rather than interrupted and challenged. A range of processes effectively contribute to the elevation of boys and of masculinity and the diminishing of girls and of femininity. Yet, paradoxically, despite the disadvantages they face, girls have long performed better within most subjects on the primary school curriculum. This issue of the relative performance of girls and boys in tests and examinations is returned to later, following a review of evidence on gender relations in secondary schools and in post-compulsory education and training.

Secondary education

At the age of eleven or so, children complete their primary education and become secondary school pupils. This progression entails leaving a particular school, a particular set of teachers and, often, friends, and entering a wholly new environment. As Delamont (1990) notes, it is a transition which is anticipated with some degree of apprehension, expressed through scary stories, rumours and myths about experiences awaiting new pupils at secondary school. The transition from one level of education to another is but one element of a number of transitions children undergo during the second decade of their lives. As they approach their teenage years, children's bodies become more adult-like, and boys' and girls' bodies become more differentiated from one another. Sexuality therefore becomes a much more important issue than in earlier schooling experiences, as do the friendship groups that develop more strongly than at primary school. Finally, pupils in secondary school have entered the last level of compulsory education. Consequently, parents, teachers and the pupils themselves become much more concerned with the future, in terms of qualifications, and the beckoning world of further education, paid work and adult life in general. Secondary education is an important context within which this key stage of transition in the life course is experienced, and so researchers have paid particular attention to the ways in which this level of the education system is productive of social inequalities, including gender inequalities.

The greater importance of friendship groups, of sexuality and of the beckoning world of 'post-school' mean that the context of secondary education differs in crucial respects from primary education. However, there are also a number of continuities in the processes that operate to distinguish between pupils according to gender. As in primary schools, the bureaucratic and spatial organisation of secondary schools may act to emphasise gender differences. Pupil records and class registers may record boy and girl pupils separately, while areas of cloakrooms or ranges of lockers might be designated for each gender. School uniforms or dress codes may be different for each gender, including clothes worn for sporting activities. Delamont (1990) reported from her study of secondary schools in Wales that it was common to ask all pupils of one gender to leave a classroom first, followed by the other. As in secondary schools in other parts of Britain, such arrangements act to segregate by gender, and represent an unnecessary emphasis on gender differences purely for administrative convenience.

Studies of secondary schools also provide evidence on the actions and attitudes of teachers. For example, Riddell (1989, 1992) studied two comprehensive schools in the mid-1980s and found that teachers held gender stereotyped views about the behaviour and attitudes of their pupils. Girls were regarded as more mature, neat and conscientious than boys. Boys were seen as aggressive, as lacking in discipline and as having a poorer academic performance than girls. These views affected the ways teachers interacted with pupils in the classroom. Riddell observed that teachers gave more attention to boys so as to maintain order and that the content of lessons was often orientated so that the interest of potentially disruptive boys was engaged. Riddell also noted that sexual humour (at the expense of girls and women) was used by some men teachers to create masculine camaraderie, as part of their strategy of controlling the behaviour of disruptive boys. On the basis of her findings, Riddell concluded that many teachers subscribed to a gendered ideology which represented all women as mothers or potential mothers, and therefore marginalised them as workers, a tendency which compromised any formal commitment on the part of the schools to equal opportunities.

Research undertaken by Mac An Ghaill (1994) in the early 1990s also found that teachers held stereotypical views about the interests, aspirations and future prospects of their white and ethnic minority boy and girl pupils. Within classroom settings, teachers were found to use gender as a strategy of control, encouraging their pupils to perform better or complete tasks more quickly through setting the girls against the boys. Abraham (1995) conducted research in the mid-1980s and similarly found that teachers' actions and attitudes reinforced gender differences. In addition to treating boy and girl pupils differently on the basis of their own gender stereotypes, Abrahams found that teachers did little to challenge gender stereotypical behaviour by the pupils themselves. Mac An Ghail (1994) also noted that the sexual harassment of girls by boys was not taken seriously by men teachers within the school he studied, whilst Measor and Sikes (1992) document cases of men teachers interacting with girl pupils in a sexualised manner. For example, making comments on the attractiveness of a girl pupil's appearance, placing their arms around the shoulders or waists of pupils and, in one extreme example, saying 'Hello, Erotica' to a pupil whose name was Erica.

This research evidence points to the number of ways teachers, largely unconsciously, convey gender-stereotyped messages to their pupils about what is normal, natural and acceptable in gender relations. Studies indicate that the gendered attitudes and actions of teachers are, though, cut across by any views they hold of the social class and ethnic backgrounds of their pupils. Mirza (1992) focused on the experiences of black British girls as they were preparing to leave school. She found that the white teachers of the girls held 'misgivings' about their aptitudes and capabilities, with many believing that black pupils were intellectually and culturally inferior. Mirza found that the black girls in her study were aware of their white teachers' negative attitudes toward them, and that, unsurprisingly, this affected the learning strategies they developed for themselves. Basit's (1997) study of British Asian Muslim girls in three schools showed that some of their teachers held stereotypical views about them, based on their gender, ethnicity and religion. In particular, teachers believed that the Muslim girls lacked self-esteem, that their parents gave them little freedom and held low expectations of their academic achievement or occupational attainment.

Studies undertaken in the 1980s showed that, despite the Sex Discrimination Act 1975, some schools continued to break the law by offering separate subjects on the curriculum according to gender. Delamont (1990), for example, reports that several schools in South Wales divided girls and boys into different craft subjects, along traditional gender lines. The introduction of the National Curriculum in English and Welsh schools from 1988 now largely prevents the degree of gender differences in option choices made by the 14-year-old pupils in the studies by Riddell (1992) and Abraham (1995). Nevertheless, evidence suggests that, because of the way it is delivered by teachers and the stereotypes within the textbooks and other materials used to teach it, the National Curriculum remains highly gendered. Mac An Ghaill's (1994) is one of the few studies of secondary schooling undertaken since the introduction of the National Curriculum and his conclusion was that the secondary school environment continues to 'systematically privilege' boys and men over girls and women, whilst Paechter's (1998) view is that girls remain 'second-class citizens' via their positioning as 'Other' within the education system.

Given the importance of friendship groups amongst teenage children, this review of the various ways secondary schooling acts to replicate and elaborate gender divisions would not be complete without examining the contribution pupils' own culture makes to this process. The first point to note here is that much more is known about the culture of boys' friendship groups than girls' friendship groups (Delamont 1990 – although see Hey 1997). Nevertheless, research has begun to reveal the complex ways pupils' own cultures are gendered. Riddell (1989, 1992), for example, shows how boy and girl pupils each challenged the authority of teachers through deliberate emphasis of stereotypical gender behaviour. For boys, this centred around the exaggeration of masculine behaviour based on violence, sexual bravado and the degrading of women. Girls manipulated codes of femininity as a means of contesting the authority of the school. As Riddell explains, girls were 'able to use the assumption that girls were quiet, helpless, emotional and very conscious of their appearance to avoid aspects of school that they found boring or difficult' (1989: 194). Generally, Riddell found that 'conservative, traditional' constructions of femininity were predominant amongst pupil cultures in the schools she studied, although a minority of 'radical' girls were actively engaged in forming new gender codes of behaviour, centred around the centrality of academic attainment with a view to future careers rather than only being a wife and mother (Riddell, 1992). Mac An Ghaill's (1994) research similarly shows that girl pupils are not passive in the face of masculine dominance within schools. In order to deal with, for example, the gendered hierarchy that operated within the school playground, Mac An Ghaill found that girls developed a variety of responses including co-operation, negotiation and outright resistance.

Post-16 education and training

Researchers have paid much less attention to the ways in which post-compulsory education and training acts to (re)produce gender divisions. However, Stanworth's (1983) study of 'A' level sixth formers confirmed that the various processes identified within primary and secondary schools are also present within post-compulsory education. In short, 'girls appear to exist on the periphery of classroom life; their marginalisation in the classroom, and the lesser attention they receive from teachers, results in girls appearing to others – and more importantly, to themselves – as less capable than they really are' (1983: 52).

Evidence suggests that, once young people are free to make choices about which subjects to pursue within their post-compulsory education and training, such choices are made along gender-stereotyped lines. This means that, at 'A' level, more boys than girls choose science subjects, and more girls than boys choose social science subjects. Vocational training is also chosen along gender lines, and as Cockburn (1987) showed for the Youth Training Scheme, young people choosing non-traditional training areas for their gender face great difficulties, both from their 'trainers' and from their fellow trainees. For girls and young women, these barriers are particularly significant since they hinder access to types of paid work which is regarded and financially rewarded as 'skilled'. A study of a postgraduate journalism course by Parry (1990) suggests that, even at higher levels of education and training, women face difficulties in areas which are non-traditional for their gender. Parry found that men teachers on the course displayed openly sexist attitudes, via their use of derogatory stereotypes and their views on the suitability of journalism as a career for women. Both men and women students on the course were conscious that, as a result, women students and femininity were marginalised.

I have reviewed a range of evidence, which shows that, irrespective of the level of education and training, a number of processes operate to prioritise boys and masculinity and marginalise girls and femininity. One measurable outcome of education, formal and informal, that pupils are exposed to are the qualifications they gain. The evidence that educational institutions largely unconsciously (re)produce gender inequalities to the detriment of girls appears overwhelming. Next, I consider the effects these processes have on the educational attainment of girls and women.

Participation and attainment in education and training

Statistical evidence on educational attainment suggests that, whilst children from economically advantaged backgrounds have higher achievements, educational performance is also differentiated by gender (in combination with ethnicity). Gender differences in attainment are present from within the first years of schooling. Earlier, it was noted that girls at primary school have long been recognised to perform better, in most subjects, than boys. This has been confirmed since the introduction of national testing of children (in England and Wales from 1988). Results indicate that, at age 7, girls achieve higher performances than boys, particularly in English. Boys are more likely to perform at the extremes, that is, by doing very well or doing very badly, especially in mathematics and science (Equal Opportunities Commission [EOC] 1996a).

Analyses of examination performance in English and Welsh schools by David, Weiner and Arnot (1997) found marked improvements by gender between the years 1984 and 1994. Girls now have higher rates of entry to GCSE exams than previously and their performance has improved markedly. In 1995–6, girls did much better than boys at GCSE, with 51 per cent gaining at least 5 grades A* – C compared to 41 per cent of boys (Office for National Statistics [ONS] 1998a). Girls have long done well in certain subjects compared to boys, particularly in English and modern foreign languages, and they continue to do so. However, in recent years, girls have also begun to outperform boys in science, mathematics and technology at GCSE level (EOC 1997a).

An element of gender stereotyping remains, with boys more likely than girls to take examinations in chemistry and economics and girls more likely than boys to take social studies (EOC 1996a). Since 1994, secondary school pupils have been able to follow a vocational course of study under the General National Vocational Qualification scheme (GNVQ), and gender stereotyping of subject choice is apparent here also (EOC 1997a). In fact, evidence suggests that as soon as pupils are able to choose which subjects they study, gender stereotyping re-establishes itself. This is linked to gender differences in occupational aspirations.

Young women aged 16 and 17, particularly ethnic minority young women, are more likely to be in education and training than young men of the same age. However, the type of qualification they study and the subjects they choose differ in important ways. Subjects studied and levels of entry at 'A' level, for example, showed marked differences by gender. Girls are more likely than boys to take and pass 'A' levels. In 1995–6, 23 per cent of girls aged 17–18 obtained two or more 'A' levels compared to 20 per cent of boys of the same age (ONS 1998a). However, boys had higher levels of performance than girls in nearly all subjects, in that they obtained higher grades (Department For Education [DFE] 1993). Subjects studied at 'A' level show marked differences by gender. More males than females take 'A' levels in mathematics and in most of the science subjects, including physics and chemistry. More females than males take subjects in humanities, arts and social studies (EOC 1996a), including English and modern foreign languages. Some subjects are becoming increasing male dominated, such as computer studies and economics (EOC 1997a). Young people following vocational education and training courses after the age of 16 are also highly likely to be studying for subjects traditionally linked with their gender. Young women follow courses in hairdressing and beauty, and caring services, whilst young men choose engineering, construction and science subjects (EOC 1996a). The pattern of gender stereotyping in the Youth Training Scheme documented by Cockburn (1987) largely continues to feature in its current form of Youth Training (EOC 1997a).

In higher education, young women have made significant advances in terms of their rates of participation. In 1992, for the first time, the proportion of women aged under 21 entering higher education overtook the proportion of men of the same age (DFE 1993). In 1995–6, there were more women than men students in higher education, whereas in 1970–1, there were twice as many men as women students (ONS 1998a). However, the subjects studied at undergraduate level differ by gender. In 1995–6, women were only 36 per cent of students in physical sciences, 24 per cent of students in mathematics and 15 per cent of students in engineering and technology. In education and languages, though, women represented over 70 per cent of all students and were over 50 per cent of students taking biological sciences, social sciences and creative arts (ONS 1998a).

Survey data show that amongst women and men of working age, more women (21 per cent) than men (16 per cent) hold no qualifications at all (ONS 1998a). The extent of this disparity varies, though, by age. The difference is greater amongst older women and men than it is amongst younger women and men. There are also important variations by ethnic origin. In spring 1997, 35 per cent of working-age women of Indian, Pakistani or Bangladeshi ethnic origin held no qualifications, compared to 15 per cent of women of black origin (ONS 1998a). Black women are more likely to hold an educational qualification than white women. Moreover, young people of African-Caribbean ethnic origin are more likely than young white people to remain in further education between the ages of 16 and 19. Their educational success has been achieved despite school-based racism, such as that experienced by the black young women in Mirza's (1992) study, and evidence that young people from ethnic minorities do not enjoy equal chances of gaining a place at university (Gillborn and Gipps 1996).

The issue of gender disparities in qualifications held by women and men in the workforce was addressed by Felstead, Goodwin and Green (1995). They analysed the Labour Force Survey and found that whilst 45 per cent of men in the workforce had a qualification, only 33 per cent of women did so. This difference in attainment was especially due to the fact that women in the workforce held fewer vocational qualifications than men in the workforce. In Wales and Scotland, the gap was found to be more pronounced than for the United Kingdom as a whole. Rather than reflecting women's lesser abilities, Felstead and his colleagues argue that the gender gap in attainment of qualifications, especially vocational qualifications, is a consequence of the greater barriers women face. Rees (1992) suggests that one of the barriers to women gaining qualifications is the way the 'training infrastructure' is geared toward training men, or women without any domestic responsibilities. Green (1993) similarly identifies family responsibilities and working part time as factors which significantly reduce the likelihood of obtaining training. Both these factors are especially significant for women workers (see Chapter 3).

A Paradox? Marginalised but successful

In this chapter, I have presented the findings of studies which reveal the various ways education and training, at all levels, act to (re)produce gender differences, with the effect that boys, men, masculine cultures and values predominate whilst girls, women and femininities are circumscribed and placed at the margins. Yet, statistical evidence shows that girls have significantly improved their educational attainment, measured by their greater participation and success in formal examinations, especially in national tests at age 7 and GCSEs at age 16, but also at 'A' levels and under-graduate degree level. As Darling and Glendinning.(1996) note, there is a tension between, on the one hand, the evidence on girls' improved academic performance and, on the other, research findings which show that girls are marginalised by the masculine domination of educational institutions.

There are a variety of possible explanations for the disparity between the research evidence on gender relations within education and training and the improved performance of girls. One is simply that the research evidence is dated. Much of the research conducted on the reproduction of gender inequalities within primary and secondary schools was undertaken in the 1980s and, therefore, might not adequately reflect gender relations characteristic of schools in the 1990s. Certainly it is true that, since the 1980s, a number of fundamental policy changes have transformed education. Especially important was the introduction of the National Curriculum in 1988, which introduced a core set of subjects including science, to be studied by all pupils at state schools in England and Wales. Also significant was the Technical and Vocational Education Initiative, which had the avoidance of gender stereotyping as one of its criteria. Alongside these changes, the 1980s was a decade of a series of initiatives especially designed to address the problem of gender inequalities within aspects of education. These included Girls Into Science and Technology, Gender Watch (see Measor and Sikes 1992 for review), and Women's Training Roadshows (see Delamont 1990). Concerns over the quality of education provided within state schools also led to the introduction of regular inspections by the Office for Standards in Education (OFSTED), which included assessing schools on gender equality criteria. All in all, over the last decade, the culture of education has become increasingly 'gender fair' (David, Weiner and Arnot 1997), and the studies reviewed in this chapter may not fully reflect this.

However, whilst there is a pressing need for new studies of primary education to update Clarricoates (1987a and b) and more studies to complement Mac An Ghaill's (1994) and Paechter's (1998) work on secondary schools, the available evidence cannot be dismissed out of hand. Social change occurs slowly and incrementally. Many of the processes contributing to the (re)production of gender inequalities within education and training are likely to be as prevalent and effective in the 1990s as they were previously. The physical structures of school buildings are probably the same, and the teachers teaching children via the formal and hidden curriculum are still living in a highly gendered world, where their own training continues to pay little attention to equal opportunity issues (Hill, Cole and Williams 1997). Given the funding difficulties faced by most schools, many of the teaching materials and textbooks and so on in use in the 1980s have survived through to the 1990s. Moreover, Delamont (1990) is critical of many of the initiatives designed to reduce gender stereotyping in education, arguing (amongst other things) that they have been only partial in their geographical coverage. They have been concentrated in England, rather than Wales or Scotland and have mainly taken place in urban rather than rural settings. Similarly, Measor and Sikes (1992), whilst acknowledging significant advances in the development of policies, argue that governments have been insufficiently committed to equal opportunities in education, with the result that many strategies for change have been experimental, ad hoc and heavily dependent upon the commitment of individuals. That there remain continuing gender inequalities within educational institutions is indicated by *The Gender Divide* (EOC and OFSTED 1996). Published jointly by the Equal Opportunities Commission and the Office for Standards in Education, this booklet is aimed at local education authorities and senior managers and governing bodies of schools. It summarises findings on gender relations in schools gained through official inspections, and highlights areas of concern. Importantly, it provides suggestions for ways schools can improve their equal treatment of girls and boys. Clearly, if gender inequality were not a continuing problem within education, neither the EOC nor OFSTED would have it as a key concern.

A second explanation for the disparity between the research evidence stressing the systematic disadvantages faced by girls and their improving academic performance is offered by Darling and Glendinning (1996). They suggest that studies which report that girls get less attention than boys from teachers are making an assumption that frequent pupil-teacher interaction is desirable. For Darling and Glendinning, less teacher-centred 'progressive' teaching methods (including project work and self-directed learning) may be particularly advantageous for girls. The dominance of boys in class inter-actions, coupled with more 'progressive' teaching strategies, may therefore positively benefit girls, through creating an educational environment where they can learn more effectively.

A quite different approach to explaining the paradox between evidence on girls' educational experiences and outcomes in terms of their attainment is taken by David, Weiner and Arnot (1997). First, they acknowledge that in the last decade or so the culture of education has been 'transformed' into one where equal opportunity issues are more central than previously. In a survey of schools in England, David, Weiner and Arnot found that most had developed their equal opportunity policies after 1988 (for data on Wales, see Salisbury 1996; for Scotland, see Turner, Riddell and Brown 1995). This is an important indication of a shift toward what David and her colleagues call a 'gender fair' culture of education, which may be reflected in the improved performance of girls in examinations. A second factor identified by David and her colleagues are changes in the curriculum, especially the introduction of the National Curriculum in England and Wales from 1988 onwards. This is argued to have counteracted previous tendencies toward gender stereotyped subject choice.

Despite acknowledging the positive and significant impact of the National Curriculum, David and her colleagues claim that it has only partially extended equal opportunities in education. They note that its effects are limited to the academic route that pupils follow within schools (GVNQ courses followed by some pupils from the age of 14 show a strong degree of gender stereotyping) and that it only makes a difference up until age 16. Post-compulsory education and training, both vocational (such as advanced GNVQs and City and Guilds qualifications) and academic ('A' levels and degrees) continue to show marked patterns of gender-stereotyped subject choice. Similarly, they argue that, although girls have significantly improved their levels of attainment, this too represents only a partial change. Importantly, girls are not outperforming boys overall. Girls are now performing equally as well as boys at GCSE level, and, in a few subjects, better than boys. But the evidence of improvement in the achievements of girls in post-compulsory education is more mixed. At 'A' level, there remains gender stereotyping in subject entry and in performance. In vocational qualifications, stereotyping is an 'enduring' feature, with boys doing better on the whole. David, Weiner and Arnot (1997) argue that recent 'moral panics' about the apparent 'under-achievement' of boys, which have grown up in the light of girls' improved performance, are mistaken in emphasis. Those expressing concern over boys' disadvantage often neglect to consider the outcomes of compulsory schooling, specifically the continuing disadvantages faced by girls and women in vocational and academic routes after the age of 16 and, ultimately, in paid work itself. In raising these issues, David and her colleagues are not denying that real changes have taken place in education over the last twenty years, as measured by a shift toward a 'gender fair' culture and by significant improvements in examination entry and performance of girls. Rather, they are seeking to caution against complacency, by pointing to areas of education where further improvements need to be made if girls and boys are to enjoy equal opportunities across all levels and types of education and training, and thereby eventually, in paid work.

Policy changes do not take place in a vacuum. Whatever the cumulative impact of the various policies and initiatives intended to remove disadvantages faced by girls and young women in education and training that have been introduced over the last twenty years, it is important to remember that wider social changes are also likely to have made a difference. In fact, David, Weiner and Arnot (1997) conclude that policy changes are not the main reason why girls have been more successful in education and training than previously. Instead, they point to changes in the labour market, and in family forms and the influence of feminism, arguing that social change in these areas may have encouraged girls to succeed in their secondary education. This wider social context, where women's status has altered significantly, may have encouraged girls and young women to place greater emphasis on their own careers, rather than assuming that their future lives are to be secured through marriage and reliance on a male breadwinner (David, Weiner and Arnot, 1997). This more broad-ranging explanation of why girls have begun to improve their educational attainment is supported by other writers. Sharpe (1994) studied a group of girls in the 1970s and found that their expectations for their future lives centred around, in descending order of importance, love, marriage, husbands, children and a stereotypically female job and patterns of work. A similar group of girls studied by Sharpe in the 1990s held quite different priorities; jobs and careers were their main concerns and, consequently, education was much more important to them. Baker and Jones (1992) used cross-national data to explore why it is that girls have improved their performance (it is a trend found in most western countries). Focusing on levels of attainment in mathematics, Baker and Jones showed that this was linked to the educational and occupational status of adult women in the various countries. Simply put, the more opportunities there were for women in a country, the better girls in that country performed (see also Walkerdine 1998). This finding suggests that girls' perceptions of their future opportunities as women in wider society strongly influences the 'choices' they make at school and their motivation to succeed. In the next chapter, the focus of attention moves to paid work, and here we will consider whether there are any grounds for the optimism young women are apparently showing, in terms of the opportunities and prospects they hope to enjoy in the labour market.

Chapter 3

In a man's world? Women and paid work

Sociologists routinely undertake historical comparisons as part of their effort to understand contemporary society. When analysing women's experiences of paid work, however, this has often proved difficult. Due to the longstanding subordination of women to men, and the interests and values of historians themselves, women have been 'hidden from history'. This means that women's involvement in the production and distribution of food, goods and services has been much less visible than men's. With this point in mind, I begin this chapter with a brief overview of the historical contexts which have shaped women's involvement in paid work. The main part of the chapter identifies the key features of women's paid work experiences in contemporary British society. I also look at explanations for change, and continuity, in women's experiences of paid work compared to men's.

Historical contexts

Prior to the Industrial Revolution, most households provided for their daily needs as a collective unit, via a range of activities centred around food, clothing and other basic necessities. These activities mainly took place within or around the home, and all members of a household were involved (although who did what varied according to gender and age – see, for example, Gittins 1993). The development of large-scale manufacturing centres under the factory system, as industrialisation progressed, meant that, gradually, a sharper separation emerged between home and work. This had particular consequences for the visibility and social valuing of women's paid and unpaid work. One manifestation of this marginalisation of women's contribution to productive activity is discussed by Rees (1992). She argues that, ever since its inception in 1801, the Census of Population systematically under-recorded women's economic activity, due to assumptions about what counted as paid work, where it took place and who did it. Some historians have compared work activities officially recorded by the Census-takers with what they originally wrote in their notebooks. Analyses have shown that, although women were described in the notebooks as under-taking a range of activities in return for money, this was not always categorised as 'paid work' by the Census-takers and so did not appear in the official Census records. 'Married women were often defined as just that: any involvement in paid work, either inside or outside the home, was not necessarily recorded' (Rees 1992: 14).

Interpretations of what counted as 'paid work' and 'a paid worker' have to be understood in the context of the prevailing gender ideologies which developed during the transition to a modern, industrial society. The ideology of 'separate spheres' firmly equated men and masculinity with paid work outside the home and women and femininity with unpaid work within the home – especially if they were married women. The pervasiveness of this gender ideology meant that, as the nineteenth century progressed, women's involvement in paid work came to be defined as a social problem. Alexander (1976) describes how women, particularly working-class women, became the touchstone of Victorian middle- and upper-class concerns about the 'dislocations' in society caused by its transformation from a pre-modern to a modern economy.

> Because of women's very special responsibility for society's well-being, it was the woman working outside the home who received most attention from parliamentary commissioners . . . emphasis was placed on the moral and spiritual degradation said to accompany female employment; especially the mingling of the sexes and the neglect of domestic comforts.
>
> (Alexander 1976: 61)

In the light of such concerns, women gradually became excluded from a range of types of paid work and their officially recorded rate of economic activity declined. According to Hunt (1988), the 1901 Census showed that only 13 per cent of married women were in paid employment, compared to 52 per cent of single women. By 1921, only 9 per cent of married women were working. As Hunt explains, many employers dismissed their female employees on marriage, although often women left of their own accord, under pressure from strong social norms which emphasised their new responsibilities as wife and mother (Hunt 1988: 5). Such practices continued, despite the Sex Disqualification (Removal) Act, 1919. This stated that neither sex nor marriage should disqualify anyone from public or civil appointments or the professions. Dyhouse (1989), however, describes the legislation as 'wholly ineffectual' and documents how, subsequent to the Act, a marriage bar operated in both public and private industry, and indeed continued to do so throughout the inter-war years (Hunt 1988). The Second World War saw women encouraged and later, obliged, to enter the formal world of work, especially in jobs that had traditionally been seen as 'men's jobs'.

However, as had occurred after the First World War, at the cessation of hostilities women were encouraged back into the home in order to leave such jobs for the returning servicemen (Braybon and Summerfield 1987).

The association of men rather than women with paid work was reflected in their representation in the labour force. From the beginning of the twentieth century, up until the 1960s, Census data indicate that women made up less than one-third of the total labour force (Hakim 1979). Particularly from the 1960s onwards, women's representation in the labour force began to rise, reaching 47 per cent of all employees in 1997 (*Labour Market Trends* January 1998). Women's increased representation in the labour force has taken place against a background of significant shifts in the formal promotion of equality with men. The Equal Pay Act, 1970 (and its 1984 amendment) requires employers to give 'equal treatment' for pay, terms and conditions of employment to men and women working in the same plant, who are employed on 'like work' (i.e. 'of the same or broadly similar nature'), or who are employed on work which, though different, has been given an 'equal value' under a job evaluation scheme (Snell 1986). The 1975 *Sex Discrimination Act* made it illegal to discriminate on the grounds of sex in employment, education and the provision of services. The Equal Opportunities Commission was set up to oversee the workings of the Act. Also passed in 1975 was the Employment Protection Act, which made it unlawful to dismiss a woman due to pregnancy. It established the right to maternity leave, maternity pay and the right to return to the job. In 1986, the Sex Discrimination Act was amended so that workplaces of five or less employees were no longer exempt from the terms of the legislation.

Using the near equal representation of women with men in the labour force and the fact that women have had formal equality with men in paid work for twenty years or so as measures, one might be tempted to conclude that the optimism about their future career prospects expressed by the girls in Sharpe's study (1994) is justified (see Chapter 2). However, my argument in this chapter is that the statistics on women's improved representation in the labour force in fact mask a whole series of ways in which experiences of paid work remain highly gendered, and that despite the legislation, women continue to face inequality and discrimination. Moreover, although the ideology of separate spheres may have waned, evidence presented in this chapter suggests that women's involvement in and experiences of paid work remain heavily influenced by their assumed and actual responsibility for unpaid work in the home.

Men's work and women's work in the 1990s

Despite representing nearly half of all employees, women's relationship to and experience of paid work continue to be very different from men's. First, women and men participate in different forms of paid work and to differing extents. Second, women and men work to differing extents in certain industries and certain occupations. Third, within an occupational hierarchy, women and men tend to work at different levels. Fourth, women and men have differing patterns of participation in paid work over their life courses, with women's activities being especially influenced by the presence and age of dependent children. Finally, women and men continue to receive contrasting financial rewards for the paid work they do, with women earning significantly less than men, on average. In all these ways, paid work is both gendered (an institution marked by gender difference), and gendering (an activity through which masculinities and femininities are actively created and constituted).

Forms of paid work

There are a number of forms of paid work. Crompton (1997) makes a twofold distinction between the 'standard' form of paid work (that is, full-time continuous employment from first entry into the labour market until withdrawal at the official retirement age), and 'non-standard' forms. Included here are part-time work, self-employment, temporary and casual paid work, and homeworking. In the last few decades, the standard form of paid work has been in decline and non-standard forms have proliferated. Statistical evidence shows that participation in both standard and non-standard forms of employment varies by gender. Full-time paid work is especially associated with men. In 1997, of all those working full time, 67 per cent were men and 33 per cent were women. Part-time paid work is especially associated with women. In 1997, of all those working part time, 81 per cent were women and 19 per cent were men (Sly, Thair and Risdon 1998). Part-time work is a crucial element of women's paid work experiences and is discussed in more detail shortly. Self-employment is one of only a few forms of non-standard paid work especially associated with men. In 1995, of all self-employed people of working age, 77 per cent were men and 23 per cent were women (Sly 1996). In contrast to the autonomy, prestige and direct financial rewards associated with self-employment, homeworking is a form of non-standard paid work commonly associated with extremely poor terms and conditions and very low rates of pay (Felstead and Jewson 1996). In 1996, 70 per cent of people working at home were women (EOC 1997b).

Industries and occupations

The industries and occupations within which women and men work also tend to be associated more with one gender than the other. Hakim (1979) describes this as 'horizontal segregation' of paid work by gender. For example, in 1997, service sector industries accounted for 86 per cent of employed women, compared with 59 per cent of employed men. Women workers were particularly predominant within the health (81 per cent women), education (69 per cent women) and hotels and restaurants (59 per cent) categories of the service industries. Within industry sectors, women and men also tend to work in different groups of occupations, with women clustered into three in particular. These are: clerical and secretarial, personal services (nursing, catering, hairdressing) and sales. In 1997, 53 per cent of women in employment worked in these three occupational groupings compared to 19 per cent of men. The concentration of women within particular types of paid work is even more advanced at the level of occupation. In 1997, women represented 87 per cent of nursing staff, 75 per cent of clerks and secretaries and 63 per cent of teaching staff. In contrast, women were only 10 per cent of science and engineering professionals, 8.5 per cent of those in skilled craft occupations, and 13 per cent of protective services staff such as police and fire officers (Sly, Thair and Risdon 1998).

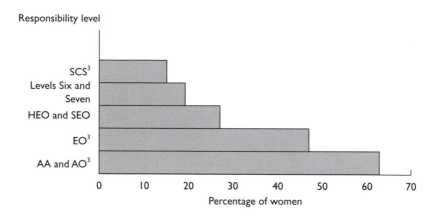

Figure 3.1 Women as a percentage of civil servants,[1] by responsibility level,[2] 1997

Notes
1   Non-industrial home civil servants, including staff of executive agencies such as the Child Support Agency.
2   Responsibility levels are an approximate equivalent to the former 'grades' within the Civil Service and are based on considerations of salary and other indicators.
3   AA and AO are Administrative Assistant and Administrative Officer, representing the lowest levels of responsibility. EO is Executive Officer. HEO and SEO are Higher Executive Officer and Senior Executive Officer. SCS is Senior Civil Service, including Permanent Secretaries, Chief Executives of executive agencies and senior diplomatic personnel. This represents the highest level of responsibility.
Source: Adapted from GSS (1988), Figure 20

Occupational hierarchies

The tendency for women and men to hold contrasting positions in the hierarchy of an occupation, with women at the bottom and men at the top, is called 'vertical segregation' (Hakim 1979). For example, in 1993, even though women represented 81 per cent of all teachers in nursery and primary schools, they represented only 50 per cent of head teachers (COI 1996). The higher the level of education, the more women's representation decreases. In 1994–5, women were 28 per cent of full-time academic staff in universities and higher education colleges and 7 per cent of full-time professors (EOC 1997c). Figure 3.1 shows that, although women predominate in the lower levels of the Civil Service, their representation decreases at the higher levels. In 1997, 51 per cent of Civil Service staff were women, but they were only 15 per cent of staff at the Senior Civil Servant level (Government Statistical Service [GSS] 1998). There have been improvements in women's representation at the higher levels over the last two decades. For example, in 1984 there were no women Permanent Secretaries (the highest level of responsibility in the Civil Service). In 1996, there were three (COI 1996).

Patterns of participation

Women's participation in paid work is fundamentally related to their stage in the family life course, particularly whether or not they have children and the age of those children (Table 3.1). Women of working age without any dependent children are the most likely to be economically active and the most likely to be working full time. Women of working age with a pre-school-age child are the most likely to be economically inactive and the least likely to work full time. As the age of the youngest dependent child

Table 3.1 Economic activity status of women aged 16–59 by age of youngest dependent child, spring 1997, UK

Economic activity status	Age of youngest dependent child			No. of dependent children	All women
	0–4	5–10	11–15		
Working full-time	18	23	34	48	38
Working part-time	33	43	40	24	29
Unemployed	4	4	4	4	4
Economically inactive	45	29	22	25	29

Source: ONS (1998a), adapted from Table 4.12

increases, so does women's participation in both full-time and part-time work (ONS 1998a). The participation of men in paid work is much less related to their parental status, or stage in their family's life course. Unlike women, men tend to be continuously engaged in full-time paid work throughout their adult lives, with interruptions caused by unemployment and ill health rather than the presence or age of dependent children. In 1995, 94 per cent of men with children aged 4 and under were economically active compared to 54 per cent of women with children of the same age (EOC 1997d). The distinctive profile of women's participation in paid work (with periods of complete withdrawal and engagement in part-time work associated with the presence of dependent children) also means that their lifetime earnings are much less than men's, as is their access to pension entitlements in retirement (EOC 1997e).

Pay

Despite the Equal Pay Act, 1970 and its 1984 amendment, women continue to earn less than men. For example, women working full time earn 72 per cent of men's average full-time weekly earnings (EOC 1996b). The gap in pay between women and men is the result of a number of factors. Amongst full-time employees, men tend to work longer hours than women and are more likely to benefit from overtime and similar payments. The major reason for the gap in pay, however, is the fact that women and men tend to be employed in different forms of paid work, in different industries and in different occupations; and, within the same occupation, at different levels. Invariably, the paid work that men do accrues higher wages and salaries than that which women do (EOC, 1996b). As Crompton (1997) explains, 'This is because jobs where there are many (or only) women tend to be poorly paid, often because they are considered to be 'women's jobs', and women's skills are undervalued' (1997: 42).

Siltanen (1994a, 1994b) makes a distinction between 'full' and 'component' wage jobs. Full wage jobs enable individuals solely to support an independent household, and any members of it who are not in paid employment. Component wage jobs enable individuals to contribute to the financial income of households, but where earnings are not enough to maintain it single-handedly. Siltanen analysed data from the New Earnings Survey and found that 50 per cent of women in full-time employment earned 'component' wages, compared to 21 per cent of men in full-time employment (1994b).

Women's work: part-time paid work

As a non-standard form of paid work, part-time work can be said to be 'feminine': most part-time workers are women (81 per cent in 1997) and, of all women employees, 44 per cent work part time rather than full time (Sly, Thair and Risdon 1998). The increased representation of women in the labour force after the 1960s is especially accounted for by their taking up of part-time rather than full-time jobs. The changed patterns of participation in paid work amongst married women and women with dependent children are also largely attributable to part-time work. For a number of reasons, then, an examination of the characteristics of part-time work is crucial if a full understanding of women's paid work experiences in contemporary Britain is to be reached.

In Britain, the significance of the distinction between full-time jobs and part-time jobs lies not in the number of hours worked, but rather in the vastly differing terms, conditions and overall status associated with each form of employment. In almost every respect, part-time workers tend to be in a much less advantageous position than full-time workers. In terms of rates of pay, part-time workers earn less per hour (£5.44) than male full-time employees (£9.39) and female full-time employees (£7.50) (EOC 1996b). Part-time workers often face poorer terms and conditions of employment (Burchell, Dale and Joshi 1997; Fagan and O'Reilly 1998; Rubery, Horrell and Burchell 1994). They may be less likely than full timers to have access to overtime payments and premium payments related to working unsocial hours. They may be less likely to enjoy benefits such as subsidised meals, and have more limited access to membership of sick pay schemes and occupational pension schemes. In 1996, while 75 per cent of men and 65 per cent of women who worked full time were in a personal or occupational pension scheme, just 33 per cent of women who worked part time were in such a scheme (ONS 1998b). Only in 1995 did certain categories of part-time worker become eligible for employment rights enjoyed by full-time workers. Previously, employees who worked less than eight hours, and those who worked between eight and sixteen hours a week, but who had not worked for the same employer for five years, did not have rights to claim unfair dismissal, to receive notice of dismissal, to receive statutory redundancy pay or to maternity leave (*Employment Gazette* 1995: 43). Part-time workers also have more limited prospects for training and promotion than full-time workers (Rubery, Horrell and Burchell 1994).

The importance of part-time working for economically active women with dependent children has already been noted. Evidence suggests that many women who return to paid work on a part-time basis after having a child experience downward occupational mobility. The *Women and Employment Survey* found that 45 per cent of those women who returned to part-time paid work returned to a lower-level occupation, compared with 19 per cent of those who returned full time (Martin and Roberts 1984). More recent evidence is provided by McRae (1991), who similarly found that women who returned to work full time were less likely to experience downward occupational mobility than women who returned on a part-time basis.

However, women in professional occupations who returned part time were less likely to experience a downward move (9 per cent) than those who were previously managers or administrators (29 per cent) or who were in clerical and secretarial jobs (26 per cent). As noted by Burchell, Dale and Joshi (1997: 222), 'From this evidence, it would appear that women may have been less likely to experience downward occupational mobility following childbirth than ten years earlier (Martin and Roberts 1984), but that, at the least, for some occupational groups, a return to part-time work still results in a fall in occupational status.'

Part-time work is 'women's work'. Most part-time workers are women and most part-time jobs are in lower-paid occupations and industries, especially in the service sector. In personal service occupations and sales occupations, for example, there are more part-time jobs than full-time jobs and these are all occupations with a majority of women employees (Sly, Thair and Risdon 1998). The reasons why part-time work is women's work are complex, but especially important factors are the 'needs' of employers and the 'needs' of women, especially those with dependent children. For employers, hiring workers on a part-time basis rather than a full-time basis, allows them 'flexibility'. Part-time workers are cheaper to employ and until recently held fewer employment rights, characteristics attractive to employers striving to succeed in a highly competitive economy. However, the concern of employers to attain a flexible workforce does not fully explain why part-time jobs are created. Smith, Fagan and Rubery (1998) argue that the type of flexibility adopted by firms is gendered. In other words, employers choose particular forms of flexible working arrangements according to whether their current or future workforce is predominantly male or female. When seeking flexibility in women's jobs, employers follow a part-time strategy. When seeking flexibility in men's occupations, other strategies are used, including overtime and shift work. As Beechey and Perkins (1987) argued, employers are not gender-blind in their recruitment practices or in their valuing and rewarding of the paid work they offer to employees, including the form in which it is offered. The creation of jobs as full-time or part-time is very closely related to conceptions employers hold about gender. Jobs which are regarded as low grade, low skilled, with no opportunities for advancement and which are low paid, are 'women's jobs' and so flexibility is achieved through the part-time route rather than other available strategies (Smith, Fagan and Rubery 1998).

Despite the many disadvantages of part-time paid work, survey data show that women who work part-time express a preference for this form of economic activity. In 1997, 78 per cent of women who worked part-time said that they did not want a full-time job, compared to 28 per cent of men who worked part-time. The proportion of women who said they did not want a full-time job was higher amongst those with children, and amongst those with younger children compared to those with older children (Sly, Thair and

Risdon 1998). A study by Rubery, Horrell and Burchell (1994) found that women part-time workers were more likely to say that they were 'satisfied' with their jobs than women full-time workers (see also Burchell, Dale and Joshi 1997). Given that evidence suggests women part-time workers express both a preference for and satisfaction with this form of employment, despite its many disadvantages, one might be tempted to conclude that part-time work represents an ideal compromise between employers' needs on the one hand and women's needs on the other. However, as Crompton (1997) cautions, women's 'needs', preferences and apparent satisfaction have to be placed within a broader context.

> We have to remember, however, that women's 'preferences' will be shaped by their available options, and it has often been pointed out that, as Britain has the lowest level of state (national or local) provision of childcare in Europe, then it is very likely that women with caring responsibilities will have a 'preference' for part-time work.
>
> (Crompton 1997: 35)

Moreover, Crompton argues that expressions of satisfaction amongst women part-timers may reflect their valuing of the convenience of the hours they work, rather than their liking for the job itself or their belief that their job is appropriate to their skills and qualifications.

Diversity and difference

So far in this chapter, I have described the paid employment experiences of women as if 'women' were a unitary category. My aim has been to provide an overview of the generality of women's experiences compared to men's. However, it is equally important to examine the way experiences of paid work may vary according to social characteristics in addition to gender. Women are not a unitary category, but face contrasting sets of opportunities and disadvantages. Age, ethnicity, social class and location are especially significant bases of diversity and difference amongst women, alongside those of marital and parental status. The impact of the latter on economic activity rates and forms of paid work has already been noted, via the discussion of the importance of the presence and age of dependent children. In the 1990s, marital status continues to act as a differentiator of women's paid work experiences, although not necessarily in a way one might expect. Data from the 1997 Labour Force Survey showed that married women have higher rates of economic activity than non-married women. This difference is mainly due to non-married women being younger (and therefore participating in full-time education rather than paid work), or being lone mothers or older women, both of whom have relatively low levels of economic activity (Sly, Thair and Risdon 1998). In 1994–6, lone mothers with dependent children were less likely than married women with dependent children to be working either part time (25 per cent compared to 42 per cent) or full time (16 per cent compared to 24 per cent) (ONS 1998b). This is a reflection of the greater difficulty lone mothers' face in accessing affordable childcare (Ford 1998; see also Chapter 4).

Age

Age is a complex source of diversity, involving variations in stage of life course and cohort experiences, as well as restrictions arising from numerical age (which might mean that a person is too 'young' or too 'old' to do a particular job). Women aged 16–19 and those aged 50–64 have lower rates of economic activity (60 per cent and 52 per cent) than other women aged between 16 and 65 (over 70 per cent) (EOC 1997f). The reasons for this reflect their contrasting positions in the life course. The economic activity rate for women aged 16–19, and for women in their early twenties, is lower (and has been declining in the 1990s) because of their (increasing) participation in further and higher education. The economic activity rate for women aged 50–64 is lower because women of this age group are either approaching the retirement age (of 60) or have actually retired. In Walby's (1997) recent analysis, however, the most important aspect of age differentiation between women arises from their contrasting cohort memberships. Older women are greatly disadvantaged in paid work compared to contemporary young women, due to the restricted education and employment opportunities they had earlier in their lives. In Walby's terms, contemporary women may appear to face the same 'gendered opportunity structures' in paid work, but their age and the cohort experiences this signifies means that their 'realistic range of options' is quite different (1997: 11). As noted in the previous chapter, recent cohorts of young women have significantly improved their attainment of educational qualifications and extended their participation in further and higher education, both vocational and academic. This means that, compared to older women, younger women hold more educational qualifications, at a higher level and across a broader range. Because of the importance of educational qualifications as a passport to higher-status and well rewarded paid work, this means that younger women are much more advantageously placed in the labour market than older women are. Using data from the 1991 Census, Walby shows that younger women are much more likely than older women to be in managerial and professional jobs and are more likely to work full time than part time. In contrast, older women predominated in lower occupational grades, including cleaners and shop assistants and, if working in such lower-level jobs, were very likely to be working on a part-time basis (Walby 1997: 56–7). In short, in contemporary Britain, there are significant contrasts in the paid work experiences of women according to their age: 'It is largely younger women who have gained educational qualifications, [and] who are entering higher level jobs, while older women are typically confined to the less well-remunerated and less secure part-time jobs' (Walby 1997: 26).

Ethnicity

Women's experiences of paid work varies greatly by their ethnicity. Census data show that in 1991, amongst women of working age, white women had higher rates of economic activity (71 per cent) than ethnic minority women (58 per cent). However, there were significant differences in activity rates according to particular ethnic minority groups. Black-Caribbean women had the highest rate of economic activity (75 per cent), whilst Pakistani and Bangladeshi women had the lowest rates (29 per cent and 22 per cent) of all ethnic groups. Conversely, Pakistani and Bangladeshi women had relatively high rates of economic inactivity due especially to their looking after a home or family on a full-time basis (Owen 1994: 51–2). Amongst women with dependent children, economic activity rates for ethnic minority women are generally lower than that for whites, and especially so amongst women of Pakistani or Bangladeshi origin (EOC 1997d).

The forms of paid work women are involved in also varies by ethnicity. Census data for 1991 show that the proportion of white women employees who work part-time (37 per cent) is much higher than for ethnic minority women employees (22 per cent). Conversely, working women from minority ethnic groups were more likely than white working women to be employed full-time (70 per cent compared to 57 per cent). In particular, Black-Caribbean women were the most likely to be full-time employees (77 per cent) of any ethnic group (Owen 1994: 84).

Ethnic minority women also experience different patterns of segregation in paid work compared to white women. Owen's (1994) analysis of the Labour Force Survey showed that, whilst three-quarters of white women work in the service sector, this sector is even more important for black-Caribbean women. For Chinese women, the distribution industry (which includes retail and catering) is important, whilst the manufacturing sector is important for women of Pakistani and Indian ethnicities. At the level of occupation, 'clerical and secretarial' is the single largest category for most ethnic groups, including whites. Non-manual occupations of a higher status, including managers and professionals, tended to account for a larger share of employment for women from ethnic minority groups than for white women (Owen 1994: 82).

Differences in forms of paid work and variations in industrial and occupational locations mean that some ethnic minority women may face poorer conditions of employment. Bhavnani (1994) argues that black women are more likely than white women to have poor working conditions, arising from shift working in manufacturing and catering, for example. Black women are also overrepresented in smaller firms, and thereby enjoy fewer fringe benefits and rely more heavily on basic statutory rights.

Evidence from the Census and from the Labour Force Survey, as well as studies by sociologists such as Phizacklea (1990), suggest the range of ways women's experiences of paid work vary by their ethnicity. As Walby (1997) explains, these differences result from a number of factors, including racism. Also important, however, are the contrasts in the age structure between whites and other ethnic groups, and differences in patterns of geographical residence. When interpreting data on ethnic variations in experiences of paid work, these factors need to be borne in mind. For example, data from the Labour Force Survey show that black women who work full-time have higher earnings on average than white women who work full-time. However, this may be due to a number of factors. First, the age profile on the black population is younger than that of the white population, and these relatively well paid black women tend to be younger women. Second, these younger black women, like other younger women, are likely to be better qualified. Third, their higher earnings may be linked to geographical location; a higher proportion of black women work in London, where average earnings are highest (EOC 1996b).

Social class

Sociologists tend to use occupation as a marker for a person's socio-economic position, as categorised under the *Standard Occupational Classification* (Office of Population Census and Surveys [OPCS] 1991). There are numerous problems when using this occupational-based scheme to classify a women's class position (Abbott and Sapsford 1987), but these cannot concern us here. Using this scheme, women are crowded into a few socio-economic categories, particularly 'skilled non-manual' (via their jobs as secretaries and word processor operators, for example), whereas men are more evenly spread. Arising from cohort differences in the possession of higher-level educational qualifications, and their related entry into higher level jobs, Walby (1997) argues that younger women are now more likely to be in the upper socio-economic groups than older women. Moreover, women in higher socio-economic groups are more likely to be in employment and are more likely to be employed on a full-time rather than a part-time basis. If there are dependent children, women in the higher socio-economic groups seem more able to pay for childcare and thereby sustain their work histories. In short, Walby's argument is that it is women with higher levels of education and qualifications who have the highest rates of economic activity. It is these same women who tend to be engaged in higher- rather than lower-level occupations, and it is these women who are best placed to sustain their work histories, through paying for full-time childcare, if they have dependent children (Walby 1997: 61).

Sexuality

Women's experiences of paid work are heavily structured by their sexuality, as the widespread incidence of workplace sexual harassment shows (see pages 50–51). In addition, Dunne's (1997) research shows that lesbian women have to negotiate their working lives within workplace cultures which are overwhelmingly heterosexist and often discriminatory against homosexuals. At the same time, their sexuality places demands upon them to be self-supporting economically throughout their adult lives.

Geographical location

The rate of economic activity of women aged 16 and over varies between the various countries of Britain, being lower in Scotland (52 per cent), and especially in Wales (48 per cent), than in England (54 per cent) (EOC 1997f). This is a reflection of contrasting industrial histories and variations in contemporary economic conditions, factors which also affect rates of part-time work and average earnings within the countries of Britain. Thus, the lower rate of women's economic activity in Wales, their higher rates of part-time work and their lower average earnings (EOC 1996b, 1997b) are consequences of the historically limited opportunities for women's employment in an economy once dominated by heavy industries, such as steel and mining (Rees 1994; Winckler 1987) and the low-wage nature of the contemporary Welsh economy.

Evidence on diversity and difference in experiences of paid work emphasises that women are not uniformly disadvantaged. Gender interacts with age, ethnicity, class, sexuality, the possession of educational qualifications, and geographical location (amongst other social characteristics) to position women differently in the structure of paid work, making some women (young, white, English) less disadvantaged than others (old, black, unqualified).

Changes . . .

It is undeniable that, during the course of the twentieth century, improvements have occurred in women's positioning in the structure of paid work: inequality has reduced and women now are better placed as paid workers than previously. Women's economic activity rate has increased from 43 per cent in 1951 (Hakim 1979), to 56 per cent in 1971, to 71 per cent in 1997 (ONS 1998a).

Occupational segregation, both vertical and horizontal, has decreased since the 1970s. Of course, the types and numbers of jobs available to both women and men have changed considerably over the last few decades, with some occupations declining and others expanding. Nevertheless, women have made real advances. Between 1975 and 1994, the proportion of economically active women who were professionals, employers and managers increased from 5 per cent to 13 per cent (Walby 1997: 35). From 1981 to 1996, the number of women employed in all occupations increased, with the exception of craft and skilled manual and plant and machine operatives (EOC 1997b). Walby's analysis of Census data shows that between 1981 and 1991, women significantly increased their representation in non-manual occupations, including a 72 per cent increase in women in the 'professional and related science, engineering and technology' category (Walby 1997: 36–7).

Women's patterns of participation in paid work have also been changing. Earlier this century women commonly gave up paid work on marriage. By the 1960s, women more commonly stopped working when they had their first child and stayed out of the labour force until their youngest child was at school. In recent years, more women are returning to work in between the births of their children (Main 1988; Martin and Roberts 1984). There has been a reduction in the amount of time women take out of paid work due to having children. An analysis by Joshi shows that women born in 1946 took on average 5.5 years out of employment after the birth of their first child, whereas women born in 1958 took 2.2 years out. However, this varied by level of education, occupation and age at birth of first child (*Labour Market Trends* 1998: 87). Overall, women with dependent children were more likely to be working in the 1990s than they were in the 1970s. In 1977–9, 52 per cent of married and cohabiting women with children under 16 were working compared to 66 per cent in 1994–6 (ONS 1998b). The increase in economic activity has been especially sharp amongst women with children under 4 years old. In 1973, 27 per cent of women with a pre-school child were economically active (Walby 1997: 50). By 1997, well over half (55 per cent) of mothers with a child under 4 were economically active (ONS 1998a). In contrast to the first half of this century, when women left paid work in their twenties as a consequence of their marriage and often never returned, contemporary young women are likely to be more or less continuously involved in paid work throughout their lives.

Inequalities in pay have also reduced since the 1970s. In 1970, five years before the implementation of the Equal Pay Act, women full-time employees earned 63 per cent of the hourly pay earned by men full-time employees. Between 1970 and 1977, the hourly pay gap reduced by 11 per cent, and between 1977 and 1995, by a further 6 per cent (Walby 1997: 31). Women full-time employees now earn 80 per cent of the hourly pay earned by men full-time employees (EOC 1996b). Over a period of 25 years, therefore, the gender gap in hourly pay for full-time employees has reduced from 37 per cent to 20 per cent.

. . . And why

The changes in women's experiences of paid work, described above, are the result of a complex intermeshing of a number of factors, each of comparable importance to the other.

First, changes in women's experiences of paid work have been one element of much broader processes of *economic change* in the second half of the twentieth century, which have also affected men. The British economy has shifted away from a primary emphasis on heavy industry and manufacturing (where men were the bulk of the employees) towards service sector industries (where women predominate). Under pressures from an increasingly competitive global economy, and with encouragement from Conservative political policies from 1979 onwards, forms of employment have themselves become restructured. In order for employers to achieve maximum 'flexibility' in their businesses, forms of employment have increasingly shifted from 'standard' (full-time and 'masculine') to 'non-standard' forms (especially part-time and 'feminine').

Second, *political processes* have transformed women's legal rights and opportunities in paid work. Under pressure from feminist campaigners, and in the context of Britain's membership of the European Union, a legal framework has been introduced which is intended to prevent discrimination against women workers. Key pieces of legislation include the Equal Pay Act, 1970 and the Sex Discrimination Act, 1975, with strengthening of the equal pay provision and extensions to the rights of part-time workers coming about under legal pressure from the European Union (Walby 1997: 38–9). Since the 1970s, employers, trades unions and other organisations have developed equal opportunity policies, and initiatives such as Opportunity 2000 have had high profile support from government ministers and leaders of the business community. As Walby concludes, 'Equal Opportunities has become a 'normal' discourse; it has moved from being a feminist issue to one which has entered the mainstream' (1997: 46). This 'diffusion' of the feminist principle of equality into society's institutions and organisations is discussed further in Chapter 9.

A third reason why women's experiences of paid employment have changed is because *women* themselves have changed. For a number of reasons, including the economic and political changes previously described, women have shifted their focus away from a primary and wholesale orientation to family and domestic life. Increasingly, women have prioritised their working lives, and have become economically active throughout their adult years. Women's improved level and range of educational qualifications has facilitated this shift, as has the widespread availability of reliable contraception, which enables women to control their fertility, and the increased availability of childcare. Changes in women's orientations toward paid work and away from family and domestic life are closely bound up with the restructuring of family and domestic life itself. As described in Chapter 5, marriage rates have fallen, divorce rates have risen, fewer people are choosing to have children, family size is declining, and women are having their first babies later. These trends form part of a broader set of social, political and economic changes affecting gender relations and which together have contributed to women's improving position in the structure of paid work.

Continuities

The measures of representation in the labour force, occupational segregation, patterns of participation and pay together suggest that women's position and status within paid work has significantly improved over the past 25 years. However, other measures suggest that such changes, albeit significant, are only partial.

While women have increased their representation in the labour force and are more likely to be economically active throughout their adult lives, these changes have largely been facilitated through the growth of part-time forms of paid work. Walby has calculated that between 1971 and 1995, the proportion of women employees working full-time rose by only 3 per cent, compared to a growth in women employees working part-time of 75 per cent (Walby 1997: 31). In 1997, 44 per cent of women in employment worked part-time, compared to 8 per cent of men in employment (Sly, Thair and Risdon 1998). As shown in Table 3.1 (p. 37), part-time work is the major form of economic activity for women with dependent children. Some shifts in vertical and horizontal segregation have occurred, but 'significant sex segregation in employment still remains' (Walby 1997: 37). This is indicated by the fact that, in 1996, most employed women were in occupations where at least 60 per cent of their fellow workers were women. Furthermore, 65 per cent of employed men worked in occupations where at least 60 per cent of their colleagues were men (EOC 1997f). Women may have increased their representation in higher-level jobs and in jobs non-traditional for their gender, but from very low bases. For example, the increase of 72 per cent of women working in the 'professional and related in science, engineering and technology' category between 1981 and 1991 is undeniably large, but women still only represented 14 per cent of all persons in that category in 1991 (Walby 1997: 36).

Improvements in pay inequalities between women and men have taken place, although the gender gap in hourly pay of full-time employees remains at 20 per cent. Yet, the gap is even greater when other measures are used. Female full-time employees earn only 72 per cent of the weekly earnings of male full-time employees (EOC 1996b). The disparity between hourly earnings of women working part-time compared with men working full time is even greater. In 1996, while male full-time employees on average earned

£9.39 per hour, female part-time employees earned on average £5.44 per hour. This gender gap of nearly 50 per cent has remained virtually the same since the 1970s. Part-time women workers have not, therefore, enjoyed reductions in pay inequalities to the same extent as female full-time workers (EOC 1996b).

Clearly, although women represent almost half of all employees, this near-equality in representation masks a range of fundamental and enduring divisions between women and men in paid work. Women's and men's experiences of paid work remain substantially different, and women remain consistently and systematically disadvantaged compared to men. Theories which aim to account for women's continued disadvantage in paid work are considered next.

Explaining gender inequalities in paid work

After the resurgence of second-wave feminism in the 1960s and 1970s, the experiences of women in paid work increasingly began to be recognised as a problem to be explained, rather than merely a natural, inevitable and inconsequential aspect of difference between women and men. A number of theories seeking to explain the various inequalities between women and men have subsequently developed, each emphasising different factors as especially important and each having some value in enhancing understanding of why experiences of paid work are gendered. Accessible, detailed accounts of the various theoretical approaches, accompanied by pointed critiques of their shortcomings, can be found in Walby (1990), Rees (1992) and especially Crompton and Sanderson (1990). More recently, Crompton (1997) has drawn a useful distinction between those theories which emphasise *constraint* (via structures and institutions, including the economic system, the state and widespread masculine discriminatory practices) and those theories which emphasise *choice* (through a focus on orientations, preferences and the individual characteristics of women and men as paid workers).

Structural constraints

Marxist-influenced approaches represent one grouping of theories which emphasise the importance of structural constraints. Such theories propose that women's disadvantaged position in paid work meets the 'needs' of the capitalist economic system. For example, women's disadvantaged position has been argued to be an element in the 'deskilling' of the labour force (Braverman, 1974), in increasing the 'flexibility' of the labour force (Barron and Norris 1976; Bruegel 1979) and as a strategy of controlling the labour force (Edwards, Gordon and Reich 1975) through diluting its homogeneity and thereby fragmenting its class consciousness and collective power.

Recently, the most influential grouping of constraints theories have been dual-systems theories, so-called because they emphasise two systems in their explanations of women's disadvantage: capitalism and patriarchy. In other words, dual-systems theories incorporate arguments from Marxist theories (that the capitalist economy and employers benefit from women's inferior status) and feminist theories which emphasise the benefits which accrue to men as a dominant social grouping (see also Chapter 1). Hartmann (1979) argues that women's disadvantaged position in paid work, whilst benefiting capitalist employers, also benefits men as a social grouping. Following the mass expansion of wage labour that accompanied industrialisation, and the sharper separation of home and work, men had to develop new mechanisms for controlling women and sustaining their dominance over them. For Hartmann, the primary mechanism of masculine control and domination is the gender segregation of types and forms of paid work, a segregation principally achieved through organised men in trade unions with the support of the capitalist state. The resulting location of women in low-valued and therefore low-waged jobs, and men in higher-valued and therefore well paid jobs, underpins the unequal power relations between the genders. Women's lower wages encourage their dependence on men and their subordinate position is subsequently reflected in the disproportionate responsibility they hold for unpaid domestic work. In Hartmann's analysis, a 'vicious circle' is created, whereby responsibility for unpaid domestic work in turn greatly constrains women's position in paid work.

Walby (1990) argues that the forms and types of paid work women tend to be found in are the result of long-term conflicts between capitalist employers and men as a dominant group. Both groupings have an interest in exploiting women's labour and have had to reach compromises that allow for their often conflicting demands to be met. Over time, with the state playing a crucial role, these compromises have seen women excluded from certain types of paid work (under the Factory Acts of the nineteenth century, for example), drawn in as a reserve labour supply during the World Wars, but then removed after the cessation of hostilities, or allowed to enter paid work, but mostly restricted to lower levels and inferior forms of it (vertical and horizontal segregation). Part-time work is the ultimate compromise between the demands of capitalist employers and the demands of men, since it simultaneously allows women's exploitation in paid work and in unpaid domestic work.

Walby suggests that sexual harassment is an important strategy men use to sustain the exclusion and segregation of women in paid work, even though, under pressure from feminism, the state via legislation has formally removed other barriers to women's participation. Evidence suggests that men's sexual harassment of women may be particularly blatantly sustained and vicious when women are working in jobs non-traditional for their gender; in other words when they have 'invaded' men's jobs. One study in

1983 found that 96 per cent of women in non-traditional spheres of paid work and 48 per cent of women in traditional areas had experienced sexual harassment of one form or another. More recently, in 1993, an Industrial Society survey found that 54 per cent of women were victims of workplace sexual harassment (for details of these and other studies, see Houghton-James 1995: 32–4). As Crompton concludes, 'sexual harassment continues to play an important part in keeping women in subordinate positions' in paid work (1997: 117).

Choice and preferences

In contrast to theories which emphasise the constraints women face in paid employment (resulting from capitalist economic restructuring and the practices of employers, the actions and behaviour of men organised in trade unions and as individuals or groups who sexually harass women, the policies and practices of governments and the state, for example), a second type of explanation emphasises free choice and preference as reasons why women predominate in some types of paid work and men in others. Most arguments of this sort are versions of human capital or rational choice theories. These propose that people's paid work experiences reflect the qualifications, skills and experiences they possess (their 'human capital'); the type of work people do and the pay they receive reflect their value to employers. Women have less human capital than men because their qualifications, skills and experience have been shaped initially by their *expectation* of responsibility for housework and childcare, and subsequently by their *actual* responsibility for it. It is therefore a 'rational choice' for men to specialise in paid work and women in unpaid domestic work; such a gendered division of labour is mutually advantageous, and represents the specialisation of each partner in the type of work in which they have the most human capital. Women engage in occupations and in forms of paid work that reflect the lower value of the human capital they offer to employers. Although this type of theorising has been subject to heavy criticism (see, for example, Walby 1990), a version of it has resurfaced via the work of Hakim (1991, 1995, 1996). Hakim's main argument is that women's experiences of paid work are largely the result of decisions taken by women themselves. Women, more so than men, 'have genuine choices to make between different styles of life' (1996: 207–8), a fact which contributes to heterogeneity amongst women and the polarisation of women's paid work experiences. Arising from their contrasting orientations to the 'modern' version of the domestic division of labour, Hakim identifies two broad categories of women. 'Homemakers' (or 'secondary earners') are women who choose to engage in employment that is subordinate to their domestic responsibilities. These women accept ideologies about the sexual division of labour and sexual difference, prefer to bring up their children themselves and prefer to work in female-dominated occupations. For a 'homemaker', 'wage work is an *extension* of her homemaking role, not an *alternative* to it' (1996: 207, original emphasis) and thus such women actively and freely choose types and forms of employment which accommodate their primary orientation to domestic responsibilities. In Hakim's controversial terms, such women are 'grateful slaves' (1991) and, according to Hakim, their orientation to paid work is the majority one (1996: 206). The second type of woman identified by Hakim is the 'career woman', who represents a minority orientation. Such women challenge the sexual division of labour and the sex stereotyping of occupations that constrain their choice of occupation, invest in educational qualifications and seek personal development and fulfilment through paid work, 'competing on the same terms as men' (1996: 207). The heterogeneity in women's preferences, for either 'homemaking' or 'careers', represents the 'source' of the polarisation in women's paid work behaviour (1996: 202). In other words, Hakim argues that the forms and types of paid work women do are a reflection of the choices they make. Since most women are 'homemakers' in their orientation, women's paid work is mostly low paid, low valued, low skilled and part-time, and in occupations such as clerical work, shop work, caring, cleaning and catering which best reflect their interests, experiences and qualifications.

For purposes of comparison, I have deliberately made a sharp distinction between those theories of women's paid work experiences which emphasise structure and constraint on the one hand, and those which emphasise agency and choice on the other. However, as was evident in the explanation of why improvements have occurred, the complexity of the lived reality of women's paid work experiences requires that theoretical explanations must incorporate *both* constraint *and* choice. In fact, this point is readily accepted by theorists representing both positions in the debate. Hakim (1996), although placing a heavy emphasis on choice, does recognise constraint. She describes the ways work cultures may be gendered, and are often experienced as 'exclusionary', including by those in jobs non-traditional for their gender (1996: 163–4). She also provides an extended discussion of the role of legislation as a form of 'social engineering' (1996: Chapter 7). Overall Hakim concludes that evidence supports a number of theories of women's experiences, including structural theories, 'so that they must be seen as complementary rather than competing' (1996: 203).

Crompton (1997), although stressing the importance of structural constraints, also allows for the part played by the choices women make. She writes (1997: 19), 'the gender division of labour is the outcome of a number of factors, and 'choice' is one of them'. Crompton's understanding of choice is though a more qualified one than that held by Hakim. For Crompton (and others like Connell 1987; Rees 1992; Walby 1997), women do make choices but within an overall context of constraint caused by the structural disadvantages they face. As an example, Crompton highlights the fact that Britain has the lowest levels of state-provided childcare in Europe. Women with children who wish to engage in paid work on a full-time and continuous basis therefore have to arrange childcare privately, which often means that it takes up a disproportionate amount of their earnings. Under such circumstances of constraint it may well be a 'rational choice' to disengage from full-time paid work and orientate toward 'homemaking'. Crompton has undertaken cross-national research, with a particular focus on differences in state policies and legislation between countries. Her comparative research reveals the importance of such structural contexts and constraints in shaping women's paid work experiences (Crompton 1996). State policies in France, for example, make it easier for women to 'choose' to work full-time, whereas state policies in Norway show that part-time work is not inherently a disadvantaged form of employment (Crompton 1997: Chapter 3).

There is a degree of consensus, then, between structural constraints theorists and choice theorists. Both allow for structure and agency, but each tend to heavily emphasise one rather than the other. Whichever type of theoretical explanation is favoured, however, it is clear that women's experiences of paid work cannot be understood in isolation from their experiences of unpaid household work. In the next chapter, therefore, I review evidence and arguments about women's involvement in, and experiences of, housework and caring work, with an especial focus on the extent to which its distribution between women and men has become more equal in recent decades.

Chapter 4

A labour of love? Household work and caring

Cleaning, cooking, washing clothes, and caring for children or other family members are just some of a wide range of tasks, performed on a daily or near-daily basis, that are termed 'household work'. More infrequently performed tasks, such as decorating, car maintenance and gardening, are also types of household work. Whilst a very few households employ a staff of paid workers to complete such tasks, and others may pay a cleaner or a childminder or use a gardening service, evidence shows that, in the great majority of households, daily, routine housework and caring work are completed on a 'do-it-yourself', unpaid basis. As shown below, historical evidence indicates that, rather than all members of a household sharing routine housework and caring work equally, these are tasks which have traditionally been completed mainly by women. Especially since the Industrial Revolution, paid work outside the home has been associated with men, whilst unpaid household work has largely been the preserve of women. As argued in the previous chapter, however, the historical association of men, rather than women, with paid work has weakened since the middle years of the twentieth century. In 1997, women represented nearly half of all employees. Most women now have a lifetime attachment to the labour market, engaging in paid employment throughout their adult lives with ever shortening periods of withdrawal arising from childrearing. To this extent, it may be argued that there has been a shift in the distribution of paid work between women and men, particularly in comparison to the first half of the twentieth century. In this chapter, I focus on unpaid household work and examine the extent to which change has occurred in its distribution between women and men.

From 'separate spheres' to the 'symmetrical family'?

In the early part of the twentieth century, evidence suggests that for most families, a gendered division of labour was the norm. Men primarily had responsibility for financial provision of the household via their paid work and women had responsibility for the management and performance of housework and caring work necessary for the day-to-day running of the household (for comprehensive reviews of the evidence see Morris 1990; Pahl 1984). Some oral history evidence reveals that men did participate in routine household work but this was infrequent and generally restricted to periods of temporary crises (for example, Lummis 1982; Roberts 1984; Thompson 1975). Evidence from sociological studies that were undertaken in the late 1940s and 1950s suggests that there remained a clear demarcation of the roles of men and women, with men as 'breadwinners' and women as housewives and mothers (for example, Dennis, Henriques and Slaughter [1956] 1969; Mogey 1956). Zweig (1952) looked at women's 'life and labour', via interviews with over two hundred women working in factories and other workplaces. Some of these working women did expect their husbands to help with the household work (1952: 21), and indeed, a few received it (p. 158). Nevertheless, Zweig's research showed that, even though a woman may have been contributing to household expenses as much as her husband, she still would 'regard it as her duty to wait on him and to serve him and to free him from household duties', despite this 'often overtaxing her strength and spirit' (1952: 148–9).

As was noted in the previous chapter, the 1960s in particular saw an unprecedented rise in the proportion of married women in paid employment. Studies of family life began to suggest that the pattern of the household division of labour was undergoing change. The work of Elizabeth Bott ([1957] 1971), especially her distinction between 'segregated' and 'joint' gender roles, has been recognised as a key starting point. Later research picked up on Bott's theme of a newly emerging division of labour, with the work of Young and Willmott ([1973] 1975) most often cited in this respect. Young and Willmott argued that the process of change in family structure had begun to enter a new stage, characterised by a decreasing segregation of roles between women and men. They described this new stage as the 'symmetrical' family (rather than say, 'egalitarian') because the term preserves a notion of difference, whilst also suggesting a greater degree of equality than at earlier stages of family structures (1975: 32). Young and Willmott emphasised, rather more cautiously than later commentators have sometimes suggested, that their argument concerned the *direction* of change from separate to joint roles. 'Division of labour is still the rule, with the husband doing the "man's" work and the wife taking prime responsibility for the housekeeping and the children' (1975: 31). Their data show that 72 per cent of the men in their sample reported helping their wives at least once a week, and that such help was more frequently given when wives worked outside the home (1975: 115). Studies by Rosser and Harris (1965) and Gavron ([1966] 1983) similarly showed that men were increasingly undertaking household work. In short, research evidence on family life in the 1960s and early 1970s suggested that changes were well underway in terms of gender roles and the household division of labour. Jointness and equality had become, or would shortly become, the predominant pattern. However, more recent evidence has thrown doubt on the extent and significance of change in the household division of labour.

A key piece of research was Oakley's (1974) seminal study of housework. Oakley found that 60 per cent of the husbands in her study rated low, 25 per cent medium, and 15 per cent high in terms of their participation in household work (1974: 137). She concluded that such findings cast doubt on claims of marriage being an egalitarian relationship, since in only a small number of marriages were the husbands 'notably domesticated'. Only a minority of the women in the sample were engaged in any paid work. Thus, for Oakley, 'the importance of women's enduring role as housewives and as the main rearers of children continues' (1974: 164–5). Edgell's (1980) research on middle-class couples consciously addressed itself to claims regarding a decrease in segregation and an increase in equality in relationships between the sexes (1980: 1–4). Edgell assessed whether his research couples were 'segregated', 'intermediate' or 'joint' in their gender roles. He found, on household tasks, that 47 per cent were segregated, 53 per cent were intermediate and none were joint (1980: 36). Edgell concluded that there was a 'marked lack of conjugal role jointness in domestic task behaviour' and that high levels of husband participation in household tasks were 'conspicuously absent'. Around a quarter of the wives were engaged in paid work, mostly on a part-time basis. Edgell describes his findings as demonstrating 'overwhelming evidence of conjugal role segregation' (1980: 35). Mansfield and Collard's study (1988) of newly wed couples had as its focus 65 couples aged under 30 and interviewed in London in 1979. In nearly all of these newly formed households, the wives worked full time, yet they were also the major housekeepers. Over two-thirds of them performed at least three quarters of the household chores (1988: 132). In only one-fifth of the marriages did both partners make more or less equal contributions to the household work (1988: 120).

Taken together, the body of research evidence from the later 1970s strongly suggests that, if family life was moving towards 'symmetricality' as claimed by Young and Willmott (1975), the rate of change was very slow: unpaid household work largely remained women's work, even when women did some paid work and even amongst younger people in newly formed households.

Shifts toward sharing? Household work in the 1980s and 1990s

In the 1970s, the idea of the 'symmetrical family' acted as a symbol for the changes which were assumed to be taking place in the distribution of paid work and household work between women and men. More recently, the idea of the 'New Man' has had a similar function. The idea of the 'New Man' is a reflection of concern about the recent economic and social circumstances men have experienced. It can be argued that rapid social changes since the 1960s and 1970s have placed older, 'traditional' forms of masculinity under pressure. Economic restructuring, unemployment, the rise of 'flexible working' and women's increased representation in the labour force are factors which, in the last few decades especially, have contributed to the weakening of the association of masculinity with paid work and a 'breadwinning' role. At the same time, feminist discourses have increasingly problematised a range of masculine beliefs and practices, via identifying the various ways these disadvantage women. In response to such pressures, 'New Men' are argued to be more 'feminine' in their masculinity. They are more open with feelings and emotions, have a more sexualised body image and an interest in fashion and skincare products. They are anti-sexist in words and deeds, and, most importantly for our purposes, are said to make an equal contribution to housework and childcare (for critique, see Morgan 1992). The 'New Man' is a idea popularised by magazine and newspaper journalists, but its widespread use is an indication of the extent to which masculinity is in a state of flux (see also discussion of 'New Laddism' in Chapter 7). In the remainder of this chapter, sociological evidence on household work from the 1980s to the present is examined to see how widespread the 'caring, sharing New Man' has really become.

Morris (1990) argues that the general proposition at the back of much recent research on divisions of labour is that a reorganisation of paid and unpaid work is taking place, through structural shifts in the economy, the participation of married women in paid work and the rise in unemployment. Wheelock's (1990) study of 'the domestic economy in a post-industrial society' certainly falls within this category, via its focus on couples in the North East of England where the man was unemployed and the woman was in paid work. Wheelock calculated that nearly 70 per cent of her sample households had undergone change to a less rigid division of labour since the man's unemployment, with men increasing their participation in housework and childcare. However, less than 25 per cent had undergone 'substantial' change (Wheelock 1990: 119). Research conducted by Morris (1985a, 1985b) in South Wales similarly examined the impact of male redundancy on the household division of labour, but found less extensive change than Wheelock. Men who experienced unemployment after their redundancy did slightly increase their participation in household work. However, for Morris, this merely represented a 'blurring' of responsibilities and was in no way sufficiently extensive as to constitute a fundamental challenge to the established pattern, even where the woman partner was herself in employment. Most often, any assistance given by the men in the household was in the form of occasional help (Morris 1985a).

A larger-scale survey on divisions of labour was conducted by Pahl (1984) in the south east of England. Of the 526 couples surveyed by Pahl, 81 per cent were 'conventional' households where the woman partner did most of the household work and only 10 per cent were households where men were more likely to take a greater share of household tasks. Pahl found that where both partners were in full-time work, there was the least likelihood of a 'conventional' pattern. However, even amongst such couples, 61 per cent had a 'conventional' distribution of household work (1984: 274–5). Pahl's findings led him to conclude that 'the domestic division of labour is more unequally shared by women' (1984: 270).

Further evidence on patterns of the division of household labour when both partners are employed full time is provided by Brannen and Moss (1991), in their research on dual earner couples with children living in the Greater London area. Brannen and Moss found that men were equal participants in the household work in only 7 per cent of the dual earner couples. In 36 per cent of the couples, the woman partner performed the majority of the work. Brannen and Moss concluded that, 'Although our data show that men with employed partners did more "family work" than those without, the most striking reality was that on every indicator studied, mothers with full time jobs did the main part of this work' (1991: 179).

Warde and Hetherington (1993) surveyed over 300 households in the Greater Manchester area in 1990. Despite significant participation in paid work by the women in the sample, Warde and Hetherington found that it was the women who did the vast proportion of routine housework and child-care – tasks done on a ongoing, daily basis. Husbands tended to do tasks associated with household and car maintenance, and other tasks that are done relatively infrequently. Warde and Hetherington calculated that a wife was 14 times more likely than her husband to have been the last one to do the ironing, 30 times more likely the clothes washing, 9 times the tidying up, 7 times the cooking and twice the washing up. In contrast, a husband was 4 times more likely to be the last one to have done painting or car washing, 3 times cutting the lawn and 20 times more likely to have last done any plastering of walls or ceilings (1993: 32). Overall, they found there was 'a continuing and pervasive conventional division of labour between women and men' (1993: 43).

Warde and Hetherington's survey also provides data on the gendering of household work between children aged over 15 in these households. The evidence shows a lesser degree of inequality amongst sons and daughters than amongst husband and wives, but nevertheless, similar patterns of gender stereotyping of tasks occurred. Figure 4.1 shows that, amongst young people aged 14–25, women are much more likely than men usually to do a range of household tasks. Such data suggest that, in the future, changes in the distribution of household work between women and men may occur only slowly: young people have a history of gendered participation in household work even before they set up their own households.

England & Wales
Percentages

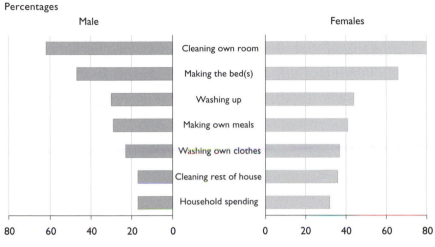

Figure 4.1 Young people who usually perform certain household tasks[1]: by gender 1992–93.[2]

Notes
1 People aged 14–25 who said that they usually or always did each of these household tasks.
2 November 1992–February 1993
Source: Youth Lifestyles Survey, Home Office © Crown Copyright 1998

Most of the evidence discussed so far has come from relatively small-scale studies. Some have been criticised on methodological grounds (see criticisms noted by Warde and Hetherington 1993 and Hakim 1996, for example). More generally, making comparisons over time and between studies is problematic. Different studies have used different definitions of what counts as household work, and some may underestimate the amount men do because tasks such as household and car repairs are not included. As Warde and Hetherington (1993: 42) note, 'Different research designs and alternative lines of questioning produce evidence [which is] to some degree discrepant'.

There is also a question as to whether findings from local studies are generalisable to the national context. In contrast, one of the largest and most nationally representative sources of data on household divisions of labour are the *British Social Attitudes* surveys. In 1991, respondents were asked who in their household was mainly responsible for general domestic duties. In 75 per cent of cases, the woman was said to be responsible and in 16 per cent duties were said to be shared equally. Responsibility for domestic duties was found to vary by the paid work status of the woman partner. For example, where the woman was not in paid work, the woman was responsible for domestic duties in 89 per cent of cases and duties were shared equally in only 6 per cent of cases. However, even in households where the woman worked full time, women were said to be mainly responsible for domestic tasks in 67 per cent of cases (24 per cent shared equally), a finding in line with those of the other studies. These data suggest that the distribution of household work between women and men is unequal, irrespective of the women's paid work status. Nevertheless, a shift towards more egalitarian arrangements since the 1987 survey had occurred. In 1987, women were said to be responsible for domestic duties in 72 per cent of households where both partners worked full time, compared to 67 per cent in the 1991 survey (Kiernan 1992: 101). As shown in Table 4.1, however, women who work full time continue to hold disproportionate responsibility for the completion of ongoing housework, especially making an evening meal, doing the household cleaning and the washing and ironing of clothes.

Data on the distribution of household work amongst couple households in the mid-1990s is provided by Gershuny (1997a, 1997b) in his analyses of evidence from another large-scale, nationally representative study, the *British Household Panel Survey*. He found that where women are employed full time, they average about 15 per cent less paid work time than their men partners. However, this is compensated for by their doing nearly three times as much household work (14 hours per week). Moreover, amongst couples where each partner worked the *same* full-time hours, the woman continued to have the main responsibility for household work. In such cases, women's total workload (paid and unpaid) was around 9 hours more per week than men's (see also Mihill 1997). Evidence from the Office for National Statistics shows similar disparities between the total (paid and household) work time of women and men (Murgatroyd and Neuburger 1997; see also Elliott 1997). As shown in Table 4.2, in 1995 women spent 85 minutes fewer per day in paid work than men. However, women spent 124 more minutes per day on housework (including home improvements, or DIY) and childcare than men. When the total work hours (paid and unpaid household) of women and men are compared, women spent 39 minutes more per day working than men.

Objectively, the fact that women do more household work than men (even allowing for differences in their hours in paid work) is unfair. What evidence is there on whether the distribution of household work is *perceived* to be fair amongst couples? Warde and Hetherington (1993) asked their respondents whether they thought they did a 'fair share' of five routine tasks, including washing up, cleaning the toilet and hoovering. Men were more likely than women to say that they did a fair share (59 per cent compared to 33 per cent). Women were more likely than men to say that they did more than their fair share (65 per cent compared to 8 per cent). These findings suggest that a high proportion of women regard the distribution of routine housework in their homes as inequitable, whereas men are much more satisfied: clearly there is a lack of agreement between women and men as to what constitutes a 'fair' distribution of household work. However, Warde and Hetherington (1993) report that 33 per cent of men felt that they did

Table 4.1 Gender distribution of household tasks, by woman's employment status, UK, 1991

	All households %	Households where man works and ...		
		... woman works full-time %	... woman works part-time %	... woman is not in paid work %
Who:				
does household shopping?				
mainly man	8	4	5	5
mainly woman	45	42	51	57
shared equally	47	53	44	37
makes evening meal?				
mainly man	9	7	5	3
mainly woman	70	60	75	81
shared equally	20	32	20	16
does evening dishes?				
mainly man	28	28	20	18
mainly woman	33	24	41	37
shared equally	37	46	38	42
does household cleaning?				
mainly man	4	5	–	–
mainly woman	68	63	82	82
shared equally	27	30	18	17
does washing and ironing?				
mainly man	3	3	–	1
mainly woman	84	78	91	91
shared equally	12	17	9	8
repairs household equipment?				
mainly man	82	84	85	81
mainly woman	6	3	7	8
shared equally	10	10	8	10
organises household money and bills?				
mainly man	31	27	29	40
mainly woman	40	44	41	36
shared equally	28	28	30	23

Source: Kiernan, 1992: 102. Copyright © Social and Community Planning Research

less than their fair share, a finding suggesting a degree of guilt about their under-involvement in domestic work.

Caring work

Given the important links between the presence of children and women's paid work experiences (see Chapter 3), a separate examination of evidence

Table 4.2 Time use activities by gender: minutes per day (UK, adults aged 16 and over), 1995

	All	Men	Women	Women + or −
Household work				
Food preparation	49	28	68	+40
Care of family (including childcare)	71	55	86	+31
Clothing care	14	3	25	+22
Shopping	36	26	46	+20
Care of home	56	43	70	+27
Home improvement	14	22	6	−16
Total household work:	240	177	301	+124
Paid work	168	212	127	−85
Paid work and household work total:	408	389	428	+39
Other[1]:	1032	1051	1012	−39
Total per day:	1440[2]	1440	1440	−

Source: Adapted from table in Annex of Murgatroyd and Neuburger (1997), using data from Office of National Statistics Omnibus Survey

Notes
1 Includes travel, education and study, voluntary work, sleeping, leisure, eating, exercise and sports.
2 There are 1440 minutes in a 24-hour day.

on childcare work within the household is necessary. Moreover, with the increasing numbers of elderly people in society, and government policies which encourage families to 'look after their own' rather than relying on the state to do so, it has also become important to examine the distribution between women and men of other forms of caring work.

Childcare

Most women have at least one child at some point in their life course. It has been estimated that, of women born in 1967, just under 80 per cent will have a child by the time they are aged 40 (Central Statistical Office [CSO] 1995). Data from the National Child Development Study [NCDS] (which has studied all individuals born in a particular week in 1958) shows that by the age of 33, 77 per cent of women have already had one child (Ferri and Smith 1996). Motherhood is, therefore, an important aspect of the great majority of women's lives. Of course, most men have children too. According to the NCDS data, 66 per cent of men had at least one child by the age of 33. However, as we saw in the previous chapter, having children impacts much more significantly on women's paid work histories than men's.

Given the centrality of motherhood in most women's lives, and the way that the *expectation* that women are, or should be, mothers affects all women whether they actually have children or not (Phoenix, Woollet and Lloyd 1991), there is a surprising lack of evidence on women's experiences of motherhood (Ribbens 1994). There is some evidence on women's experiences of the childcare work that mothering entails. Boulton (1983) studied 50 London women, who had exclusive responsibility for their pre-school child(ren). She found that two-thirds experienced a sense of meaning and purpose in their lives as mothers, but that half also found childcare to be a predominantly frustrating and irritating experience. Piachaud (1984) studied 55 mothers of pre-school children in Yorkshire. He described the nature of the childcare work that the mothers performed. He noted that, on average, 7 hours per day or 50 hours per week were spent on childcare and that most mothers lacked any time free from childcare responsibilities. Moreover, many of the basic caring tasks were 'physically exhausting, repetitive and frequently boring and dirty' (1984: 19). Graham (1993) argues that the nature of childcare work is highly routinised and spatially restricting. She found, amongst mothers with pre-school children, 80 per cent of the day was taken up by everyday routine activities and tasks, and 75 per cent of each day was spent in the house.

Evidence on the time use of men and women (see Table 4.2) shows the greater time women spend engaged in childcare work than men. This disparity clearly varies according to the age of the youngest child and paid work status, especially of the woman, but differences remain significant even after these factors are taken into account. Brannen and Moss (1991) found that amongst dual earner couples with children, where *both* partners worked full time, it was the woman who had the main responsibility for childcare. In other words, it was the mother rather than the father who made arrangements for the care of the child during the working day, who took the child to the arranged childcare and who collected them at the end of the day. Once home with the child, it was the mother who then had the main responsibility for the child. Even with both partners working full time, Brannen and Moss found that less than half the fathers 'frequently' changed their child's nappy, less than half 'frequently' fed their children and less than 40 per cent got up at night to the child. Amongst men and women in the NCDS sample, the most egalitarian arrangements for childcare responsibilities were found in dual earner couples where both partners worked full time. However, even amongst such couples, 24 per cent of men and 32 per cent of women surveyed said that general childcare was mainly the woman's responsibility (Ferri and Smith 1996).

What do women feel about their disproportionate responsibility for childcare? Research suggests that a woman's paid work status is an important influence on their views about childcare responsibilities. For example, the 1990 *British Social Attitudes Survey* found 94 per cent of women with a child under 12 gave as an 'important' reason why they were *not* in paid work that 'it is better for children to have their mother at home', whilst 91 per cent said that an important reason was that enjoyment gained from spending time with children was greater than that gained from working (Witherspoon and Prior 1991). In general, such women gave more positive than negative reasons for not being in a paid job, and for having primary responsibility for care of children. Ferri and Smith (1996) found, however, that the extent to which husbands shared in the care of children was a key factor in *working* women's expressed satisfaction with their marital relationship and with life more generally. Those with uninvolved, or under-involved, partners were more likely to say they were unhappy in their marital relationship, to report higher levels of disagreement over responsibility for domestic work and to say they were dissatisfied with their life in general. Levels of reported dissatisfaction and discord increased with the number of hours women worked, findings which indicate the stress many mothers experience in coping with paid work and unpaid work (Ferri and Smith 1996: 43).

When women with children are at their paid work (whether full-time or part-time), evidence from a range of sources shows that it is informal sources of childcare which are more extensively used. Witherspoon and Prior (1991) found that for 59 per cent of part-time women workers and 55 per cent of full-timers, relatives were the main source of childcare. Data from the NCDS study showed that 36 per cent of working mothers with a child under 12 used their husband, 35 per cent used their parents or in-laws, and 35 per cent used other relatives. Friends and neighbours were much less important, being used in only 8 per cent and 9 per cent of cases respectively (Ferri and Smith 1996: Table 8). Finlayson, Ford and Marsh (1996) found that of those working women using any form of childcare for their dependent children, just under one quarter (23 per cent) used formal or professional care. Of working mothers who use formal or professional care, childminders are the most frequent form of care (around 9 per cent), followed by day nurseries (around 7 per cent), and nannies or au pairs (around 4 per cent) (Ferri and Smith 1996; Witherspoon and Prior 1991).

Evidence suggests that women's greater responsibility for children extends to paying the costs of childcare themselves (Brannen and Moss 1991). Over 90 per cent of working mothers using formal or professional childcare in 1991 paid for most of it, or all of it, themselves (Corti, Laurie and Dex 1994). Women who work full time are more likely than those working part-time to use formal or professional care, and therefore are more likely to pay for it. Nevertheless, where part-time women workers do pay for childcare, they spend a disproportionate amount of their hourly earnings as a consequence (Finlayson, Ford and Marsh 1996). Over the last decade, the use of formal, and therefore paid, childcare has increased (Corti, Laurie and Dex 1994), and women are paying more in real terms for it. Between 1991 and 1994, for example, spending on childcare increased by 26 per cent, a rise which remains significant even after controlling for wage inflation

(Finlayson, Ford and Marsh 1996). More working mothers are, therefore, spending increasing proportions of their earnings on childcare. According to calculations by Marsh and McKay (1993), women paying for childcare spend around 25 per cent of their earnings on average, although part-time workers and low paid workers spend more. As Finlayson, Ford and Marsh conclude, women with children often have to 'buy their way back into the labour market' (1996: 300). For the great majority of women (65 per cent), however, informal unpaid sources are the most important source of child-care while they are at work. This finding indicates that in the context of the relatively low-paid nature of most women's paid work, it is access to this type of childcare which makes the taking on of paid employment financially viable (Corti, Laurie and Dex 1994). However, it also reflects women's pref-erences for home-based and family-based childcare (Thomson 1995).

Other caring work

The increasing proportion of elderly people in the population, combined with government 'care in the community' policies, have led to a heightened awareness of the important role played by individuals who care for elderly, sick or disabled people on an informal, unpaid basis. A nationally repre-sentative survey of informal care was incorporated in the 1985 *General Household Survey*, which suggested that there were 6 million carers in Britain, 3.5 million of them women (Parker and Lawton 1994). A more recent source of nationally representative data on informal carers is the 1991 *British Household Panel Study*. This survey also found that, amongst the adult population, more women (17 per cent) than men (12 per cent) said they looked after or gave special help to a sick, elderly or disabled person either inside or outside their own household. Adults aged 45–64 were the most likely of any age group to be carers, especially women (27 per cent compared to 19 per cent of men in this age group). The survey found that an equal proportion (4 per cent) of men and women defined themselves as 'co-resident carers' (i.e. caring for someone they lived with, most often a spouse). However, women were more likely than men to care for someone outside their own home. In the 45–65 age group, 22 per cent of women and 14 per cent of men were 'extra resident' carers, most often caring for par-ents. Significantly, female providers of informal care, whether co- or extra-resident, spend more time than men on caring. Of co-resident caring women, 41 per cent spent at least 50 hours per week caring, compared to 28 per cent of men (Corti, Laurie and Dex 1994). Therefore, although men provide significant amounts, and the biggest source of care for people aged over 65 are elderly themselves (Arber and Ginn 1991 cited in Brannen *et al.* 1994), women are more likely to be providers of informal care than men (Corti, Laurie and Dex 1994: 5). Moreover, Arber and Ginn's (1995) analy-sis of *General Household Survey* data shows that, amongst those providing informal care, the norm is to provide such care whilst also engaging in paid work.

Explaining the distribution of household work

The evidence on informal care, together with that on housework and child-care, reveals that women perform a disproportionate amount of household work in contemporary Britain. Women's responsibility for household work has continued despite the changed nature of housework and childcare during the twentieth century. The introduction and increased availability of a wide range of domestic 'labour saving' technology has not directly reduced the time women spend on housework (Wajcman 1991: 87; see also Cowan 1989). Higher standards of hygiene and childcare have mediated any 'liberating' effects of technology. Nor has domestic technology weakened the gendered division of household tasks. Evidence suggests that, despite the automatic washing machine and 'easy care' fabrics, 'clothes care' remains a household task which women are much more likely to do than men (see Table 4.2 for example). Similarly, Warde and Hetherington's (1993) data show that women were nearly five times more likely than men to have been the last one to do the vacuum cleaning, whilst men tended to have done household maintenance tasks, presumably involving the use of 'power tools'.

Why do women do more, and have the greater responsibility for, household work than men? A number of explanations have been proposed. First, women may do more household work than men because of time available for them to do it. On average, men do spend more hours in paid employment than women. However, the time spent by women doing household work more than makes up for their lower average hours of paid work and means that women spend more hours working (paid and household) than men (see Table 4.2). Moreover, Gershuny (1997a, 1997b) has shown that even when women and men spend exactly the same amount of time in paid work, women still do more household work than men.

A second explanation is that women's greater involvement in household work is a reflection of their lack of economic resources and power, compared to men. Women's paid work tends to be low in status and poorly paid, relative to men's. This may mean that, between couples, the man's attachment to paid work is regarded as the primary one, via his higher status, and relatively well-paid job, with knock-on effects for power relations within the household. Women's weaker material position, via their more limited access to economic resources from paid work, is reflected in their greater responsibility for household work. In her review of research evidence on the control and management of money within households, Crompton concludes that the 'findings lend support to the resource theory of power . . . that is, the more resources a woman brings into the household, the more likely she is to experience an equal relationship within it' (Crompton 1997: 98).

However, even amongst dual-earner, full-time working couples (who are more likely to have similar incomes from paid work), Brannen and Moss (1991) found inequitable distributions of household work. Moreover, Gregson and Lowe's (1994a, 1994b) research on waged domestic labour and the redistribution of household work within dual career couples shows that, when women have greater economic power, this does not mean that *men* do more housework and childcare; rather that *other* women (cleaners and nannies, for example) are paid to do it.

A third explanation for women's more extensive participation in, and responsibility for, housework and caring work centres around the role of gender ideology, particularly attitudes and beliefs about men as breadwinners, and women as housewives and mothers. As noted earlier, Warde and Hetherington (1993) found that daughters and sons do differing amounts of household work. They argued that this reveals the importance of the *ideological* bases of gendered allocations of household work, since there were no material or time reasons to account for the difference (1993: 37). Brannen and colleagues (1994) note that attitudes to gender roles are argued to be at the heart of the issue of women's combining of employment and family responsibilities (see also Thomson 1995). Particularly important are attitudes to the participation of mothers in paid work, especially if they have pre-school children. Data from the 1990 *British Social Attitudes* survey revealed a high degree of consensus amongst women that paid work is acceptable for women after marriage and before having children (85 per cent) and after the children leave home (70 per cent). However, as shown in Table 4.3, there was much less consensus about what mothers of pre-school children should do, with important variations according to women's paid work status (Witherspoon and Prior 1991; see also Thomson 1995).

Table 4.3 Attitudes to mothers and paid work

. . . .	All	Mothers of a child under 12		
		Working full time	Working part time	Not in paid work
Should the woman work when there is a child under school-age?	%	%	%	%
Work full time	5	18	1	1
Work part time	33	35	55	27
Stay at home	51	41	34	64

Women aged 18–59

Source: Adapted from Witherspoon and Prior (1991: 150)

Kiernan (1992) analyses *British Social Attitudes* data on attitudes towards sharing housework from 1984, 1987 and 1991. She notes a trend toward greater egalitarianism during this period, since higher proportions said housework tasks should be shared in 1991 than in previous years. Figure 4.2 compares the proportion of respondents who in 1991 said that particular tasks *should* be shared equally with those who reported such task were *actually* shared. There is a clear gap between attitudes and practices, a gap which Kiernan notes has widened between 1984 and 1991. In other words, more people now think household tasks *should* be shared equally, but practices have not kept pace with changes in beliefs. Kiernan's analysis suggests that it is the attitudes of *men* which are the key to change in practices: a man with egalitarian attitudes is more likely to be egalitarian in practice and to share domestic work. However, women's attitudes seemed to have less effect; egalitarian attitudes held by a woman do not mean that her partner is more likely to share domestic work.

Other data suggest that men are more 'gender traditionalist' than women. Witherspoon and Prior (1991) note that men are 'considerably' more likely than women to believe that childcare should largely be a

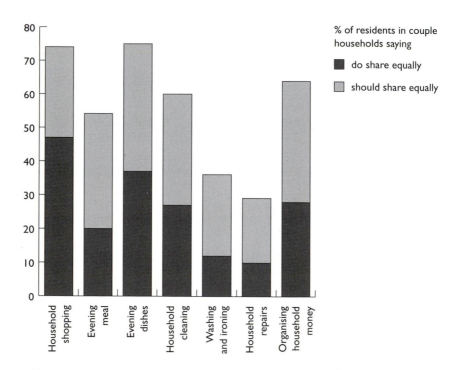

Figure 4.2 Sharing household tasks: in theory and in practice, 1991
Source: Adapted from Kiernan 1992: 105 © Social and Community Planning Research

woman's responsibility. In 1990, amongst parents with a child under 12 years old, just over a half of fathers agreed that a pre-school child would suffer if its mother worked, compared to one-third of the mothers. Nearly 60 per cent of the fathers believed that mothers of pre-school children should not work outside the home, compared to 50 per cent of mothers. As Witherspoon and Prior conclude, 'Whatever talk there is of the 'New Man', he is much rarer than the 'New Woman'' (1991: 152). Attitudinal data indicate, therefore, that men's gender attitudes, although changing, are 'lagging behind' those of women. This is important, given that it is men's attitudes which especially influence the actual distribution of household work (Kiernan 1992).

Despite the inequitable distribution of housework and childcare between their dual career couples, Brannen and Moss (1991) found that only a minority (36 per cent) of the women said they were dissatisfied with their partner's contribution. The women used a variety of strategies to minimise criticism of their partners, including excusing partners on the grounds of the primacy of their job compared to their own job, having low expectations of their housework and childcare activities, praising them for activities they did do, and retracting or down-playing any criticisms. Behind these strategies of dealing with the inequitable division of household work lay ideologies concerning traditional gender roles and marriage, which constrained women to present their relationship as a happy one and not to reveal any 'deficiencies' to those outside it (Brannen and Moss 1991: 213).

Evidence from *British Social Attitudes* suggests that substantial proportions of women either support or feel neutral about the idea that 'a wife's job is to look after the home and the family' (Kiernan 1992). If women define household work as their responsibility, even when they are also engaged in paid work, then the likelihood is that they will do more of it than their partner, and feel satisfied with this arrangement. However, Kiernan (1992) also presents data which show that women with egalitarian attitudes (who presumably do not define household work as their responsibility), are not any more likely to have a partner who does his fair share. In such households, there may be a disparity between each partner's support for traditional gender ideology, with the man being resistant to participation in household work. Baxter and Western (1998) suggest that, even in such circumstances, women are unlikely to express high levels of dissatisfaction with the distribution of paid work. Their analyses show that, when men undertake certain non-traditional household tasks, women are more satisfied, even if men's participation remains a limited and objectively unequal one. Baxter and Western explain this as a pragmatic response on the part of women, given that the only conceivable alternative is not an equal distribution of household work, but a situation in which men do even less (1998: 118). According to Thompson and Walker (1989: 857, cited in Kiernan 1992), 'Women's employment, time availability, resources, conscious ideology, and power do not account for why wives still do the bulk of family work'. As suggested by Baxter and Western (1998), perhaps women's resigned acceptance of men's intransigence does.

In the analyses of Delphy and Leonard (1992), it is not surprising that men are apparently so reluctant to do a more equitable share of household and caring work. In Delphy and Leonard's terms, household and caring work takes place within a domestic or patriarchal 'mode of production'. Men exploit (or 'appropriate') women's labour and benefit directly from it. For one thing, the routine, never-ending tasks necessary for the daily functioning of the household, and its individual members, are done by women, rather than by men themselves. Moreover, the appropriation of women's labour by men within the household means that, when it comes to selling their labour power to employers, men are 'freer' whilst women face greater restrictions and limitations.

Diversity and difference

In this chapter, I have reviewed a range of evidence which shows that, despite women's increased participation in paid work, they continue to bear primary responsibility for the completion of housework and caring work. Several contrasts between this chapter and the previous one, on paid work, are apparent. In the previous chapter, there was heavy reliance on official statistical data, whereas in the present chapter, rather more use has been made of non-governmental sources (including *British Social Attitudes* data, *British Household Panel Study* data) and smaller-scale, often qualitative, sociological studies. This is a reflection of the greater importance placed on paid work compared to household work, with effects on the types of sources available. Only recently (1997) have efforts been made officially to measure and value household work, (Murgatroyd and Neuburger 1997; see also Elliott 1997; Thomas 1997). This is linked to a second difference between the present chapter and the previous one. The limited nature of knowledge about household work compared to paid work is reflected in the paucity of information about the ways the distribution of household work varies by social factors in addition to gender. However, given that economic activity rates and patterns of participation in paid work amongst women vary by ethnicity, social class, age and geographical location (see Chapter 3), it might be expected that distributions of household work also vary.

Women of South Asian ethnicities, particularly those of Pakistani and Bangladeshi origin who are Muslim, have low rates of recorded economic activity (see Chapter 3). Most often this is argued to be a reflection of cultural and religious traditions, including *purdah* (which restricts women's participation in public life) and *izzet* (family honour). Together, such traditions prohibit women working outside the home and give them strong obligations for household work within it. However, Brah and Shaw (1992) argue that exclusively cultural explanations fail to take account of other factors which may depress the paid work activities of Muslim women, including the structure of the local labour market in areas of Muslim settlement. Brah and Shaw point out that there are regional variations in the level of Muslim women engaged in paid work (and therefore variations in economic inactivity and full-time unpaid household work). Of the Muslim women Brah and Shaw interviewed during their research, only a quarter gave the opposition of their family as the main reason why they were not doing any paid work (1992: 49). The socio-economic characteristics of women of Pakistani and Bangladeshi ethnicities may make it more difficult for such women to undertake paid work, irrespective of their cultural traditions. For example, Pakistani and Bangladeshi women tend to belong to larger than average households (making for a heavier household workload) and, due to relatively low incomes amongst their ethnic groupings, these households may also lack washing machines and other labour-saving devices. Finally, Pakistani and Bangladeshi women, when they do engage in paid work, tend to have lower average earnings than other women, a factor which may further push them to household work rather than paid work (Brah and Shaw 1992).

Bhopal (1997) studied a sample of 60 British women (aged 25–30) of South Asian ethnicity, of whom half were married (and had had arranged marriages) and 23 were cohabiting with their male partner. Bhopal found that, regardless of formal marital status, most household work tasks were mainly performed by the women. However, amongst cohabiting couples, men were more likely to 'help' (1997: 114). This difference was one of several which led Bhopal to distinguish between 'traditional' women and 'independent' women in her sample. In addition to performing most, if not all, the household work, 'traditional' women were married, had had arranged marriages, had low levels of education and low-level paid occupations (if they worked outside the home at all). 'Independent' women, whose partners were more likely to 'help' do the household tasks, had rejected the South Asian tradition of arranged marriages (and were cohabiting rather than being married), were highly educated and worked in semi- professional or professional occupations. The work of Bhopal (1997), together with that of Brah and Shaw (1992), usefully cautions against the stereotypical depiction of South Asian women in terms of the household division of labour. In general, however, evidence on ethnic variations in the household distribution of housework and caring work is extremely scarce.

The issue of social class variations in the household division of labour has received more extensive attention (Edgell 1980; Gavron 1983; Pahl 1984, for example), but there is little consensus as to its effects. In a review of the findings on the relationship between social class and shared childcare, Ferri and Smith (1996) note that some studies show working-class fathers to be more participative, while others show that middle-class fathers are more involved. Their own data showed that working-class fathers were more likely to play an equal part in caring for their children than middle-class fathers (1996: 27). Gregson and Lowe (1994b) report 'much the same' distribution of household work amongst their dual career middle-class couples as was found by Morris (1985a, 1985b) in her study of working-class couples. This leads them to conclude that 'social class is of minimal importance' in the distribution of household work between men and women (1994b: 56). However, their own research in fact points to emerging trends in social class differences, via the increased use of (working-class) paid domestic workers by dual career (middle-class) couples. More generally, if it is correct to argue that the more economic resources a women has from her paid work, the more equitable the distribution of household work (as suggested by Crompton 1997), then social class *is* likely to have an effect. Women in higher-status, professional and relatively well paid middle-class occupations may face less inequitable distributions of household work than women in low status, semi or unskilled, relatively poorly paid occupations.

Attitudinal evidence shows that older women are more likely to be supportive of traditional gender roles than younger women (Kiernan 1992; Pilcher 1998a; Scott, Alwin and Brown 1996; Witherspoon 1985), and this is also reflected in their lower rates of economic activity (see Chapter 3). Older women in contemporary Britain have lived most of their lives in a society which encouraged them to invest their identities heavily in housework and motherhood, rather than in paid work. Certainly, Mason's (1987) study of long married couples aged between 50 and 70 showed that women tended to do most of the household work and retained responsibility for these tasks, despite their husband's retirement from paid work.

In summary, the available evidence on variations in the gendered distribution of household work according to ethnicity, social class and age (limited though it is) does suggest that some women face a more unequal division of labour between themselves and their men partners than others. What happens in couple households where both partners are the same gender? There is very little evidence on this interesting issue. Peace's (1993) small-scale study sought to explore the organisation of housework and caring work in lesbian households. Half of the couples had children living at home with them. However, this did not lead to the biological mother doing all the housework, nor all the childcare. Peace found that the couples in her sample divided the housework and childcare according to what they were best at, or enjoyed doing or what was the most practical arrangement. Each couple discussed and then worked out the division of responsibility for tasks in order to ensure that both shared fully in the household work, whilst also allowing each partner to engage in paid work, education or training. Dunne's (1997) study also suggests that in lesbian households, the performance of routine tasks is organised in a much more 'even handed' way than is often the case in many heterosexual couple households. Amongst her sample of lesbian couples, Dunne found that there was little 'specialisation' in terms of who did what around the house. Instead, flexibility was a key characteristic, and most often, neither partner felt that they had primary responsibility for the running of the household. Dunne concluded that the women in her sample had an 'egalitarian' approach to the division of household work, a reflection of the absence of 'an ideology that legitimises the domination of one partner over the other', amongst contemporary lesbians (1997: 214). Taken together, the studies by Peace (1993) and Dunne (1997) suggest that, in couple households without a man partner, the division of household work may be much more equal.

Lagged adaptation

The general picture that emerges from this review of recent research evidence on patterns of the household division of labour is summarised by Morris. She writes that ' . . . none of the data seem to warrant any suggestion that the traditional female responsibility for household work has been substantially eroded, or that male participation has substantially increased' (1990: 102). Gershuny, Godwin and Jones (1994) argue that over time, women's increased participation in paid work has only partly been offset by men's increased participation in unpaid work. They suggest that a process of 'lagged adaptation' is underway, whereby men have been slower to respond to women's changed attitudes and practices. These arguments about a process of 'lagged adaptation' seem to be supported by evidence showing that, over time, men have been gradually increasing their share of housework and caring work. However, men are still 'lagging behind' women in terms of both egalitarian attitudes and egalitarian practices. Women continue to spend much more time on unpaid household work than men and continue to be primarily responsible for it. This is an unequal distribution which contributes directly to the disadvantages women face in their paid work and to the advantages men face in theirs.

One potential solution to lagged adaptation primarily on the part of men, which results in the problem of women's continuing disproportionate responsibility for household work, may be to hire someone else to do it. Gregson and Lowe (1994a) have shown that during the 1980s, demand for waged domestic labour underwent a 'resurgence', especially in the areas of childcare for pre-school children and general household cleaning. The resurgence in demand emanated particularly from middle-class households with both partners in full-time professional occupations. 'On the basis of our survey findings, we suggest that between 30 per cent and 40 per cent of dual career households in contemporary Britain employ waged domestic labour in some form', with the employment of a cleaner (nearly 75 per cent) being especially prevalent (1994: 50). As might be expected from evidence on job gendering (Chapter 3), and the gendering of household work (this chapter),

Gregson and Lowe's evidence suggests that waged domestic labour amounts to the buying in of *other* women to undertake housework and childcare that would otherwise be the responsibility of the *woman* partner.

Arguably, there remains 'lagged adaptation' too on the part of state policy and public and private provision which might otherwise facilitate a more equal distribution of household work. Despite significant and rapid increases in the numbers of childcare places available in the private sector (Brannen *et al.* 1994), Britain continues to have the lowest level of publicly funded childcare provision in Europe. Maternity leave and paternity leave provision also lags behind that of many European countries (Brannen *et al.* 1994). Some shifts in state policy have occurred in the last decade, particularly in relation to allowances and benefits disregards for the costs of childcare. In the March 1998 Budget, for example, new measures were introduced to enable more women to enter paid work, if they wish to do so. Low-income families are to be eligible to claim a tax credit which would provide up to 70 per cent of their childcare costs, to a maximum of £150 per week (Buckingham and Finch 1998). Other recent policies aimed at improving access to childcare, included tax relief on workplace nursery places (1990) and funding of £300 million for out-of-school childcare places (1997). The provision of free places in nurseries, playgroups or schools for every 4-year-old child from September 1998 may also be interpreted as a shift in policy on state-funded childcare (Chaudhary 1998).

Evidence discussed in this chapter clearly shows that women's increased participation in paid work has had some knock-on effects for the distribution of the household work that they were formerly largely solely responsible for. Part of this household work has been redistributed to men, but 'New Man' remains a rare species, even amongst dual earner households with both partners in full-time work. Household work has also been redistributed to individuals outside the household – either relatives providing informal care of children, or paid domestics, hired to clean the house or do the laundry, or childcare professionals providing care as nannies or in nurseries, or as childminders in their own home. In short, a significant amount of responsibility for household work has remained with women. When engaged in paid work, many women continue to complete household work mainly on a do-it-yourself basis (in that they literally *do* do it themselves), whilst increasing numbers are paying others (primarily other *women*) to do it for them. Women's changed relationship with paid work and its effects on their relationship with household work, are suggestive of shifts in household relations of another sort, since they bring into play personal, loving relationships between women, men and children. In the next chapter, the focus of attention shifts to personal, intimate relationships, particularly (although not exclusively) those between women and men which centre around family formation and dissolution.

Chapter 5

Love and sexuality: women and personal relationships

Despite their increased participation in paid work, women's traditional roles as wives and mothers remain fundamentally significant, both socially and to women themselves. As shown in the previous chapter, evidence on the distribution of household work reveals the extent to which housework and caring work (including caring for children) remains 'women's work'. Thus far, household work has been examined as 'work', for example its distribution between members of a household, the allocation of particular tasks, and the time spent performing tasks. However, being a wife and a mother clearly amounts to much more than the performance of routine housework and caring tasks: it also involves relationships with other people (partners or husbands and children), based on emotional attachments. It is not enough, therefore, to examine household relationships merely in terms of the work that living together generates. Household relationships must also be examined as personal, intimate bonds with love, happiness and sexuality as central features. In this chapter, therefore, the focus shifts away from women and work, to evidence and debates about the personal relationships that women enter, via sexual relationships, cohabitation, marriage and having children.

What's love got to do with it?

Unlike poets, songwriters, scriptwriters and novelists, who write extensively about love, sociologists have had little interest in it until recently. For Jackson (1993), sociology's neglect of love as an emotion is surprising given that contemporary culture is inundated with representations of love and the extent to which relationships based on love shape people's movement through the life course. Childhood, youth and adulthood all involve personal relationships with other people: parents, girlfriends, boyfriends and lovers, whether short-term, or long-term, institutionalised by marriage or more informally through cohabitation. Sociologists have examined manifestations of love and sexuality at the macro, societal level, via official statistical data on rates of conception, birth, marriage, cohabitation and divorce, for example. As shown later in this chapter, such data are useful for tracing social trends in personal relationships, but they tell us little about emotions, feelings and sexuality in people's everyday lives.

Some sociologists have begun to examine love as an emotion, arguing that it is a crucial element in the reproduction of gender inequalities between women and men. According to Jackson, 'feminists and non-feminists alike have recognised the centrality of the concept of "love" to familial ideology, to the maintenance of heterosexual monogamy and patriarchal marriage' (1993: 202). Jackson goes on to recount a well-known feminist slogan, which points to love as an ideology, legitimising women's oppression, and trapping them in exploitative heterosexual relationships: 'It begins when you sink into his arms and ends with your arms in his sink'. For Rich (1980), the ideology of love and romance is one of the social forces which 'compel' women toward sexual relationships with men. Rich argues that men are *not* the obvious sexual partners for women, since they are bearers of the patriarchal culture which oppresses women. Instead, for Rich, the most obvious sexual partners for women are *other* women, since they share a distinct culture or set of experiences in common with one another. Women's heterosexuality is a 'choice' that has to be explained, according to Rich, and the ideology of romance and love is a key part of that explanation.

Other writers have been concerned with examining the culture of love and romance, and the way interaction with this culture is gendered. Jackson (1993) points to the representations of love and romance in literature and popular culture, including in fairy stories, teenage magazines and romantic novels. These 'cultural products' are aimed particularly at girls and women and contribute to women's more developed 'emotional literacy' (or emotional skill), compared to men. Jackson argues that, in Anglo-Saxon culture, traditional definitions of masculinity do not encourage men to be open and free with their emotions, whereas femininity is constructed as caring, nurturing and expressive. Evidence discussed by Duncombe and Marsden (1993) suggests that, within heterosexual couple relationships, tension and discord may occur due to the ways emotional expression is gendered. Their study of 60 married or cohabiting couples in long-term relationships revealed a failure of men to relate emotionally to their partners. Similar findings were reported by Mansfield and Collard (1988) in their study of newly married couples. Three months after their marriage, most wives in the study expressed disappointment with the emotional content of their relationship with their husbands. The wives felt there was inequality in the exchange of intimacy and openness of emotions, with husbands failing fully to reciprocate.

The extent to which traditional constructions of masculinity mean that men are discouraged from developing emotional literacy is evident in the characteristics of the 'New Man'. As noted in the previous chapter, the 'New Man' represents a more 'feminised' masculinity involving a greater willingness to be open with feelings and emotions. Duncombe and Marsden (1993) similarly point to the proliferation of popular accounts of men's 'emotional disabilities', including books such as *Men are from Mars, Women are from Venus* (J. Gray 1992), and *You Just Don't Understand* (Tannen 1991). Such developments suggest that gender differences in emotional literacy are becoming problematised, and Duncombe and Marsden (1993) explain this as an outcome of the increased cultural emphasis on personal, intimate, loving relationships as the ultimate source of self-fulfilment in contemporary society. In this context, they argue that the study of intimate emotional behaviour is a topic of major sociological importance: 'Men's difficulties in expressing intimate emotions will emerge as a major source of the "private troubles" underlying the "public issues" of rising divorce and family breakdown, or the instability of cohabitation among couples who may often be parents' (1993: 233). It is to the 'public issues' of changes in intimate, personal relationships between women and men, as measured by rates of marriage, cohabitation, births outside marriage, divorce and such like, that we will turn shortly. First, though, it is necessary to consider the wider context of such trends, via a focus on changes in sexual ideology and behaviour.

The 'liberalisation' of sexuality

Elliot notes that, 'In everyday thought, the decade of the 1960s stands out as a key moment of change in family values and sexual mores' (1996: 5). Yet, writers such as Weeks (1986) and Wellings *et al.* (1994) argue that the complexity of processes of change in family life and sexual morality mean that some shifts in attitudes and behaviour occurred before, and others after, the 1960s. Moreover, not all groupings of the population were affected by changes at the same time, nor to the same extent. Nevertheless, between the 1950s and the 1970s, a number of factors combined to place traditional ways of organising sexual, parental and marital relationships under great strain.

Elliot identifies the emergence of 'divergent but mutually reinforcing revolutionary discourses and tendencies' as an important pressure for change (1996: 10). For example, socialist groupings, the student protest movement, the 'counter culture' (the commune movement and the hippies) and, importantly, the women's liberation movement, all shared 'a common emphasis on equality, individual autonomy, and self-realisation' and a 'perception of the conventional . . . family as limiting freedom, impeding self-realisation and confining intimacy' (Elliot 1996: 9). Economic prosperity, full employment, the rise in women's paid employment, the expansion of the welfare state and increased geographical mobility are a further set of factors which arguably weakened aspects of conventional family and sexual moralities during this period (Elliot 1996: 10–12).

Whatever the reasons for the birth of the so-called 'permissive society', there are a number of distinctive developments which occurred in the 1960s (or thereabouts) which mark it out as an important period of change. There were key pieces of legislation, which both reflected changes in attitudes and behaviour, and contributed to further changes. The Divorce Reform Act, 1969 extended the grounds on which a divorce could be obtained, via the concept of 'irretrievable breakdown'. Under the Abortion Act, 1967 the artificial termination of a pregnancy was legalised, according to certain provisos. The terms of the Sexual Offences Act, 1967 allowed for (male) homosexuality, subject to the activities taking place in private and between consenting adults (lesbian relationships have never been recognised by legislative regulation of them – see Smith 1992). Legal controls over cultural representations of sexuality were reduced, including in the theatre, on film and television and in printed media. The development and introduction of the oral contraceptive pill from the early 1960s represented a significant advance in women's ability to control their own fertility. Until 1972, the pill was only prescribed to women who were married and was not available regardless of ability to pay until 1975.

In her assessment of its significance, Hawkes (1996) argues that there *was* something distinctively different about the 1960s in terms of a shift in the construction of sexuality. Taken together, the legislation on divorce, homosexuality, censorship, abortion and that which facilitated the distribution of the Pill, meant that the state effectively condoned the separation of sex from both marriage and reproduction. In this sense, the 1960s represents a key period in the weakening of a sexual morality dominated by Christian ideology, where sex was something of an evil, necessary for procreation, and therefore tolerable only between women and men and, moreover, only within the confines of marriage.

Are arguments about a post-war trend toward greater sexual freedom supported by survey data on people's sexual behaviour? Wellings *et al.'s* (1994) large, nationally representative survey of people aged 16–59 does provide evidence of change in sexual behaviour over time. For example, the age at which women and men first have heterosexual intercourse has gradually fallen. The survey found that, for women born in the early 1930s, the median average age at which they first had heterosexual intercourse was 21, whilst for those born in the early 1940s, it was 19. Younger cohorts of women, born between 1966 and 1975, first had heterosexual intercourse, on average, at age 17. The pattern for men shows a similar reduction over time in age at first heterosexual intercourse, although men tend to have this experience at a younger age on average than women (Wellings *et al.* 1994: 37–44). A second area of sexual behaviour has also changed over time. The survey found that younger birth cohorts report having had more sexual partners than older birth cohorts. The increase in the number of sexual partners represents a change from life-long monogamous sexual relationships within marriage, to serial sexual relationships. The increase in divorce and remarriage (see page 84) has obviously had an effect here, but so too has the greater acceptability of pre-marital and non-marital sexual relationships. Wellings *et al.* found that the acceptance of pre-marital sex is now nearly universal, with around 90 per cent of respondents to their survey saying it is not wrong at all. Young people aged 16–24 years old were even more accepting of pre-marital sex, with only 5 per cent saying that sex before marriage is wrong (1994: 244–8).

In addition to evidence on people's changing sexual behaviour over time, there are other indications of an increased degree of sexual freedom in contemporary society. Hawkes (1996) refers to the way sexuality has become a product or a commodity, marketed to consumers. She suggests that, in a society where personal relationships (and especially intimate, sexual relationships) are widely regarded as the key to self-fulfilment, 'selling sexuality' has become increasingly important. From 'how to do it' and 'how to do it better' books and videos, to the emphasis on sex in women's magazines and men's magazines (see also Chapter 7), sexual matters and sexual lifestyles are presented in a more prominent and open way than in earlier decades.

Survey data on people's changed sexual behaviour and beliefs, along with the extent to which sexuality has become an important sector of the consumer market, can be taken as evidence in support of sexual liberalisation. Has this process of social change in sexual morality been of benefit to women? A number of developments could be identified as having particular relevance for women. For example, the gradual expansion of women's access to the contraceptive pill, regardless of their age, marital status or ability to pay, means that more women than ever before have a reliable means of preventing pregnancy. Therefore, the technological development of the pill combined with official shifts in opinion as to who should benefit from it, mean that women are better placed to enjoy sex with a man without fear of pregnancy. The increased availability of abortion has enabled more women to end unplanned, unwanted pregnancies. The reduction in censorship, combined with the 'commodification of sexuality', might be argued to have opened up a cultural space for women to be more freely expressive in aspects of their sexuality. There are now pornographic magazines for women (as there have long been for men) and some publishers have found success through marketing 'erotic novels' to women readers. Moreover, as portrayed in the film *The Full Monty*, men dancers or strippers, with overtly sexual routines, regularly perform to audiences comprised mainly of women. All of this is a long way from 'lying on your back and thinking of England', once women's strategy for coping with the 'necessary evil' of procreative sex with husbands whose sexual desires were 'naturally' much stronger than their own.

It is undeniable that a shift in sexual morality *has* occurred during the second half of the twentieth century, with the 1960s representing a particularly important period of change. However, within contemporary Britain, there remain strong social norms which regulate sexual behaviour: things *are* freer now than previously, but there is not a moral 'free for all'. For example, despite increased liberalisation, Wellings *et al.* (1994) found that 70 per cent of men and 58 per cent of women disapproved of male homosexuality. Respondents were slightly less disapproving of female homosexuality (or lesbianism). The survey also provides data on people's reported sexual preferences, with 92 per cent of men and 95 per cent of women saying that their sexual experiences had been 'exclusively' heterosexual. Only 1 per cent of men and 0.25 per cent of women surveyed said that their sexual experience was 'mostly' or 'exclusively' with others of the same gender as themselves. However, around 3 per cent of men and nearly 2 per cent of women said that they had had some sexual contact with a person of the same gender as themselves within the last two years (Wellings *et al.* 1994: 182–8). Findings on the high levels of disapproval of homosexuality and the low level of predominantly homosexual and lesbian sexuality point to the resilience of heterosexuality in contemporary Britain, despite 'sexual permissiveness'. In other words, heterosexuality remains the 'hegemonic' form of sexuality (Hawkes 1996).

The 'double standard' of sexuality

In examining the ways sexual desire remains socially patterned and regulated, sociologists have also noted that important differences persist between the rules governing women's sexuality on the one hand and men's sexuality on the other. There exists a gendered 'double standard' of heterosexuality, which means that women's sexuality is subject to greater regulation compared to men's. There are a number of sources of evidence to support this claim. For example, Wellings *et al.* report on several aspects of the 'double standard' of sexuality. Men of all ages were found to report having had a higher number of heterosexual partners than women. This finding was argued to reflect a tendency for men's prolific sexual activities to be condoned, whilst women with many sexual partners are viewed much more negatively (1994: 102). A further aspect of the 'double standard' revealed by the survey was the 'sexual redundancy' of older women. Older women were found to be more likely than older men to have no sexual partner. Men, on the other hand, were found to be more likely to form a sexual relationship with a younger woman (1994: 119). For Sontag (1979) and Itzin (cited in Arber and Ginn 1991), such findings reflect the fact that women are primarily valued for their youthful, physical attractiveness, attributes which do not stand up well to increasing age. A well-known example of this aspect of the 'double standard' of sexuality is the stronger disapproval shown toward a sexual relationship between an older woman and a younger man, than is the case vice versa.

Wellings *et al.* also found marked differences between women and men in attitudes to casual sex. Whilst 63 per cent of women surveyed said that 'one night stands' were wrong, only 36 per cent of men said so (1994: 252). Arguably, this finding reflects the gendering of emotion, described earlier, and particularly the extent to which women are more heavily exposed to discourses of love and romance. In contrast, for men, 'it is through the idiom of sexual bravado and conquest, not the language of romance, that masculinity is asserted' (Jackson 1993: 214).

Studies of young people's sexuality show the resilience of the sexual double standard in contemporary Britain, some 20 to 30 years after sexual liberalisation and its supposed effects on traditional sexual morality. Lees (1989) interviewed a sample of girls aged 15 to 16 in the early 1980s (see also Lees 1986). Her findings show the importance of sexual reputation to the status of girls, which differs in important ways than that for boys. 'A girl's standing can be destroyed by insinuations about her sexual morality, a boy's reputation in contrast is usually enhanced by his sexual exploits' (1989: 19). Terms like 'slag' and 'tart' were especially important ways through which girls' sexuality was socially controlled and regulated. Lees found that this language of sexual reputation was applied exclusively to girls and there was no equivalent label set applied to boys. Her interviews with girls revealed that few were able to define a slag or a tart in any precise or consistent way. In other words, such labels were found to lack specific meaning, but were all the more powerful as a means of social control precisely because of their vagueness. In their efforts to avoid being labelled as a slag or a tart, girls had permanently to monitor and check their sexuality, including their style of dress, their friendliness with boys and their number and frequency of sexual encounters. However, girls simultaneously had to avoid appearing too uninterested and unattractive to boys, because the only sure way to avoid a negative sexual reputation was to get a steady boyfriend (1989: 26).

Research amongst 16–21-year-olds by Holland and her colleagues (1996) also revealed that similar sexual behaviour by young women and young men tends to result in different sexual reputations. In the words of one of the young women they interviewed, 'If you sleep around you're a slag, if a bloke sleeps around he's lucky' (1996: 242). Holland and her colleagues argue that the sexuality of young people in their study was regulated by what they called 'the male in the head'. In other words, both young women and young men constructed their sexuality in response to the rules of male-dominated heterosexuality. For young women, this meant they had to safeguard their sexual reputation and avoid being labelled as sexually promiscuous. For young men, the 'male in the head' meant that they had to demonstrate their sexual reputation in order to enhance their standing with their male peer group. Holland *et al.* did find evidence that some young people attempt to resist conforming to the rules of male-dominated sexuality, with women becoming more sexually assertive and men becoming more caring and emotionally involved, but nevertheless most continued to be very aware of its constraining power.

Holland *et al.*'s concept of 'the male in the head' is an attempt to describe the way in which sexuality is subject to the 'surveillance' of a hegemonic heterosexuality, which is male-dominated. It is a notion which suggests the extent to which women's sexuality continues to be constructed as 'belonging to' or being the property of, men (Richardson 1993). Although the use of chastity belts to control women's sexuality is now a part of history, it was only fairly recently (1991) that rape within marriage became unlawful. More peripheral evidence also points to men's ownership of women's bodies and sexuality. For example, those who participate in 'wife swapping' still refer to it as such, rather than 'husband swapping'. Within wedding ceremonies, fathers (most often) still give their daughters away, a custom which can be argued to represent the passing on of property between two men (Richardson 1993). Moreover, most women give up their surname on marriage and take the name of their husband (McRae 1993). The hegemony of masculine dominated heterosexuality might also explain why lesbianism is regarded as a non-authentic form of sexuality. It implies sexual activity not based around a sexual act or organ regarded as central to dominant sexual ideology, i.e. penetrative sex and the penis. An important consequence of male dominated rules of heterosexuality for women is discussed in Chapter 8, in the context of the legal processing of men's sexual violence.

For many writers, feminist and non-feminist, sexual liberalisation has not led to women and men becoming fully equal 'sexual citizens'. Yet, the real changes that have occurred in sexual morality and behaviour can be argued to have made people more aware of the constraining power of male dominated heterosexuality, and its important role in sustaining gender inequalities. In many feminist analyses, sexual liberalisation means that women are now *more* constrained: to be 'liberated' sexual beings, to be *more* sexually available for men and are consequently 'more vulnerable to exploitation in the name of (male-defined) sexual freedom' (Hawkes 1996: 11). Walby (1990) highlights two examples. First, she says that the reduction of censorship as part of the process of liberalisation has allowed the expansion of pornography (see also Chapter 7), a development which is highly problematic for women. Second, Walby argues that, in a context where heterosexual activity is now seen as desirable, normal and central to a happy, healthy and fulfilled life, 'the pressures on women to marry or cohabit with a man, with all the consequent form of servicing [including housework and childcare], are increased' (Walby 1990: 127). Such pressures further exacerbate the invisibility of lesbianism as an authentic form of sexuality (Smith 1992).

In one sense, the morally conservative New Right would agree that sexual liberalisation has made women more vulnerable than previously (Abbott and Wallace 1992). However, whilst for Walby (1990) pressures to enter a long-term heterosexual relationship have increased, moral conservatives argue instead that sexual liberalisation has encouraged an unwelcome decline in the stability of family life based around marriage and children. As a result, they argue, women are less secure and more vulnerable and so have become increasingly reliant on the welfare state to support themselves and their children. It is to changes in marriage, cohabitation and having children that we turn next. Via a focus on official statistics showing trends in patterns of family formation and marital breakdown, the issue of the ways women's personal relationships based on love and intimacy have changed can be addressed further.

(Un)tying the knot? Trends in marriage, cohabitation and divorce

According to the famous song, love and marriage 'go together like a horse and carriage', a reference to the way romantic love has long been institutionalised through marriage vows 'until death do us part'. In this section, I consider the extent to which there has been a weakening in lifelong unions formalised through marriage ceremonies. Are 'love and marriage' as old-fashioned a form of relationship as 'horses and carriages' are forms of transport?

Marriage behaviour has certainly changed significantly in the years since the Second World War. From 1945 onwards, those marrying for the first time began to do so at younger ages. In 1946, the average age at first marriage for women was 24, declining steadily until the late 1960s, when it reached 21 for women (Haskey 1995). At around this time, rates of marriage reached a post-war peak. Since the early 1970s, however, marriage rates have fallen and age at first marriage has risen. In 1993, the average age at first marriage for women was 25 years (Haskey 1995). In 1995, there were 322,000 marriages recorded in the United Kingdom, the lowest since 1926 (ONS 1998a). Moreover, the numbers of first marriages (where neither partner has been married before) are at the lowest recorded level since 1889, when the population was much smaller (Haskey 1995).

In contrast to the falling popularity of marriage, rates of cohabitation have significantly increased in the post-war decades. Cohabiting couples are a growing minority in contemporary Britain. In 1986, of all couples under the age of 60, 6 per cent were cohabiting, but by 1994, this had risen to 13 per cent (Craig 1997). Cohabitation prior to marriage has become normal in contemporary Britain. About 5 per cent of women who married in the 1960s lived with their future husbands prior to marriage, compared to about 70 per cent of those who were married in the early 1990s (Haskey 1995). One of the reasons for the rise in age at first marriage, noted above, is that women and men are living together *prior* to their marriage. Moreover, evidence suggests that the period between starting to live together and eventual marriage is becoming ever longer in duration (Haskey 1995). Nevertheless, most cohabiting couples do, eventually, legally formalise their relationship through participating in a marriage ceremony (McRae, 1993). To a considerable extent, marriage remains the predominant form of heterosexual 'coupledom'. Cohabiting or 'living together' does not seem to be an *alternative* to marriage for most people, but rather a *preliminary* stage of a marriage itself.

A third way marriage behaviour has changed is in the increasing propensity of people to end an unsatisfactory marriage, through obtaining a divorce. Of course, this has been facilitated through changes in the divorce law, including the Divorce Reform Act, 1969 and the Matrimonial and Family Proceedings Act, 1984, which mean that divorce is now more easily and more quickly obtained. In 1956–60, there was a yearly rate of two divorces per thousand married persons, but by 1980 this had risen to 12 divorces per thousand married persons (Elliot 1991). Subsequently, the divorce rate gradually rose further, reaching a peak in 1993 and has fallen only slightly since then (ONS 1998a). It has been calculated that, if present trends continue, around 40 per cent of marriages will end in divorce (Craig 1997). As divorce law has become more liberal, it has become increasingly likely that the petition for a divorce is filed by the wife, rather than by the husband. In the immediate post-war years, less than half of divorce petitions were filed by women. By the late 1970s, wives filed 73 per cent of divorce petitions and this pattern continues (Elliot 1991).

A further change in marriage behaviour is the increase in remarriages, from 20 per cent of all marriages in 1950 to 36 per cent in 1987 (Elliot 1991). In 1995, remarriages accounted for around two-fifths of the total number of marriages (ONS 1998a). Importantly, remarriages are mostly between partners where one or the other (and often both) have previously been divorced, rather than, say, widowed.

Data on marriage rates (both first marriages and remarriages), cohabitation rates and rates of divorce together suggest the resilience of marriage as an institution in contemporary Britain, albeit one that has undergone transformation since the first half of the twentieth century. Women and men are not rejecting marriage. Rather, they are cohabiting prior to marriage, perhaps on a trial basis, and if after a period of marriage things turn sour, women (in particular) are ending their unsatisfactory marital relationships. Rates of remarriage, and cohabitation prior to remarriage, suggest that many hope to find happiness and fulfilment in another heterosexual union, based around a new marital relationship. For most women and men in contemporary Britain, love and marriage still 'go together', but not in such an exclusive a way as previously. Nowadays, love also 'goes together' with pre-marital sex, cohabitation and remarriage. The extent of change in

Table 5.1 Women aged 18–49 by marital status, 1979–96, UK

Status	Year	
	1979	*1996*
Married	74%	57%
Single	18%	29%
Divorced	4%	9%
Cohabiting	11%	26%

Source: *General Household Survey 1996* (ONS 1998b)

women's personal relationships with men is shown in Table 5.1, which contrasts 1979 with 1996. During this period, the proportion of women who are married has fallen by 17 per cent, whilst the proportions who are single, divorced or cohabiting have risen by 11 per cent, 5 per cent and 15 per cent respectively.

Having and not having children: trends in births and conceptions

In the familial ideology dominant in twentieth-century Britain, first comes love, love leads to marriage, and marriage to having children. For much of the century, this has also been the order of things in practice for most people. In the previous section, changes in people's marriage behaviour were described, via a focus on marriage, cohabitation and divorce rates. Here, we consider changes in the marital status within which women have children, along with other trends in their fertility behaviour.

Having children

One of the most significant changes in patterns of family formation during the twentieth century is the sharp increase in births outside marriage. In the middle of the nineteenth century, around 6 per cent of all births were 'illegitimate', declining to 4 per cent by 1900. The proportion of births outside marriage rose during the two World Wars (1914–18 and 1939–45), but fell again to reach around 6 per cent in the 1950s–60s (Werner 1987). Since then, as shown in Table 5.2, there has been a rapid increase in the proportion of births that take place outside marriage, particularly since the late 1970s. In 1996, around 35 per cent of births were outside marriage (ONS 1998a). Nearly 30 per cent of births outside marriage were registered by both parents, and of these almost three quarters were registered by parents who shared the same address (ONS 1998a). In other words, a significant proportion of 'extra-marital' births are, in fact, births to couples who are cohabiting with one another. Half of those women who are unmarried at

Table 5.2 Births outside marriage as a percentage of all births, 1964–93, England and Wales

1964	7.2%
1977	9.7%
1988	25.6%
1993	32.2%

Source: Adapted from Table 1, Babb and Bethune (1995)

the time of their first child, moreover, are likely to be married by the time of their second (Babb and Bethune 1995). The increase in births outside marriage is linked to the changes that have occurred in marriage behaviour, especially in cohabitation. Arguably, extra-marital *conception* and *pregnancy* are now much less likely to lead to a marriage than previously. Rather than participate in 'shotgun' weddings, more couples wait until after their child is *born* before marrying, others marry after second or subsequent children and still others never marry at all (McRae 1993).

The increase in births outside marriage is linked to a second area of change in the marital contexts within which women have and raise their children: the rise in lone motherhood. In the early 1970s, lone parent families represented 8 per cent of all families with dependent children. By 1996, their proportion had increased to 21 per cent (ONS 1998b). Lone parent families are defined as a mother or father, living without a spouse and not cohabiting, with her/his dependent children (Haskey 1998). Most lone parent families are, in fact, lone *mother* families, and increasingly so. In 1971 there were 7 lone mothers for each lone father, compared to 14 in 1994 (Haskey 1996).

Up until the mid-1980s, a large part of the (gradual) increase in lone parent families was accounted for by increased divorce and separation. After the mid-1980s, the largest part of the (more rapid) increase was due to a rise in single lone motherhood (ONS 1998a). Between 1971 and 1996, the proportion of all families with dependent children headed by a single mother (that is, never married and non-cohabiting) increased from 1 per cent to 7 per cent. During the same period, the proportion of all families with dependent children headed by a divorced lone mother or a separated lone mother increased in each case from 2 per cent to 6 per cent and 5 per cent respectively (ONS 1998b). As a whole, most lone mothers have, at some point, been married (i.e. they are now divorced, separated or widowed) and many others have probably lived with their partner informally. Only 15 per cent of lone mothers have never married nor lived in a partnership outside marriage (Haskey 1998).

Since the late 1970s, there has been a trend for women to have their babies at an older age than previously. In other words, more women are deferring childbearing. In general, fertility rates for women aged over 30 have been rising, whilst those for the under 30s have been falling (Craig 1997). By the early 1990s, for the first time women aged in their early thirties were more likely to give birth than women aged in their early twenties. For example, in 1993 there were 87 births per thousand women aged 30–34, compared with 82 births per thousand women aged 20–24. (Women aged 25–29 are the most likely age group to give birth, at 114 births per thousand). Fertility rates are also rising amongst women aged 35–39, and amongst those who are aged 40 and over. For example, in 1983 there were 4.5 births per thousand women aged 40–44, compared with 5.8 births per thousand women of this age in 1993 (CSO 1995). The fact that more women are delaying having children has led to an increase in the average age of first time mothers, from 26 years old in 1976 to 29 years old in 1996 (ONS 1998a).

Not having children

General rates of fertility (that is, live births per thousand women aged 15–44) are calculated to have fallen by over 40 per cent between the 1960s and the late 1970s, in part reflecting women's greater control over fertility due to the contraceptive pill (Armitage and Babb 1996). There was a slight rise in the general fertility rate after 1977, but during the 1980s the rate remained fairly stable (ONS 1998a). In the 1990s, there has, however, been an overall fall in the total fertility rate (Craig 1997). In other words, there is an emerging trend for fewer women to have fewer children, and some are choosing not to have any children at all. Table 5.3 shows that the proportion of women without children is predicted to increase in the near future. It has been calculated that 20 per cent of women born in the 1960s will not have children (*Population Trends* 1996), compared with only 13 per cent of women born in 1947 who had not had a child by the age of 40 (CSO 1995). As Craig notes, 'Assuming that involuntary fertility has not changed, this means that childlessness by choice has increased . . . sharply' (1997: 9).

Table 5.3 Percentage of women without any live-born children

Women born in:	By age 45	Approximate end of childbearing
1924	16	1969
1934	11	1979
1944	10	1989
1954	17	1999
1964	22	2009
1969	22	2014

Source: Adapted from *Population Trends* 1996, Vol. 85: p 1–2.

Diversity and difference

Earlier in this chapter, I noted that processes of change in sexual, marital and parental relationships have not affected all groupings of the population equally. Importantly, it is young people who have shown the greatest changes in patterns of marriage and cohabitation (Haskey 1995).

Social class variations are also significant. For example, those in the highest social class have their first experience of sexual intercourse up to three years later than those in the lowest social class (Wellings *et al*. 1994), and marry at a later age, on average. The incidence of divorce and separation also varies by occupational social class, with those in higher professional and intermediate groupings having a lower rate of divorce than those in semi or unskilled groupings (Elliot 1991). Women from manual occupational class backgrounds are two and a half times more likely to have a baby outside of a marriage than women from a non-manual background (Babb and Bethune 1995).

Sexual behaviour, patterns of family formation and childbearing also show marked variations by ethnic group. Survey data provided by Wellings *et al*. show that those of Pakistani, Bangladeshi and Indian (or 'South Asian') origin are much less likely to report having had sexual intercourse before the age of 16 than other ethnic groups, including whites. This is especially true for women, with only 1 per cent of women of 'South Asian' origin reporting experiencing sexual intercourse before the age of 16, compared with 8 per cent of white women and 10 per cent of black women. Average age at first sexual intercourse also varies by ethnic origin, at 18 years for both black and white women and 21 years for 'South Asian' women (Wellings *et al*. 1994: 54).

As Jackson (1997) notes, the centrality of the ideology of love to the western tradition of marriage means that the South Asian custom of 'arranged marriages' is viewed negatively by dominant white culture. The common image is of a reluctant young woman forced into marrying a man selected by her parents. Modood *et al*. (1997) provide evidence which counters this stereotype. Whilst a majority of South Asians over the age of 35 had had their spouse chosen by their parents, this was a less common experience for younger groups, particularly amongst Hindus and Sikhs. Moreover, Modood *et al*. found that young people reported that they had varying degrees of choice over their marriage partner. In general, the survey found that the attitudes of young South Asians on arranged marriages are different to those held by their parents. Modood *et al*. concluded that, 'the traditional parentally arranged marriage is in decline, consultation and negotiation are prevalent and most young Hindus and Sikhs are now, at least in their own estimation, the final arbiters in the choice of their marriage partner' (1997: 319. See also Anwar 1998).

Berrington uses data from the *Labour Force Surveys* 1989–91 to illustrate the 'striking differences in marriage and family formation patterns among the white and ethnic minority populations in Britain' (1994: 542). First, age at marriage. Women of 'South Asian' origin are likely to marry at between two and three years earlier (at age 22–23) than whites (age 25), and between six and seven years earlier than women of Black Caribbean origin, whose average age at marriage is 30 years. The propensity of South Asians to marry relatively early means that over 80 per cent of such women aged 25–29 were currently married, compared to 60 per cent of white women. At the same age, 66 per cent of Black Caribbean women reported they were single.

Second, divorce and separation rates are relatively high amongst individuals of Black Caribbean origin, compared to other groups. Of women aged 35–39, 19 per cent reported they were currently separated or divorced, compared with 10 per cent of white women and 5 per cent of women of Pakistani and Bangladeshi origin.

Third, rates of cohabitation show marked variations by ethnicity. Between 1989 and 1991, 11 per cent of white women aged 20–29 were cohabiting, the highest proportion of any ethnic group (apart from the 'mixed' category). The proportion of women of South Asian origin aged 20–29 who were cohabiting was extremely low (2 per cent for those of Indian origin and 0 per cent for those of Pakistani and Bangladeshi origin – although, see Bhopal 1997), in part a reflection of their greater propensity to marry by the age of 30. Around 8 per cent of women aged 20–29 of Black Caribbean origin were cohabiting in 1989–91.

Turning now to childbearing and the marital status within which children are reared, the propensity to marry at early ages amongst South Asians also means the earlier onset of childbearing. However, it also means that such women have very low rates of birth outside marriage. In 1994, amongst women born in Pakistan or Bangladesh, rates of birth outside marriage were 1.3 per cent and 2.5 per cent respectively (Armitage and Babb 1996). Lone parent families, who are invariably headed by a lone mother, are especially common amongst Black Caribbeans, representing 27 per cent of such family units, compared to 8 per cent of whites and 6 per cent of those of Indian origin.

I noted in Chapter 3 that caution must be exercised when interpreting data on ethnic differences. As with patterns of participation in paid work, patterns of marital behaviour and parenting status may reflect the significant differences in the age structure of ethnic minority groupings in comparison to the white population, rather than, say, the influence of cultural traditions or the impact of racism. For example, 63 per cent of family units of Pakistani origin and 58 per cent of Indian origin are made up of a married couple with their children, compared to 32 per cent of family units in the white population. As Berrington explains, the 'preponderance of married couples with children' among these ethnic minority populations reflects their overall age profile, of a large number of 30–39-year-olds with their children now aged under 15 years old (1994: 540). Nevertheless, analyses which take this factor into account by drawing comparisons between ethnic groups for a particular age group (as above, where comparisons were made between women aged 20–29, 25–29 and 35–39) reveal significant differences in sexual and marriage behaviour, and in having children.

Elliot argues that characteristics such as the low rate of cohabitation, divorce and extra-marital births among those of 'South Asian' origin are strongly suggestive of the 'continuing integrity' of South Asian family values, particularly ideals of family honour, obligation, the primacy of mothering for women and the dominance of male authority (1996: 57). Such features lead Walby to describe Muslim Asian women in contemporary Britain as experiencing 'private patriarchy', where women are controlled individually and directly by men within the home and family environment (1990: 181. See also Bhopal 1997).

The marriage and parental status of women of Black Caribbean origin are very different, as are their patterns of participation in paid work (see Chapter 3). For Berrington, the low rates of marriage and high levels of 'independent living' (in lone parent families, for example) displayed by Black Caribbean women, support arguments that these women have a distinctive commitment to 'emotional and economic independence' from a male partner (1994: 541). Similarly, for Walby, whilst Muslim Asians are closer to the private form of patriarchy, Black Caribbean women are closer to the public form, where women have greater access to the public arena but are nevertheless subordinated within it (for a fuller discussion of Walby's theory of patriarchy, see Chapter 1). White women are positioned somewhere between Muslim Asian women and Black Caribbean women, although due to their changing participation in paid work and their changing marital and family formation behaviour, they appear to be moving more towards the Black Caribbean position (1990: 181).

Interpreting changes in personal relationships

In this chapter, I have argued that real changes have taken place during the post-war decades in women's personal, intimate relationships, as indicated by, for example, trends in rates of marriage and divorce, cohabitation and births outside marriage. These changes in sexual and family relationships are the outcome of a number of factors, including shifts in sexual and familial ideology, the increased participation of women in paid work, the availability of reliable contraception, the extension of legislation (on divorce and abortion, for example) and the expansion of the welfare state. There is little debate as to the fact that change has occurred and that these factors have been significant causes of change. There is, however, rather less consensus as to the *extent* of change and the *significance* of this change for gender relations (Elliot 1996: 34–9).

One position in the debate is that, whilst some real changes have taken place in sexual, marriage and parental behaviour, major *continuities* persist. Here, we might cite evidence that the great majority of women claim to be heterosexual in preference and practice (Wellings *et al.* 1994), that the majority of women are married with at least one child by the age of 33 (Ferri 1993) and that most births still take place within a heterosexual couple relationship (ONS 1998a).

A second position in the debate is that the changes *have* been major ones, if not in scale then in ideological or symbolic significance. Changes in sexual, marriage and parental behaviour are argued by sections of the political New Right to represent a 'regrettable' erosion of 'traditional' family forms and as contributing to a range of social problems, including lone mothers, childhood delinquency, rising welfare spending and the marginalisation of men (Abbott and Wallace 1992). For some feminists, such as Barrett and McIntosh (1982), shifts away from marriage and other 'conventional' family and parental relationships might be welcomed as signs that women are increasingly being liberated from oppressive and exploitative relationships with men and that they now have a greater degree of choice, freedom and independence (albeit often restricted by poverty and their continuing responsibility for children).

A third position in the debate proposes that there are *both* marked changes *and* continuities in contemporary sexual, marriage and parental relationships between women and men. Having reviewed each of the three positions in the debate, Elliot herself lends support to the third one, arguing that the range of available evidence suggests 'traditional' and 'liberated' sexual, marital and parental relations *coexist* with one another (1996: 38). Variations in sexual preference, age, social class and ethnicity further contribute to this 'plurality' of personal, intimate and loving relationships and make contemporary Britain a society where a much wider range of relationships are tolerated than previously. Overall, women have gained from this move towards plurality and the greater toleration of diversity. However, women's positioning in the structures of paid work (Chapter 3) and unpaid household work (Chapter 4), along with their more intensive exposure to the ideology of love and romance and the persistence of the sexual ' double standard', together mean that they remain less powerful and more constrained in their sexual and loving relationships than men. As shown in the following chapters, it is also possible to argue that some aspects of 'liberalisation', in the form of the development of technologies of conception and contraception, and the increased sexualisation of women's bodies, represent a narrowing rather than an expansion of versions of femininity for women.

Chapter 6

Body matters: technology and women's bodies

Historically, science and technology have been constructed as areas of masculine interest and expertise (Harding 1986), part of the 'public sphere' outside the home from which girls and women were excluded. In contemporary Britain, the gendering of science and technology is reflected in subject choices made by girls and boys in further and higher education (see Chapter 2) and in the structure of paid work (see Chapter 3). Masculinity continues to be partly defined through rational thought, technological competence and 'mastery over machines'. By contrast, femininity continues to be partly defined as irrational/emotional, technologically incompetent, and via women's reproductive capacities and mothering roles, as closer to 'nature' than to science (Harding 1986; Wajcman 1991). The persistence of such associations in the late twentieth century is highly significant, given both the value placed on technological 'progress' and 'advancement' and the rapid pace and widespread nature of technological developments. From genetically modified food and the cloning of sheep, to the computer and telecommunications technologies which transform the use of space, time and modes of interpersonal contact, human (mainly masculine) control over the 'natural world' is extending ever further.

For some sociologists, advances in technology are an important element in a wider set of economic, political, social and cultural changes. These changes have transformed Britain from a modern society to a 'late modern' or 'postmodern' society, characterised by risk and uncertainty and, as a consequence, a heightened search for value and meaning (Beck 1992; Giddens 1991). In the context of this disorder, insecurity, unpredictability and the search for meaning, there has been a rise in the importance of bodies as signifiers of status and as a means through which self-identity or subjectivity is expressed (Shilling 1993). People have always had some degree of control over their bodies; their intake of food and the extent of physical activity, for example, their use of tattoos, clothing and other bodily adornments, their abstinence from sex or their use of simple contraceptive devices or techniques. However, in the post-war decades especially, technological developments have greatly extended the possibility for people to control and even transform their 'natural' bodies.

In this chapter, I consider some aspects of both advances in technology and the increased preoccupation with the presentation of self via the body, through a particular focus on women's bodies. The first part of the chapter examines the issue of reproductive technologies; in other words technological interventions in biological reproduction, specifically birth control technologies (which prevent or end pregnancy) and technologies of conception (which help women to have babies). The second part of the chapter is concerned with gendered aspects of bodily presentations of self. It focuses on techniques some women use to transform their 'natural' bodies and mould them in the shape of the culturally dominant images of ideal feminine bodies, including dieting, cosmetic surgery and hormone replacement therapy (or HRT).

Choice and control in reproductive technologies

Stanworth (1987) identifies four categories of reproductive technologies. First, technologies concerned with the control of fertility, either through the prevention of conception (the condom and the Pill, for example) or the termination of a pregnancy (that is, abortion). Second, technologies used in the management of labour or childbirth, such as drugs which induce labour, caesareans and episiotomies, forceps and foetal monitoring. A third category of reproductive technologies are designed to improve the health and genetic characteristics of foetuses and babies, and include amniocentesis tests and other screening tests, and ultrasound scans. A fourth category of reproductive technologies is concerned with assisting conception, via overcoming or bypassing infertility. Examples of these 'technologies of conception' include artificial insemination, in vitro fertilisation and drugs which stimulate ovulation.

The idea that reproductive technologies have greatly benefited women is widespread. The 'medicalisation' of pregnancy and birth is generally regarded as the primary factor in the reduction of risks for the health and life of both mothers and babies. Moreover, the 'liberating' effect of contraception is frequently cited as a factor in the improved status enjoyed by women in contemporary western, industrialised societies (see Chapter 5, for example). Certainly, feminists themselves have long campaigned on the issue of birth control. It was a concern of the early feminists (Dyhouse 1989) and featured prominently in the campaigns of the 1970s Women's Liberation Movement. Of the seven 'demands' formulated to eradicate the oppression of women, two related directly to reproductive choice: 'free contraception' and 'abortion on demand' (Coote and Campbell 1987). Feminist demands for ready access to technologies of birth control stem from the belief that the striving for equality with men is heavily dependent upon women having control over their own fertility.

A radical feminist analysis of the liberating potential of reproductive technology was made by Shulamith Firestone in the early 1970s. For Firestone (1971), inequalities between women and men are biologically based, with the different reproductive capacities of women and men being especially important. Prior to the advent of birth control, women's capacity to conceive, carry, give birth to and breastfeed a child meant that women were 'at the continual mercy' of their biology and hence they became dependent upon men for survival (1971: 8–9). For Firestone, this natural difference in reproductive capacity between women and men led, over time, to the development of other, socially based gender differences. The elimination of gender differences therefore requires the replacement of natural reproduction by artificial means, through the use of technology. Firestone's argument is that all aspects of the debilitating processes of natural reproduction must be taken away from women's bodies, a strategy which would ultimately require foetuses to grow in 'artificial wombs'. Through such technology, women's ownership of their own bodies will be restored (1971: 11).

Firestone's radical analysis must have seemed bizarre and as belonging to the realms of science fiction when it was first proposed. However, from the perspective of the late 1990s, her ideas about the extent to which artificial technological reproduction can be developed seem much more within the realms of the possible. Yet scepticism over the value, purposes and effects of technological 'progress' is also much greater now than in the 1960s and 1970s. Concern over damage to the environment and characterisations of genetic engineering as 'meddling with nature' are just two examples of the loss of faith in scientific advancement and 'technological fixes'. Accordingly, more recent feminist writers have tended not to share Firestone's perspective on the liberating potential of reproductive technologies. In the next section, contrasting interpretations of two types of reproductive technologies are examined. It is shown that contemporary feminists are, at best, ambivalent about many aspects of reproductive technologies, whilst others argue that, far from liberating women, artificial interventions in the process of reproduction represent a new form of men's domination over women and their bodies.

Technologies of birth control

Birth control techniques (including the withdrawal method, primitive condoms, herbal abortifacients, pessaries, abortion and infanticide) have probably always existed, and are known to have been practised in ancient Egyptian society (Gittins 1993: 100). Nevertheless, sexually active women at risk of pregnancy in late twentieth-century Britain have a much greater choice of reliable methods of contraception and wider access to safer terminations of unwanted pregnancies than previously.

Statistical evidence presented in Chapter 5 showed that more women are deferring having children (that is, they are having babies at an older age), and more women are reaching their menopausal years without having had any children at all. Moreover, in families with dependent children, the average number of children decreased from 2.0 in 1971 to 1.8 in 1996 (ONS 1998b). Evidence on trends in women's fertility and the average number of children in families suggest both that women have become more *enabled* to control their fertility and that they *are* actually doing so. In the 1990s, rates of conception per thousand women aged 15–44 fell, as did rates of birth (Filakti 1997). Evidence suggests that these trends in conceptions and births reflected the more widespread use of technologies of birth control, specifically contraception and abortion. Between 1989 and 1995, the proportion of women using at least one form of contraception rose from 69 per cent to 73 per cent (ONS 1997a). The form of contraception women use varies by their age and marital status. Generally, however, amongst women aged 16–49, the pill was the most frequently used form of contraception (used by 25 per cent of women), followed by sterilisation, either of the woman or her partner (24 per cent), and the male condom (18 per cent). Around 28 per cent of women aged 16–49 reported using no methods of contraception (ONS 1997a).

Despite the availability of a range of contraceptives, it has been estimated that about half of all pregnancies which occur in England and Wales are unintended, due either to the failure of a chosen method of contraception or a failure to use any method of contraception (Filakti 1997). Some of these unintended pregnancies will lead to live births, others to abortion. Since the early 1970s, there has been an increase in the proportion of conceptions leading to abortion. In 1971 in England and Wales, 12 per cent of conceptions led to abortion, rising steadily to 20 per cent in 1995 (ONS 1998a). As noted by Richardson (1993), the frequency of abortion is an indication of its importance as a means of reproductive control. Nevertheless, as with forms of contraception, not all women have equal access to abortion. Under the current law (the Abortion Act, 1967), a 'legally induced' abortion must be performed by a registered medical practitioner, in an approved establishment and certified by two medical practitioners as 'necessary' according to certain grounds. These necessary grounds centre around the risk to the mental and physical health of the woman (or any of her children) if the pregnancy was to continue; and/or the risk that, if the child was born, it would suffer from serious physical or mental handicap (ONS 1997b). These grounds for legal abortion are open to varied interpretation and, consequently, there are marked variations in access to abortion regionally and according to an individual doctor's judgement. In England and Wales, almost one in three women pay for their abortion to be performed privately, because access to National Health abortion services is restricted by general practitioners and local health authorities (Abortion Law Reform Association, no date).

The greater availability of abortion and the increased range and reliability of methods of contraception have largely been welcomed by feminists, although there remain concerns about access, the health risks and unpleasant side effects of some forms of contraception, and the use of sterilisation and contraception by injection on women in underdeveloped countries (Richardson 1993: 65–8). Other sociologists have drawn attention to the broader contexts which shape the development, availability and use of birth control. Wajcman (1991), for example, highlights the commercial interests of pharmaceutical companies who have made huge profits from the success of the contraceptive pill. She also suggests that a determining factor in the development of birth control methods has been a concern with facilitating male-centred sexual enjoyment. Similarly, Roberts (1981) identifies a 'masculine hegemony' which regulates the availability and use of birth control, operating through religious ideology, the medical profession, the law and the state, as well as the nature of women's relationships with men in the context of male-dominated rules of heterosexuality (see also Chapter 5). As shown below, recognition of the wider contexts which constrain women's reproductive 'choices' is also central to analyses of technologies of conception.

Technologies of conception

Debates about women's reproductive rights and choices must necessarily incorporate arguments for women's right *to* conceive, along with their right *not* to. An unknown number of women, for a range of physiological reasons, are themselves infertile, whilst countless others experience involuntary childlessness due to their partner's infertility. In the past, very little could be done by way of medical treatment to overcome or bypass infertility. However, in the post-war decades, a range of medical interventions have been developed which offer the hope of having a child to many women who experience difficulty conceiving 'naturally'. These techniques have proven to be highly controversial, raising complex, legal, ethical and moral issues with great significance for contemporary gender relations. Artificial insemination, for example, leads to questions about the necessity for sexual intercourse, issues of paternity, and 'lesbian mothers'.

Arguably the most controversial technique to aid conception is *in vitro* fertilisation, or IVF. In this set of procedures, eggs are fertilised by sperm outside rather than inside a woman's body. There are various stages to this process, but commonly, hormonal drugs are administered to stimulate a woman's ovulation and, following intensive monitoring and testing, surgery is then performed to 'collect' any eggs. Fertilisation of eggs by sperm takes place in a laboratory container (in the popular imagination, a 'test tube') and the fertilised eggs are then placed inside a woman's body (see Crowe 1990 for a more detailed account of IVF procedures). The first 'test tube baby' born as a result of this new conceptive technology was a girl, in 1978. IVF-related techniques include egg donation, embryo donation and the freezing of embryos, eggs and sperm.

In response to concerns raised by technological interventions in 'natural' processes of reproduction, new legislation governing the area was introduced in 1990, and the Human Fertilisation and Embryology Authority (HFEA) was set up to regulate developments. Recent controversies it has overseen include the use of IVF-related techniques to enable women aged in their fifties and sixties to have children (Chazan 1995; Mihill 1995), and the case of a woman who sought to obtain permission to use her husband's sperm, which was extracted from him without his written consent prior to his death (Dyer 1997).

In 1994, nationally there were 69 clinics offering IVF treatment. Between 1 January and 31 December 1994, 19,189 women received IVF treatment, resulting in 4,417 pregnancies and 3,477 live births. During this period, the great majority (95 per cent) of treatments used the woman's own eggs (4 per cent of treatments used donated eggs and 1 per cent used donated embryos). A woman may undergo several 'treatment cycles' without success. In 1994, the live birth rate per treatment cycle was 14 per cent (HFEA 1996). According to information given to prospective IVF patients by the HFEA, in 1997 the cost per IVF treatment cycle varied from between £700 to £2,500, depending upon the particular clinic and the combination of IVF techniques involved.

These are some of the facts about IVF, as a form of new conceptive technology. As noted above, IVF and related techniques have proved highly controversial and for a number of reasons. Moralists, for example, are concerned that the techniques lead to the creation of human life, via fertilised eggs or embryos. If unused, questions are then raised about the right to (further) life of these 'technological' creations. In addition to these deeply moral questions, there are also complex ethical and legal issues around biological and social motherhood (and fatherhood). For example, the techniques may involve the implanting of one woman's eggs in another woman's body (perhaps having been fertilised by an unknown donor's sperm). Although sensitive to these issues, feminists have as a primary concern the analysis of technologies of conception in terms of their effects on women, in the context of a society where women already suffer inequalities of power and disadvantage relative to men.

Whilst there is a broad consensus amongst feminists that technologies of birth control have been largely beneficial to women, there is a much greater diversity of response to the technologies of conception. One interpretation of the new conceptive technologies like IVF is that they represent a positive application of scientific knowledge and techniques, which have contributed to the extension of women's rights to self-determination and control over their own bodies. Such technologies of conception provide women with the possibility of having a child, of becoming a mother, when previously this choice was not open to them, due either to their own infertility or that of their partner. Here, technology is characterised as beneficial to and empowering of women, acting to extend their reproductive choice and rights via assisting in their wish to have a child. In this view, technologies of conception liberate infertile women from the dictates of their own individual biology in the same way as technologies of birth control liberate fertile women from the dictates of their individual biology.

In other feminist analyses, however, the parallels between technologies which either prevent women from, or assist them in, having children lay more in the extent to which they represent an increase in men's control over women's bodies. In other words, rather than contributing to women's liberation, technologies like IVF amount to a new and disturbing form of oppression. The most identifiable feminist grouping who oppose development like IVF on these grounds are the Feminist International Network of Resistance to Reproductive and Genetic Engineering (or FINRRAGE). For these feminists, the science at the basis of technologies of conception could ultimately lead to men removing the 'last woman-centred process' from women's control (Hanmer 1987: 96). In this interpretation, the new technologies of conception, originally developed to assist the minority of women who are infertile, could be employed as the preferred methods of all biological reproduction. The artificial processes give men as a social grouping an unprecedented degree of control over biological repro-duction, enabling, for example, the birth of boys rather than girls (via sex selection), multiple births rather than single births, and offering guarantees of paternity. In the analyses of FINRRAGE, technologies like IVF amount to the 'taking over' of women's reproductive processes by men as an expres-sion of 'womb envy'. Far from extending women's rights and choices through liberating them from their biology (as argued by Firestone), the 'artificial invasion' of women's bodies by technology (Klein 1987: 65) represents a patriarchal strategy to take from women the one advantage they have over men. The new technologies, in this perspective, are a highly technological, medicalised form of violence against women's bodies and are to be feared and resisted as practices which continue the long-standing exploitation of women's bodies for masculine advantage (see Arditti, Klein Duelli and Minden 1989; Corea *et al.* 1987).

Neither of the interpretations of conceptive technologies (like IVF) considered so far are fully satisfactory, for they both pay insufficient attention to the wider social context which acts to shape their development, application and use. Rather than interpreting conceptive technologies as either uniformly liberating or uniformly oppressive of women, it is more satisfactory to take a nuanced view and argue that artificial techniques of reproduction have both advantages and disadvantages. Stanworth (1987) and Wajcman (1991), for example, point to the interests of the (mainly male) scientists and doctors in establishing and extending a prestigious, lucrative research and medical specialism, and note that the state has facilitated the development and application of some technologies, whilst frustrating others. Women's 'choices' and reproductive rights are therefore constrained by a shifting alliance of professional and state interests.

In assessing the impact of the new technologies on women, recognition must also be given to the fact that some women are more able to make choices than others. As noted earlier, clinics offering conceptive services are limited and the financial costs of the treatments are high. In addition to geographical location and finances, women may find that their age, marital status, sexuality, ethnicity or ablebodiedness further constrains their access to treatment. As Wajcman concludes, 'women who are already advantaged in society have been in a position to benefit from recent reproductive techniques. In this area as elsewhere, technologies operate within and reinforce pre-existing social inequalities' (1991: 78). In other words, writers like Wajcman, Stanworth and Hanmer, in her more recent writings (1993), acknowledge that the new conceptive technologies have extended some women's rights of self-determination and enabled some women to make choices to become mothers. A major concern is that the new conceptive technologies coexist with particular constructions of femininity within which motherhood is central. As Wajcman explains, 'these new technologies are about fulfilling, rather than rejecting, the traditional feminine role' (1991: 57). In the context of a powerful ideology of motherhood, the new conceptive technologies can therefore be argued to represent a further constraint on women to fulfil their 'natural' desires to have a child. Rather than accepting their infertility as a 'natural' fact of life, however unfortunate, the existence of new technologies may compel women to seek 'technological fixes'. Nonetheless, Purdy (1996) argues that recognising the socially constructed nature of women's desires for children does not reduce its power in women's everyday lives. In the context of constructions of femininity where motherhood is central, being unable to have children may be experienced as devastating and painful. Therefore, on these grounds new conceptive technologies can be argued to have a humanitarian value and to extend women's control of their bodies.

Although acknowledging the value of technologies of conception, Stanworth and Wajcman also accept parts of the FINRRAGE analyses, especially the significance of masculine domination of the scientific and medical techniques of artificial conception and the extent to which these groupings now have a greater capacity to control aspects of women's lives than previously. Stanworth (1987), however, points out that the FINRRAGE analysis is overstated. It incorporates both an over-inflated view of the powers and interests of science and medicine and a demeaning view of women as their hapless, willing, compliant and powerless victims. Moreover, through suggesting that all and any interventions in reproduction are deleterious to women, the FINRRAGE position prioritises 'natural routes' to motherhood (see also Delphy 1993) and thereby denies the real, life-enhancing benefits 'artificial methods' have brought to many thousands of women since 1978.

For Stanworth, as for other writers, advances in reproductive technologies are 'a double-edged sword' (1987: 15). In the context of men's domination of science and medicine, techniques like IVF do represent an increase in masculine control over women's bodies. Yet, in a context which constrains women to adhere to the culturally dominant construction of femininity where motherhood is central, such technologies can be argued to have extended women's 'choices' and, therefore, control over their bodies. Clearly, one of the main problems with the new conceptive technologies is that the extension of fertility through artificial means reinforces constructions of women's femininity in terms of the reproductive functions of their bodies. Technology now extends the reproductive element of femininity to the previously infertile and also to the post-fertile (or the post-menopausal). To this extent, these technologies can be argued to have encouraged a narrowing of understandings of what women can be and do in contemporary society: technology has the potential to facilitate motherhood for all women, and for ever longer periods of their lives (see also Sawicki 1993). The ways other 'technologies of femininity' can be employed to incorporate women within a narrow range of femininity, according to culturally dominant ideals, are considered next.

Technologies of femininity: managing and making feminine bodies

In everyday, common-sense explanations of gender inequality, the differences between men's bodies and women's bodies are taken as indications of the 'naturalness' of their contrasting roles and statuses in society, and are seen as the main reason why women and men can never be truly or fully equal. As noted in Chapter 1, such populist theories of gender inequality have their academic equivalents in the writings of natural scientists, socio-biologists and some feminists (e.g. Firestone 1971). For sociologists like Connell (1987), however, the bodies of women and men are not purely 'natural'. Instead, our bodies (the interiors and visible exteriors) are outcomes of both natural and social processes. As an example, Connell describes a set of social practices which, in combination, act to *negate* (or minimise) similarities between women's bodies and men's bodies, through exaggerating their differences. One important practice through which this is achieved is via gendered clothing and adornments: make-up, skirts, dresses, tights, high-heeled shoes, and handbags for women; trousers, ties, flat shoes and 'executive' briefcases for men. Connell also describes how social practices literally *transform* the body in a physical sense, (re)creating masculine bodies and feminine bodies. For example, boys and men are encouraged more than girls and women to be physically active, to develop and sustain strength, endurance and physical confidence. This social practice facilitates the differing physicality of masculine and feminine bodies and translates into muscle tone, posture, and the texture of bodies. In other words, Connell highlights the extent to which, rather than our bodies determining our masculinity or femininity through our social practices, we *make* our bodies either feminine or masculine. For Connell, negations and transformation of bodies are part of an ongoing effort 'to sustain social definitions of gender, an effort that is necessary precisely because the biological logic . . . cannot sustain the gender categories' (1987: 81).

Connell suggests that the advantageous social positioning of heterosexual men is reflected in the dominance of particular idealised body images. Evidence in support of this claim is provided by Grogan (1998), who found that heterosexual men are much happier with their bodies than either women or gay men. The power (heterosexual) men have in constructing culturally dominant images of bodies is further reflected in the extent to which, in the media, the 'ideal body' is young and female (Grogan 1998). In the culturally dominant construction of femininity, the age and sexual attractiveness of women's bodies are central. The idealised feminine body is also slim, invariably white and necessarily able-bodied.

Drawing on Connell's (1987) arguments, it is possible to identify what I shall call 'technologies of femininity', techniques employed by women to manage their 'natural' bodies and make them conform more closely to the culturally dominant images of what 'valuable' feminine bodies look like. In addition to routine practices involving clothing, make-up, jewellery and hairstyles, women may also 'negate' and 'transform' their bodies through: removing 'unfeminine body hair' on legs, face and in armpits; cosmetic surgery to enhance their breasts, remove fat or tighten sagging and wrinkling skin (see Davis 1995, 1997b); controlling their intake of food via dieting; and prolonging their 'feminine youthfulness' via hormone replacement therapy (HRT). The remainder of this chapter considers arguments and debates that have arisen around two of these technologies of femininity, namely HRT and dieting.

Managing the ageing female body: the menopause and HRT

The menopause is a physiological process which signals the end of a woman's capacity to conceive a baby, just as the onset of menstruation signals the beginning of that capacity. It involves changes in levels of hormones, particularly the 'feminine' hormone oestrogen, and symptoms experienced include rapid changes in body temperature (commonly referred to as 'hot flushes'), vaginal dryness, decreased bladder control, unpredictable vaginal bleeding, 'mood swings' and depression. In the past, the menopause was interpreted as a natural and inevitable physiological ageing process, as a loss of fertile womanhood, a sign that youthfulness had ended and old age and, eventually, death were ever closer. As suggested by Hepworth (1987), given the shorter life expectancies in past times, that negative perceptions were made of the menopause as a sign of the onset of old age, is hardly surprising. However, as life expectancy has risen during the twentieth century, and the importance of bodies as bearers of cultural value and subjectivity has increased, bodily indications of ageing, like the menopause, have been subject to reinterpretation. As Hepworth (1987) puts it, there are now a lot of years left to live after the first appearance of bodily indicators of growing old. Rather than interpreting physiological processes of ageing like the menopause as a sign that one's life is coming to an end, instead it is more likely to be regarded as a marker of a new stage of life.

Changes in interpretations of menopause, from a natural physiological transition involving loss and endings, to be accepted and endured, to more positive interpretations of it, provide the background for the controversy surrounding hormone replacement therapy, or HRT. Prescribed for women, HRT treatment replaces oestrogen lost with 'the change of life', with manufactured hormones, and thereby is intended to alleviate the unpleasant symptoms of the menopause. It is also claimed to have other beneficial effects on health and vitality, including prolonging a youthful appearance, protecting against the bone disease osteoporosis and reducing the risk of strokes and heart disease (see 'publicity' for HRT reviewed in Lupton 1996a, and Klein and Dumble 1994). In other words, HRT is 'dominantly represented as an age-retarding commodity, like expensive moisturisers or cosmetic surgery, as well as a health-protective strategy, similar to the activities of engaging in exercise or giving up salt' (Lupton 1996a: 94). Along with the various reproductive technologies discussed earlier, HRT is an example of the application of science and technology to intervene in the 'natural functions' of a woman's body. Its introduction and use has generated contrasting responses, both among feminists and others.

For pharmaceutical companies and medical scientists, as well as general medical practitioners, menopause is predominantly understood as a 'deficiency disease' for which a cure is needed – the logical remedy taking the form of hormonal supplementation or 'replacement' (Komesaroff, Rothfield and Daly 1997: 3), to be taken for the rest of a woman's life. In one popular advice book, HRT is described as 'the greatest treasure of a middle-aged woman's life', making her feel like a 20-year-old, sustaining and improving her sex life and contributing to the continuing happiness of her marriage (Gorman and Whitehead 1989). In feminist analyses, however, menopause is not characterised as a disease and so HRT is regarded as a further example of the 'medicalisation' of women's bodies and natural reproductive functions. For Klein and Dumble, for example, the prescription of HRT amounts to the 'drugging' of healthy women, and is 'yet another form of medical violence' against women which therefore 'disempowers' them (1994: 339). Klein and Dumble dispute the 'beneficial' effects of HRT, arguing that, despite the heavy promotion of it in the media and in the medical literature, only a minority of women are actually taking it, and moreover, half discontinue the treatment within one year. Klein and Dumble focus on the debilitating side-effects of HRT (including vaginal bleeding, severe headaches, increased risks of cancer, and addiction) as a major reason why women stop taking it and others choose not to, despite the pressures for them to do so. For Klein and Dumble, HRT does not represent a 'real' extension of choice and control for women, but rather an extension of patriarchal conventions of 'valuable' and 'proper' femininity (that is youthful and sexually active) to women in their later years of life. Instead of artificially prolonging their youthful femininity with medical technology, women should develop a positive attitude to their increasing age, and grow older 'naturally' with joy and dignity. Similar exhortations for women to grow old 'naturally' and gracefully are made by Greer (1991). For Greer, the menopause represents a wholly positive transition in a woman's life. It allows them to reclaim the sense of self that existed prior to the onset of menstruation, an event which constrains women to be primarily sexual and reproductive beings. Critics of the 'disease model' of the menopause, who therefore oppose the use of HRT, do recognise that the symptoms of the menopause are unpleasant and debilitating for many women. Rather than taking manufactured hormones, however, many of these writers advocate the use of 'natural' remedies, for example, alterations in diet or taking herbal medicines (Kenton 1995).

Feminist analyses of the menopause and of HRT have themselves been subject to criticism. Lupton (1996), for example, argues that in portraying the menopause as a 'transition of self discovery', and a prelude to sexual and reproductive liberation, some feminists are themselves seeking to predefine the menopause in certain ways for women. Moreover, she argues, some feminist critiques of HRT are often 'contradictory and selective' in their representations of 'natural' and 'artificial' processes and treatments. If the symptoms of the menopause are 'natural', arguably any intervention to alleviate their unpleasantness is 'unnatural', including the use of herbal remedies. Lupton further contends that there is a contradiction between feminist arguments *for* contraceptive technologies like the Pill (which is a manufactured hormonal treatment) and criticisms raised *against* HRT. Finally, Lupton argues that feminist critiques often fail fully to contextualise the 'choices' about HRT made by women in the middle years of their life. In late-modern societies, dominant cultural values place heavy pressure on individuals to act 'rationally' and follow strategies to maintain valued, that is youthful, attractive, healthy bodies. In this context, taking HRT is just another 'bodily maintenance' strategy. Lupton's assessment of feminist critiques of HRT is a useful one. Arguably, however, she herself pays insufficient attention both to the *gendered* nature of exhortations for 'body maintenance' as an expression of self and to the negative valuing of feminine *ageing*. In the context of a society where women's bodies are primarily valued for their youthful attractiveness to men and their reproductive capacities, the menopause may be experienced as a major loss of value and meaning by women. HRT as a 'bodily maintenance' treatment therefore has a heightened significance beyond the general rise in importance of bodies as the bearers of status in late-modern society. It represents a means of retaining status in a society where definitions of 'valuable' feminine bodies are narrow and constraining, and where, via the ageing of the population, the proportion of women with 'aged' bodies is set to massively increase.

Women's bodies, food and dieting

Cosmetic surgery and HRT represent fairly 'high-tech' methods of transforming 'natural' female bodies into ones which are accorded a higher cultural value. Currently, cosmetic surgery and HRT are used by only a small minority of women. A more 'low-tech' and much more widely used 'technology of femininity' is dieting, where the quantity and/or types of food eaten are deliberately limited in order to transform the size, weight and shape of the body.

Dieting amongst women is a common, almost routine practice and is much more prevalent amongst women than it is amongst men (Dolan 1994; Germov and Williams 1996). In interviews with 200 women, Charles and Kerr (1986) found that over three-quarters had dieted out of a concern with their body weight. Studies of eating habits and satisfaction with body image amongst girls suggest that the gender division of dieting as a feminine practice begins in childhood. Hill, Oliver and Rogers (1992) found that girls aged 9 and upwards were dissatisfied with their body shape and size, whether they were objectively 'overweight' or not. Grogan and Wainwright (1996) interviewed girls aged 8 who reported their current worries about being 'fat' and their desire to be thin when they were adult women. A larger-scale survey by the Schools Health Education Unit found that nearly half the 14- and 15-year-old girls mistakenly thought of themselves as overweight and that many dieted by missing out on meals. One in five girls did not eat breakfast and one in seven did not eat lunch (Carvel 1998). As Wardle *et al.* (1993: 180) conclude, such studies are revealing of the 'self-denigration and unrealistic weight goals that prejudice the well-being of many young women'.

The prevalence of dissatisfaction with body image and the practice of dieting amongst women is widely argued to reflect the constraining dominance of contemporary ideals of valuable feminine bodies. As Lupton writes, 'Given the current elision of sexual attractiveness with a slim body, many individuals make efforts to conform to this ideal' (1996b: 137). Eating disorders, such as anorexia nervosa and bulimia, are the extreme versions of the problematic relationship many women have with food and their body image, as a consequence of pressures to attain slim and sexually attractive bodies (Charles and Kerr 1986; Dolan 1994; Lupton 1996b; MacSween 1993). Although there is evidence that both self-starvation and restriction of amounts of particular types of foods have long existed, particularly as a display of religious piety (Lupton 1996b), it is likely that the scale of such practices has massively increased in the late twentieth century and that their meanings are substantially different (MacSween 1993).

One interpretation is that, in late-modern or postmodern society, controlling food intake and transforming the shape of one's body is a way of attaining value and meaning and of expressing one's sense of self, especially for women (Giddens 1991; Lupton 1996b). Others have suggested that the shift in the second half of the twentieth century away from the 'voluptuous, curvaceous' ideal to the slimmer, thinner ideal is linked to changes in women's status and position in society. No longer positioned primarily as matronly, maternal, reproductive beings where fatness equals fertility, thin bodies in women are argued to symbolise the sexuality and independence of contemporary women (for example, Dolan 1994. See also Chapter 5). Importantly, though, such analyses fully recognise that this shift in ideal body image acts to disempower women, since most women do not match up to the 'thin ideal' (Germov and Williams 1996).

Analyses of body images point to the ways in which women and girls internalise culturally dominant, masculine-defined norms of valuable feminine bodies which are relentlessly promoted in the media and through the interests of the diet, fitness and health industries (Germov and Williams 1996; Grogan and Wainwright 1996). Having reviewed evidence on the media's influence on eating problems, Walker and Shaw conclude 'it appears that the media's images have an effect upon women's self and body image, particularly if they already have a reason to be sensitive to their body size (eating disorder, unhealthy eating attitudes, adolescence and pregnancy)' (1994: 50). Significantly, these categories of women with reasons to be sensitive to their body size encompass most women and at several periods within their lives.

Evidence suggests, however, that not all groups of women are subject to the same cultural pressures to be thin. For example, eating disorders like anorexia and bulimia are more prevalent amongst middle-class women (MacSween 1993: 1) and less prevalent amongst women of Asian and African-Caribbean ethnicities than white women (see references in Wardle et al. 1993). In exploration of cultural variations in the 'thin ideal' (Germov and Williams 1996), one study compared perceptions of ideal body shape and the dieting and weight concerns held by British Asian and British white young women (Wardle *et al.* 1993). The Asian women in the study were less likely to describe themselves as 'too fat', were less likely to want to lose weight and were less restrained in their eating habits than the white women. The researchers found, though, that the Asian women were slimmer than the white women and when this factor was taken into account, differences between the two groups were reduced. However, the Asian women were not more satisfied with their bodies *because* they more closely matched the 'thin ideal'. In fact, Asian women were found to favour even slimmer body images than the white women. Instead, Wardle and her colleagues concluded that the Asian women were less negative about 'fatness' than the white women and so were more satisfied with their bodies overall. Its important to note that Wardle *et al.*'s research shows that Asian young women were only *relatively* more satisfied than white women. Levels of dissatisfaction were still significant amongst the Asian women, with over half of them saying they wanted to lose weight (compared to 70 per cent of the white women). 'Like other studies in the body image area, this investigation confirmed the negative appraisal of body size reported by a majority of normal weight young women' (Wardle *et al.* 1993: 180).

Choices, constraints, resistance

In this chapter, I have examined a range of ways through which contemporary women are constrained to adhere to culturally dominant images of femininity, and the extent to which technology is implicated in the reproduction of 'valued' feminine bodies. In debates about the impact reproductive technologies and technologies of femininity like HRT and dieting have upon women, issues of choices and constraint are central. There is a recognition that these developments do extend the right of bodily control to individual women, for whom becoming a mother, retaining a youthful femininity or conforming to the 'thin ideal' are important to their sense of self. Moreover, dieting and the other technologies of femininity may be positively experienced by women, via a sense of empowerment gained through the control they exercise over their bodies. However, there is also a recognition that women exercise their 'choices' to undergo IVF treatment, take HRT or semi-permanently monitor and restrict their intake of food, in a social context which places great pressures on them to do so. Therefore, whilst for individual women these techniques have advantages, for women as a whole they can be argued to represent a cumulative narrowing of the range of valuable femininities within a masculine-dominated culture.

Clearly, not all women uncritically accept constructions of femininity as centred around motherhood, youthful sexual attractiveness and a slim body. For example, evidence suggests that the dominant representations of the menopause as an illness to be treated are countered by some women's own more neutral constructions of it as an event of minimal importance, one

Figure 6.1 Cartoonist Kerber satirises the prevalence of the 'thin ideal' for fashion models

Figure 6.2 Dawn French (bottom right) and Jo Brand (top left) are role models for the many women whose own bodies do not conform to the 'thin ideal'

Photograph by Trevor Leighton

which does not greatly affect their sense of self or womanhood, and therefore not one which requires 'treatment', like HRT (Hunter and O'Dea 1997). More generally, there has been increasing controversy over the prevalence of 'anorexic' fashion models and the messages this conveys to girls and young women about desired and admirable body shapes (see Figure 6.1). Women may also consciously reject the 'culture of slenderness' (Grogan and Wainwright 1996), accepting and revelling in their 'voluptuous body in contrast to the thin ideal' (Germov and Williams 1996). Several authors note the growth of an anti-dieting movement or the 'fat rights' movement, especially visible in the United States of America, and the presentation of alternative feminine body images via role models such as Dawn French and Jo Brand (see Figure 6.2. For Jo Brand, see also Wagg 1998). However, it may be significant that both these women are comediennes rather than fashion models, pop stars or actresses. Within popular culture and the mass media, the overwhelming representation of the ideal female body remains the young, sexually attractive and slender body. The space for challenges to dominant constructions of femininity, although growing, remains a limited one. This theme is explored further in the next chapter.

Chapter 7

Scripting femininities: popular media culture

The role the various media of communication play in conveying ideas about gender has been noted in earlier chapters. For example, children's books and television programmes were argued to be heavily stereotyped by gender, thereby contributing to the marginalisation and disadvantage girls face within the education system (see Chapter 2). Leisure reading, in the form of girls' magazines and women's romantic novels, was argued to facilitate women's greater 'emotional literacy' and therefore the gendered construction of emotion as 'feminine'. In addition, shifts in sexual morality were noted to be reflected in the increased marketing of sexual cultural products (including men 'dancers' or strippers, erotic novels and pornography) to women consumers (Chapter 5). In the previous chapter, the media was said to exhort women to conform to particular ideals of femininity, as these are marked on the body: slim, youthful, sexually attractive. That the various media of communication are so often invoked in explanations of gender inequality is a reflection of their importance in contemporary society. For many sociologists, Britain, like other western, industrialised countries, is a 'media-saturated' society. Images and information are widely available on a mass scale, especially via television and printed media, assisted by advances in communication and computer technologies. The penetration of information and images is so extensive that it is 'interwoven' with everyday life (Abercrombie 1996: 1–3). Consequently, individuals who may wish to avoid the 'media-saturated' society have to try very hard to do so.

The overwhelming presence of the mass media in contemporary Britain is one reason why it is necessary to devote a whole chapter in consideration of their role in producing and sustaining gender inequality. A second reason is the sheer complexity of the relationship between the various media of communication and their audiences. For example, assuming (for the moment) that it *is* possible to identify a uniform representation of femininity, damaging to women's status and position, there remains a problem of establishing a *causal* relationship between the representations and their effects. To claim that there is a direct link between media representation and women's disadvantaged position involves a whole host of assumptions, not least that audiences are passive and fully accepting of the 'dominant ideology' the media uniformly communicate to them.

In this chapter, I focus on representations of femininity within several forms of popular media culture. First, I examine academic analyses of two forms of popular media culture aimed primarily at women, namely television soap operas and magazines for girls and women. Then, I review arguments and debates which surround popular media forms aimed primarily at men and which offer particular representations of women, namely pornography and the 'New Lads'' magazines, such as *Loaded*. As shown below, in some analyses, these varied forms of popular media culture are argued to reproduce subordinate femininities. In others, the complexity of the relationship between cultural products and audiences is emphasised, so that, although the media are seen to play an important role in producing and sustaining gender inequality, the processes through which this is achieved are regarded neither as simple nor as wholly effective.

Feminine genres

Feminist-influenced analyses argue that the mass media and cultural institutions more generally are dominated by men (as active managers of and actual producers of images, information and entertainment) and by masculine representations of gender. These processes often result in the prioritisation of masculinity and the marginalisation or stereotypical depiction of femininity. Consequently, in their analyses of soap operas and magazines for girls and women (cultural products purposively developed to attract female audiences) a primary concern has been whether these 'feminine genres' represent a 'ghetto' or, more positively, a valuable cultural space that is beneficial to women (Geraghty 1991: 198).

Soap operas

Soap operas originated in 1930s America, when in an effort to attract both audiences and advertisers to daytime radio, broadcasters developed programmes which would be appealing to women. Hence, 'serial stories' were developed featuring prominent women characters, focused on feminine concerns of home and family, and sponsored by companies advertising products of interest to women, especially washing (or soap) powder (see Allen 1995; Kilborn 1992). In Britain, the later development of commercial radio and television, and indeed daytime television, means that British soap opera has a slightly different history; nevertheless, it belongs to the same genre. Currently, of the five terrestrial television channels, four have programmes which are recognisably 'soap operas' and which regularly provide them with their highest viewing figures: *Eastenders* (BBC1), *Coronation Street* (ITV), *Brookside* (Channel Four), *Family Affairs* (Channel Five).

What are the distinctive features of soap opera as a genre? First, soap operas are argued to have a distinctive narrative form and structure. In other words, the way they tell their 'stories' marks them out as different from other fictional television programmes. Soap operas are 'never ending stories' and so are said to lack 'narrative closure'. They are continuous serials, comprising several different plot lines, running simultaneously. The way the passing of time is represented within soap operas is also argued to be distinctive. Soaps have their own 'history' which the multiple plot lines often draw upon. Soap opera 'time' is also organised to match daily life and the way time passes within it. This is one aspect of soap operas' 'realist convention', in that they attempt to reflect what ordinary, everyday life is like (Abercrombie 1996: 48–50). In British soaps, this has tended to mean white, urban, working-class life. The second set of distinctive features that make soap operas recognisable as such are the content of the stories they tell. The settings of soap opera are argued to be the ordinary, everyday worlds, where personal and emotional life are central. Hence, there is an emphasis on family life and the world of the home, rather than the world of paid work, and an emphasis on community and locality. This orientation to family, home and community means that women characters are central figures in soap operas, and it is their concerns and behaviour which often propel the multi-stranded plots of soap operas forward (Abercrombie 1996: 50–54). Analysts of the soap opera genre have argued that both its narrative form and its narrative themes are 'feminine'. In other words, the way the stories are told and their thematic focus make them especially popular with women. At the same time, however, these features make them less valued since they place them within 'low' (feminine) rather than 'high' (masculine) culture.

As Brunsdon (1995) explains, early feminist analysis of the mass media was 'realist' in its approach. In other words, the concern was to highlight the disparity between the narrow, stereotypical depictions of women (as either sex objects or housewives), and the reality of most women's lives. Consequently, soap operas were identified as vehicles for the perpetuation of traditional gender ideology, where women's value was as wives and mothers and their places were in the home and the local community. 'The programs were one instance of the brainwashing project of the mass media, the project to keep women thinking that all they could do was be housewives' (Brunsdon 1995: 58). Early feminist analyses were then hostile, in that soap operas were regarded as an expression of patriarchal ideology, as well as disdainful toward the women who were soap operas' main audience. In part, this analysis of soap opera reflected ideas held more generally in media and cultural studies about the relationship between media forms (or 'texts') and audiences (whether viewers or readers). In the 'dominant text' view of the relationship between media and audiences, the text (in this case soap opera) is seen to have a largely singular meaning, which acts to promote dominant ideology and thereby contributes to the maintenance of the (gender) status quo. The audience, in this perspective, is passive, open and receptive to the meaning promoted by the text (Abercrombie 1996: 200).

As Strinati (1995) notes in his review of feminist theories of popular culture, more recently there has been a criticism of the simplicity of the 'realist' approach. Instead of assuming that the mass media and popular culture can operate as mirrors reflecting the reality of everyday life, more recent feminist argument proposes that these institutions themselves actively construct 'reality'. Here, the distinction between 'real women' and 'images of women' is seen as a false one. Our understandings of what women are and how femininity is experienced are argued to be heavily mediated through symbolic representation within the media and popular culture (Brunsdon 1995: 51). As a consequence, the focus of analysis shifts away from images of women as detrimental and in need of rectification, to the ways media and cultural texts construct femininity, representing it as 'easy and naturalised' (McRobbie 1997: 172), as well as the ways women themselves are actively engaged in this process.

This shift in analytical focus was in part a reflection of changed understandings as to the nature of the relationship between media 'texts' and their audiences. More recent research within media and cultural studies has emphasised the 'dominant audience' view. Here, the text is not seen to have a singular meaning, but instead is argued to be 'polysemic' in meaning. In other words, there are a variety of meanings within a text, allowing a range of possible interpretations amongst its audience. In this model of the relationship between the text and the audience, the latter are not seen as passive, but rather as engaging actively and analytically with the former. This active, skilful, contemplative response heightens the likelihood of resistance or opposition to any dominant ideological meanings a text may promote (Abercrombie 1996: 201). Furthermore, in this approach, the audience is understood as heterogeneous, comprising persons differentiated by class, gender, ethnicity, age and sexuality (for example), social characteristics which further influence the ways a text may be interpreted. Attention is also paid to the everyday contexts within which media texts are consumed, especially the power relations that operate within families and domestic settings. These are argued to shape both access to and interpretations made of media texts. For example, Morley found that the gendered relationship women and men had to 'the home' affected their styles of watching television. For men, 'home' was associated with not being at work and so was for them primarily a space for leisure. For women, even if they also had a paid job, 'home' was also work space, because of the primary responsibility they had for housework and caring work within it. This meant that women tended to watch television whilst simultaneously doing household work, for example, ironing, cooking or feeding children (Morley

1986). Gray found that there were similar processes shaping women's consumption of television and pre-recorded videos, in her study of the 'gendering' of video recorders. One of her findings was that men retained expertise over the programming of video recorders and also control over the remote controls used to operate them (Gray 1992). Such studies show us that media consumption 'is as much an interaction between family members as it is between text and [audiences]' (Moores 1993: 59).

Such shifts in theoretical understanding and analytical focus have encouraged a re-evaluation of soap operas as a feminine genre. Instead of being hostile and disdainful of soap operas and their audiences, scholars became interested in why women found them so pleasurable. The work of Geraghty (1991) and Brown (1994) are good examples of this more positive evaluation of soap opera as a feminine form of popular media culture.

Geraghty's (1991) work focuses on soap operas broadcast in the evenings on British television in the 1980s, including American series (*Dallas, Dynasty*) and British series like *Coronation Street* and *Eastenders*. Geraghty analyses these programmes as texts, that is, in terms of the representations of women they contain and the meanings they offer to women audiences. According to Geraghty, soap operas 'offer a space for women in the television schedules which not only acknowledges their existence, but demonstrates their skills and supports their point of view' (1991: 196). It is the 'validation of women's skill in the personal sphere' which is the basis of the pleasure women gain from watching soaps, in the context of broader ideology which accord such skills little value (1991: 195–6). For Geraghty, however, the representations of women soap operas offer are contradictory ones. On the one hand, soaps recognise that not all women are the same and present different aspects of women's experiences. Women characters in soap operas are rarely all good, or all bad. They are often depicted as struggling with the competing demands on them, and are sometimes shown resisting their domestic and family responsibilities in order to pursue their other desires. Geraghty suggests that these representations of femininity are ones that women audiences can readily identify with and are a source of pleasure to them. On the other hand, soap operas do tend to project a homogenised, universal femininity based on highly conventional, traditional feminine skills and concerns, centred around the family, home and locality. Geraghty implies that the polysemic meaning around femininity within soap operas allows the differentiated female audience to variously interpret the representations of femininity they encounter. To this extent, soap operas are potentially both a ghetto, where femininity is valued but firmly based within the domestic and the personal, and a beneficial cultural space, where women audiences can actively enjoy the struggles of strong, independent women characters (Geraghty, 1991: 197–8).

The argument that soap operas can act as a beneficial cultural space for women, rather than merely as a ghetto, is central to Brown's (1994) study of soap opera fans. Brown contends that interpretations of meanings within soaps as texts are not only made at the time of viewing but, importantly, through talking about soaps with family, friends and colleagues. On the basis of her research with women soap opera fans, Brown argues that 'much of the pleasure in soap opera fanship lies in the discursive network among women that builds around these programmes' (1994: 1). Rather than soap operas 'brainwashing' women, as in earlier feminist analyses, Brown maintains that women watching and talking about soaps can represent a form of resistance to patriarchal society and their subordinate position within it. This resistance can be conceptualised on several levels. First, the very fact that women do gain pleasure from soaps is a resistive political act. In patriarchal culture, women are ideologically positioned as 'pleasure givers', rather than 'pleasure takers': their enjoyment of soap operas is contrary to this. Moreover, women who enjoy soap operas are gaining pleasure from a culturally devalued form, something that the women in Brown's study themselves made fun of (1994: 133). Second, the discursive networks among women where soap talk is central are a further form of resistance. The discussion networks involved sharing knowledge and perspectives and acted to establish communal feeling and solidarity amongst women (1994: 132). Brown distinguishes between two types or levels of pleasure women gain from soap operas. 'Active pleasure' is gained through soap operas' themes of 'the culture of the home and women's concerns'. For women in soap opera groups, their sense of identity as women is confirmed and valued through soaps in a way that it is not in dominant culture. 'Reactive pleasure' involves a re-reading of the representation of women within soaps, a recognition that women's concerns of family and home arise out of their inability to control their own lives. Pleasure is gained, then, from recognising their oppression as women and reacting to it (1994: 173). For Brown, therefore, women fans use soap opera to 'talk and joke in recognition of their subordination' and in so doing, 'they break boundaries and assert their power' (1994: 149).

Whether soap operas are politically significant as brainwashers of women, or as an acknowledgement of the value of women's traditional skills and concerns, or as a form of popular media culture which can be subverted to resist women's subordination in patriarchal society, changes to soap opera may undermine their exclusivity as a 'feminine genre'. Geraghty (1991) argues that producers of soap operas have consciously introduced new themes into these 'never ending stories', including issues of 'race', age and sexuality. These represent a move away from the 'concentrated examination of the personal sphere', which prioritises women characters and women's concerns, a shift accompanied by the 'adoption of more conventional male story lines and generic codes', including crime and violence. For Geraghty, these changes in soap operas represent a 'breaching of women's space' and may lead to a loss of the pleasures soap operas traditionally offer to women (1991: 196–7). As a consequence, both the negative and positive political significance of soaps for women may be reduced. An alternative view might be that the introduction of issues around 'race', age and sexuality extends the representation of femininity within soaps beyond the white, adult and heterosexual norm, and thereby increases the pleasure of soaps for women whose social positioning was previously under-acknowledged.

Magazines for girls and women

Weekly and monthly magazines for girls and women are, like soap operas, another 'feminine genre' in an otherwise masculine-dominated media. As with soaps, feminist media analyses of girls' and women's magazines have developed from early hostility to trying to understand why it is that their readers find them so pleasurable.

Women's magazines

In Britain in the 1950s, sales of women's magazines were higher than in any subsequent period and the magazines were apparently read by well over 60 per cent of all women (Winship 1992: 82; see also Ferguson 1983). This massive popularity of women's magazines occurred in the context of the post-war resurgence of the ideology of domesticity for women. In the Beveridge Report of 1942 (which laid the foundation for the welfare state), women were viewed primarily as wives and mothers. In Beveridge's words, women's work in the home, though unpaid, was 'vital': it allowed their husband to do 'their' paid work, as well as contributing to the furtherance of 'the British race' and the 'British ideal' in the world (see quotations in Wilson 1983; Cowgill 1994). In combination with official concerns about the low birth rate and rising divorce rates following the disruption caused by the Second World War, these factors made the 1950s a period where femininity became especially defined in terms of motherhood and domesticity (Wilson 1977; 1983; although see Philips and Haywood 1998 for an alternative view of 1950s femininity). It is in the context of a strong ideology of domesticity that the popularity of women's magazines during this period can be understood. The dominant ideology of femininity had elevated being a housewife and mother to activities of great importance, comparable to men's involvement in paid work. Women's magazines can therefore be understood as the 'trade press' of the professional housewife and mother (Winship 1992). These publications aimed to help women excel in their 'trade' within the home and so were the housewives' equivalent of *The Grocer* or *Farming Weekly*.

Early feminist media analyses of women's magazines were critical of the 'cult of femininity' (Ferguson 1983) they were seen to promote. In line with perspectives on the relationship between texts and audiences dominant at the time, women's magazines were chastised as highly influential socialising agents, conditioning women to seek happiness and fulfilment through dependent housewifery and motherhood. Indeed, as Hermes (1995) notes, this hostility to women's magazines and expressions of concern for the ideological enslavement of women who read them has been a prominent strand within feminist media analysis until quite recently. In contrast, studies by Winship (1992) and Hermes (1995), rather than condemning women's magazines as patriarchal propaganda and regarding their readers as cultural dupes, instead are centrally concerned with understanding why contemporary women continue to find them so pleasurable.

Winship's (1992) research is focused on the success of the 'new practical and domestic magazines' for women launched in Britain in the 1980s. For Winship, magazines like *Bella* and *Best*, with their practical emphasis on recipes, clothes and knitting patterns and general household tips, represent a major change in the magazine market. In some analyses, these new formula magazines have been argued to represent a return to 'old-fashioned femininity' of a type so prevalent in the magazines of the 1950s. For Winship, however, any similarity between the 1950s' magazines and the 1980s' magazines is only superficial. Whilst the 1950s' magazines can be thought of as a 'trade press', assuming and seeking to cultivate a commitment to femininity contained within the domestic sphere, Winship argues that the content and style of magazines like *Best* facilitate 'uncommittedness' to traditional feminine identities and pleasures (1992: 102). For example, *Best* contains features on women and paid work, and an emphasis on time-saving – a 'busy ethic', suggestive of the multiple roles contemporary women juggle. Articles are directed at women in a range of personal and social circumstances, rather than speaking only to the married, full-time housewife and mother. *Best* is described by Winship as having a 'bitty-style', dominated by short articles and features with pages perforated so that they are easily removed and filed away for reference purposes. These characteristics are argued by Winship to allow readers to use the magazine in different ways. Its content, with a practical, domestic emphasis, may be interpreted seriously by some readers, who use it as a key element in their more traditional femininity based around housewifery and motherhood. For others, the 'bitty-style' may facilitate a 'critical distance' to traditional feminine concerns and be used as a non-serious 'quick read'. Here, Winship suggests, the new practical magazines may represent a sort of 'wish fulfilment' for women who are too busy (with paid work, domestic responsibilities and so on) to be busy in a *Best* way, but at some level wish they could be. The success of these magazines is, then, argued to be a reflection of tensions around contemporary femininity (1992: 105), and ambivalence about what women are meant to be and do, and enjoy. Whilst the 1950s' women's magazines can be understood as a 'trade press', celebrating the cult of domesticity for women, the new women's magazines like *Best* can be understood as texts where the dominant ideology of femininity is dissolved and a multiplicity of femininities are assumed to exist (Winship 1992: 87).

Winship reached her conclusions about the meanings of the new practical women's magazines largely on the basis of a textual analysis. In contrast, Hermes (1995) interviewed readers of women's magazines in order to find out what meaning this form of popular media culture held for them. Hermes was initially disappointed to find that, not only did her interviewees talk with much less enthusiasm about women's magazines compared to *other* genres, they described their use of women's magazines as largely meaningless and insignificant. The things that made women's magazines primarily attractive to the readers in Hermes' study were that they filled up spare time, and were easy to 'pick up and put down' again. In other words, Hermes found that readers described their use in a detached and remote way, which involved a denial of the personal and cultural significance of women's magazines. Nevertheless, in the interview data, Hermes did uncover 'repertoires' or ways of talking about women's magazines which help explain why readers bother to 'pick up' these texts in the first place. Two important ways of talking about women's magazines were the 'repertoire of practical value' (where the practical value of handy tips and advice was stressed) and the 'repertoire of emotional learning' (where 'true life' stories were said to help readers interpret their own lives, personal relationships and crisis situations). Hermes argues that these and other interpretative repertoires offer readers a means by which to 'fantasise' about being 'perfect selves' (a perfect cook, lover, mother, listener, friend, or an up-to-date consumer or highly cultured person, for example – 1995: 62). Hermes concludes that the reading of women's magazines has meaning, for those who do so, at two levels. First, women's magazines are valued because they fit in with the 'busyness' of everyday life, and its complex mix of duties and obligations. Importantly, women's magazines do not get in the way of the completion of these duties and obligations, because they are easy to 'put down'. Second, it is the 'moments of empowerment', gained via fantasies about perfect selves, that make women's magazines sufficiently interesting to 'pick up' in the first place. Women's magazines are polysemic in meaning and their relevance and 'worthwhileness' will vary according to the identity of the reader, and to her fantasies, anxieties and preoccupations (1995: 64). Hermes' analysis portrays readers of women's magazines as reflective and active, rather than passive sponges soaking up the meanings they contain. Her argument that an important meaning of magazines lies in their element of fantasy echoes Winship's points about 'wish fulfilment'. Thus both authors locate the continuing popularity of women's magazines (although many have falling circulation figures – see Table 7.1) in the context of contradiction and tensions around contemporary femininities.

Table 7.1 Average circulation size of women's magazines, July–December 1997

Publication	Average circulation per issue	1996–97 % change (+/−)
Top Five weeklies[a]		
Woman	731,754	−11.6
Woman's Own	702,765	−13.1
Woman's Weekly	638,306	−8.3
Hello	574,585	+7.1
Best	511,841	−6.0
Total	2,427,497	
Top Five monthlies		
You and Yours[b]	612,413	−
Prima[b]	540,727	−4.3
Cosmopolitan[c]	461,116	0.0
Good Housekeeping[c]	440,655	−8.0
Marie Claire[c]	457,034	−9.1
Total	2,511,945	

Source: Audit Bureau of Circulation (1997)

Notes
a Audit Bureau of Circulation (ABC) category 'Women's Interest: Women's Weeklies'.
b ABC category 'Women's Interest: Women's Practical'.
c ABC category 'Women's Interest: Women's Lifestyle and Fashion'.

Girls' magazines

The shift in feminist analyses of 'feminine genres', away from the dominant text view and toward the dominant audience view, is also evident in studies of girls' magazines. This means that 'female readers are granted more power in relation to the ideological effect of the text' (McRobbie 1996: 175) and that greater attention is paid to the wider social settings within which girls' magazines as media texts are both consumed and produced.

It is possible to trace the changing understandings of representations of femininity and their effects on audiences within McRobbie's own research. Writing in 1996, McRobbie accepts criticisms made by Frazer (1987), amongst others, that her early analyses of *Jackie* magazine made simplistic assumptions about the ideology of femininity it promoted and its effects on the reader (1996: 175). Frazer's own research examined the responses of teenage girls to *Jackie* magazine and found that the ideology of femininity within it was undercut by the girls' 'reflexivity and reflectiveness' (Frazer 1987: 419).

In her more recent research, McRobbie (1996) analyses girls' magazines of the 1990s. She gives greater weight to the skilful and reflexive readers of these texts, and also highlights the role played by those media professionals who produce the magazines. McRobbie argues that the new magazines for girls and young women (such as *Just Seventeen, More!* and *19*) offer significantly different representations of femininity than was true of earlier girls' magazines. 'The more solid version of femininity – with its romantic narratives, its lessons on the art of seduction and its advice about how to hold on to your man – have faded away ... What we can see [now] is a sharp sense of transition and fluidity in these magazines as to what it is to be a young woman today' (1996: 176, 184). The new magazines are distinctive in two main ways, according to McRobbie. First, in the way they address their readers and in the assumptions they make about them. Magazines like *More!* and *Just Seventeen* are argued to be written in a ironic, mocking style which both assumes a degree of 'knowingness' and encourages a certain detachment or distance from traditional femininities on the part of the reader. For example, 'when *Just Seventeen* decided in 1994 to revive the love story, it did so with the quotation marks fully on display. No reader could be so naive as to swallow it straight' (1996: 176). The second distinctive characteristic of the new magazines for young women is their intensive focus on sexuality, so that, more than ever before, sex fills the space of the magazines' pages and is prominently proclaimed on their covers. For example, the November 1998 front cover of *More!* (whose readers are, on average, between 15 and 17 years old) read 'I'm Horny, Horny, Horny', whilst, inside the magazine, there appeared the regular feature 'Sex Directory' (subtitled '*More!*'s University of Rumpy Pumpy') and numerous pictures of semi-naked men (see also McRobbie 1996). In accounting for the emergence of these new magazines, McRobbie notes the important role played by magazine professionals, that is, the editors and writers who produce magazines aimed at young women. Her research shows that many of the young women employees of the magazines are highly educated professionals with media studies qualifications, who also have an understanding of 'gender politics'. In their journalism, the new magazine professionals simultaneously 'want to retain the pleasure and fantasy of the magazine form' whilst also drawing on their own adherence to feminism (1996: 183, 184). Through the use of irony, the 'new generation' of magazine professionals provide a space for 'critical reflection on normative femininities' on the part of their readers, and have also expanded young girls' sexual horizons (1996: 189).

For McRobbie, the new magazines for girls and young women do regulate normative femininity (through representing femininity within a masculine dominated culture of heterosexuality) but at the same time they also suggest a 'new moment in the construction of female sexual identities' (1996: 177), centred around boldness, increased knowledge and confidence and informed choices which may empower young women in their sexuality. For this reason, McRobbie claims that, 'In some ways the magazines, within the constraints of their own codifications, have (recently) extended the possibilities of what it is to be a woman' (1996: 178).

Studies by Geraghty (1991) and Brown (1994) on soap opera, and by Winship (1992), Hermes (1995) and McRobbie (1996) on girls' and women's magazines, together argue for the complexity of the relationship between 'feminine genres' and their audiences, which potentially makes them both cultural ghetto and beneficial cultural space. Whilst it is important to seek to understand the complexity of the relationship between women and 'feminine genres', how this varies by women's social status and is shaped by wider social settings of both consumption and production, academic analysis needs also to concern itself with representations of women in other forms of media, including 'serious' cultural forms (like television news, documentaries, drama and newspapers) not defined as 'women's interest'. There are limited signs that representations of femininity are expanding beyond conventional stereotypes (see also Chapter 6). For example, one might point to television dramas like *Prime Suspect* and *Silent Witness*, where the main characters are strong and independent women shown to be highly competent in their masculine-dominated professional fields of paid work (see Marshment 1997 for other examples of an increased presence and range of femininity in popular media culture). However, as discussed next, some areas of popular media culture aimed especially at men continue to cause controversy due to the representations of women they contain.

Masculine genres

One aspect of the liberalisation of sexuality in the post-war period is the reduction in censorship of sexually explicit media of communication (see also Chapter 5). It is widely recognised that legislation (for example, the Obscene Publications Act, 1959) has resulted in a growth in the availability of, and explicitness of, sexual images and information, through films, videos, magazines and books, as well as other media. Technological advances including satellite and cable television, video recorders, personal computers and the Internet have greatly expanded the range of ways in which people can gain access to sexually explicit material. Whilst there is agreement amongst various political groupings and academics that sexually explicit media have proliferated, there is much less consensus as to how this proliferation should be interpreted. For libertarians, the increased availability of sexually explicit media represents an advance in freedom of expression and a retreat by the state from interference in the private life of its citizens. For conservative moralists, the increased availability of sexually explicit media is indicative of the moral depravity of contemporary society: it has contributed to the separation of sex from procreation and thereby to the erosion of marriage and the nuclear family (see Jackson 1995 for review). Consequently, increased censorship and expanded state intervention in the private lives of individuals is an actively pursued aim, as a means of 'purifying' contemporary morals.

Feminist analyses of the meaning and significance of the proliferation of pornography, and the role of censorship, are rather more complex than either the libertarian or moral conservatist response. In the remainder of this chapter, I focus on the argument proposed by some feminists that the depiction of women's bodies within pornography is a central way in which men oppress women, along with criticisms of this view made by other feminists. Then I consider the significance of recent trends whereby erotic/pornographic representations of women's bodies are arguably spreading out of pornographic magazines into other men's magazines (the so-called 'New Lads'' magazines).

Feminism and pornography

Feminist analyses of pornography can be broadly divided into two oppositional groupings. On one side, there are 'anti-pornography' feminists, who regard pornography as central to women's oppression. Through organisations such as the Campaign Against Pornography, this grouping of feminists seeks to restrict the production and circulation of pornography, either through tighter legal regulation or through direct action (Jackson and Scott 1996). On the other side, there are 'anti-censorship' feminists who argue that pornography is not a central way in which women are oppressed, and who, through organisations like Feminists Against Censorship, oppose the greater restriction of sexually graphic material.

Anti-pornography analyses

At the forefront of the anti-pornography feminists are the American writers Dworkin (e.g. 1981) and Mackinnon (e.g. 1992) and, in Britain, Itzin (1992a). In Dworkin's view, pornography is central to the male system of domination over women (1981: 200). For Dworkin, 'the major theme of pornography as a genre' is male power over women in all its guises, including economically, physically and sexually (1981: 24–5). Within pornography, women's sexuality is devalued and objectified for male sexual pleasure. Dworkin describes the 'standard values of pornography' as the excitement of humiliation, the joy of pain, the pleasure of abuse, the centrality of the penis, and the woman who resists only to discover that she enjoys it and desires more (1981: 200). The degradation of individual women within pornography and all women by pornography is both a means by which male power over women is achieved and a celebration of that power (1981: 25).

Catherine Itzin (1992b; 1992c) proposes an analysis of pornography broadly in agreement with Dworkin. For Itzin, as for Dworkin, pornography is a means of subjugating women and a collective expression and enactment of male power. It is central to the subordination of women and in itself represents a form of sex discrimination (1992b: 3). In Itzin's analysis, pornography causes harm in a number of ways. In the production of pornography, individual women (and children) are exploited and abused, both economically and sexually. The conventions of pornography, with its themes of domination and coercion, sexualises violence and thereby legitimises sexual coercion by men against women. At the least, pornography 'conditions male sexual arousal and orgasm to sexual objectification and sexual violence: to women's subordination' (1992b: 67). At the worst, pornography may be used in the sexual abuse of women (and children) and may 'stimulate' some men to commit acts of sexual violence, including rape and murder (1992c: 67). Because of its role in perpetuating sexism (as well as racism – see also Dworkin 1981; Forna 1992), sex discrimination and sexual violence, pornography is argued by Itzin to be 'completely incompatible' with gender equality (1992c: 70).

For many anti-pornography feminists, there is a range of research evidence which overwhelmingly demonstrates that pornography causes harm. First, there are a number of laboratory-based studies which investigate the effects of exposure to pornography on men's sexual arousal, attitudes to rape and propensity to engage in aggressive or violent behaviour. Studies by the American researchers Malamuth, Zillman, Donnerstein and Linz are those most frequently cited as proving that men find sexually violent pornography arousing, that it leads to greater acceptance of rape and of sexual violence toward women and that it results in increased levels of aggressive behaviour against women in laboratory settings (a finding which is often taken to imply that exposure to pornography is linked to sexual aggression against women in general, especially rape). Some anti-pornography feminists also argue that studies of convicted rapists reveal a link between their interest in and use of pornography and their acts of sexual violence against women. Finally, evidence of the harm pornography causes has been argued to be revealed in the personal 'testimonies' of women, who have either been sexually abused by men, subsequent to their use of pornography, or who have been exploited and physically and sexually abused as workers in the pornography industry. Detailed, favourable reviews of the research evidence on the harm pornography causes are provided by Russell (1993) and Itzin (1992a).

For many anti-pornography feminists, the evidence that pornography causes harm to women, in a whole range of ways, including causing rape, is undeniable. Therefore, the curtailing or even outright prohibition of pornography becomes a key concern. For Itzin, as for others, the current legal regulation of pornography is inadequate and ineffective, primarily because within it, pornography is adjudged solely in *moral* terms rather than in *gender* terms. The representation of femininity, of women's sexuality, within pornography is not in itself regarded as problematical by the current legislation. Hence, sexually explicit material legally circulates where the degradation and objectification of women is the predominant theme. Some anti-pornography feminists, both in America and Britain, have therefore attempted to formulate a legal definition of pornography where gender is central, which can then be used in the development and implementation of legislation to end the harm that pornography causes. Attempts to introduce anti-pornography legislation include Clare Short's efforts on two separate occasions (1986 and 1988) to prohibit 'indecent displays' of naked or partially naked women in sexually provocative poses in newspapers (the so-called 'Page 3 Bills') and Dawn Primarolo's (1989) *Location of Pornographic Material Bill* (see Itzin 1992d). Neither of these Members of Parliament were successful in their attempts. The most famous attempt to reach a specific definition of pornography and to develop legislation against its production and sale was made by Dworkin and Mackinnon in America in 1983. Defining pornography as 'the graphic sexually explicit subordination of women through pictures and/or words' and where violence and coercion are included, Dworkin and Mackinnon's 'Minneapolis Ordinance' sought to legislate against pornography on the grounds that its production and distribution was discriminatory against women and thereby violated their civil rights under the United States' Constitution. Ultimately, the Ordinance failed, because freedom of speech and expression was held to have ultimate priority over the harm pornography was recognised to cause for women (see Itzin 1992d; Smart 1989).

Feminist anti-censorship analyses

Although they fully acknowledge that it is a sexist media form, where women's sexuality is consistently misrepresented in line with dominant masculine sexual values, anti-censorship feminists vehemently disagree with most other aspects of the analyses of pornography made by writers such as Dworkin and Itzin, as well as the solutions they propose. Prominent amongst British anti-censorship feminists are writers such as Segal (e.g. 1993), Wilson and McIntosh (in Rodgerson and Wilson 1991). At the outset, these writers dispute the value of focusing primarily on representations of women's sexuality within pornography as a central basis of male power. For anti-censorship feminists, prioritising pornography means that, in their view, more fundamentally important causes of women's subordination (such as the structures of paid and unpaid work) are neglected. In this view, rape and other forms of sexual violence, along with gender inequality prevalent throughout society, existed before the emergence of commercial pornography. 'Pornography may mirror the sexism of society but it did not create it' (Rodgerson and Wilson 1991: 67). Pornography in and of itself is not the cause of women's disadvantaged position in society, nor will the greater curtailment of its production and distribution on its own eliminate that disadvantage.

A key component in the anti-censorship feminist arguments is the refutation of research evidence relied upon so heavily by some anti-pornography writers. Segal (1993) disputes the assumption that violence is prevalent within pornography, and the argument that the amount of violent pornography has proliferated. Moreover, she cites research evidence which shows that, amongst men who use pornography, violence is the least arousing aspect. In addition to contesting the characterisation of pornography as violent in content and that this feature is a primary source of arousal, anti-censorship feminists are highly critical of the *methodology* of the studies which are argued to demonstrate that exposure to pornography causes sexual arousal, attitude change and behaviour change, including increased aggression to women. Studies such as those by Donnerstein, Linz, Malamuth and Zillman are argued by Segal (1993) and King (1993), amongst others, to have employed a highly contested research design (that is, social-psychological experiments in laboratory settings) with an unrepresentative sample (male students at several American Universities). For Rubin, even if the weakness of the research design are ignored, their findings do not support claims that pornography *causes* violence and rape. At the most, she says, laboratory studies show some changes in attitudes in artificial settings, which may or may not have real implications for behaviour at another time and place (1993: 38). Similarly, Segal maintains that such research has merely established that exposure to pornography has a very weak effect in a very few men under carefully controlled conditions (1993: 14. See also Howitt and Cumberbatch 1990).

Other types of evidence often used by anti-pornography feminists to argue that pornography causes harm are similarly subject to counter-interpretation by anti-censorship writers. Thus, they maintain that even if some convicted rapists have been shown to have an interest in pornography, this does not mean that pornography *caused* them to act in a sexually violent manner. Personal testimonies of harm given by workers in the pornography industry are matched by the testimonies of other workers, who defend the nature of their employment, say they enjoy their work and are empowered by it. Any attempt to prohibit pornography may, in fact, lead to a worsening of their position and represents a threat to their source of income (see Segal 1993: 16–17).

Compared to anti-pornography feminists, anti-censorship feminists tend to locate themselves more within recent trends in mainstream media and cultural studies. Anti-pornography writers tend to regard pornography as texts with a dominant, singular meaning, a perspective which therefore allows specific definitions of pornography (as formulated by Dworkin and Mackinnon) to be reached. In contrast, anti-censorship feminists favour an interpretation of pornographic texts as polysemic in meaning, as open to any number of interpretations according to the context in which they are used and according to the reflexivity of the audience (Rodgerson and Wilson 1991; Segal 1993). In this view, it is impossible to reach a specific definition of pornography since, like beauty, pornography is in the eye of the beholder. In Segal's words, 'It is never possible, whatever the image, to isolate it, to fix its meaning and predict some inevitable pattern of response, independently of assessing its wider representational context and the particular . . . context in which it is being received (1993: 15).

Anti-censorship feminists insist that a focus on pornography is mistaken, in that it distracts attention from more important issues, and unjustified, in that the evidence on the harmful effects of pornography is at best unclear and at worst, unconvincing. Consequently, anti-censorship feminists argue that efforts to define and restrict pornography are misguided with potentially unfavourable consequences for sexuality, per se. Writers like Rubin (1993) and Rodgerson and Wilson (1991) argue that feminist perspectives on sexual representations must aim to extend women's control over their bodies and their understanding of their sexual desires. Efforts to define and curtail the production and distribution of pornography are counter to this, because they will restrict or even reverse the trend towards the freer expression of women's sexuality that has evolved during the twentieth century (Segal 1993). Anti-censorship feminists point out that women make up a large proportion of the audience for pornographic material and gain sexual pleasure from it, even though it consistently misrepresents their sexuality. Rather than outlawing it, the way to change dominant representations of women's sexuality within pornography is to increase the amount of sexually explicit material produced by women and for women (Segal 1993; Rubin 1993. See also Gibson and Gibson 1993). Thereby, women's sexual citizenship rights will be extended and the central assumptions which determine dominant sexual ideology will be challenged (Rodgerson and Wilson 1991: 12).

Clearly, the research evidence on the relationship between pornography and men's sexual violence is central to the arguments of both anti-pornography feminists and anti-censorship feminists. This allows Jackson and Scott (1996) to criticise both sides in the debate. They argue that, whilst it is 'misguided' to use the research evidence to claim there are links between exposure to pornography and men's sexual violence, it is 'equally misguided to draw on research of this kind to demonstrate the absence of any relationship between pornography and the abuse of women' (1996: 23). For Cameron and Frazer (1992), feminist analyses of pornography must move beyond claim and counterclaim over causes and effects. They accept that it is 'inadequate' to argue that pornography simply and directly 'causes' violence, but insist that there are 'important and complex connections' between pornographic representations of femininity and sexual violence. In the analysis of Cameron and Frazer, pornography is a cultural resource which people draw upon as they interpret and give meaning to sexuality. It is a representation of sexuality which shapes sexual desire, expression and pleasure in a particular way, prioritising masculine dominance and feminine submission. In other words, 'pornography contributes to the cultural construction of a particular form of masculinity and sexual desire which make rape possible and which script the possibilities for its enactment'

(Jackson and Scott 1996: 23). Cameron and Fraser suggest that we must use our imaginative capacity to develop alternatives to 'pornographic fictions', where representations of sexuality are less dependent on eroticised relations of masculine dominance and feminine submission (1992: 379).

Kappeler (1986), like Cameron and Frazer, also argues that it is necessary to shift feminist debates on pornography away from disputes about causes and effect. She maintains that it is necessary to analyse pornography as a form of representation which constructs women as sexualised objects for the masculine gaze. This is an understanding of pornography shared by Coward (1987), who describes pornography as a 'regime of representation of sex'. In other words, it is a particular way of depicting bodies in writing, films, photographs and so on which mean that they are interpreted as 'pornographic' by society. This approach suggests that there is no intrinsic meaning in representations of sexuality or naked bodies. Instead, the meanings are decided by the 'codes' or 'conventions' that make particular texts meaningful. Within the pornographic regime of representation or genre, these codes centre around the fragmentation of women's bodies (via reducing the whole of women's bodies to particular parts, especially breasts and genitals) and submission as the primary expression of women's pleasure. It is these codes which are problematical for women, rather than sexually explicit representations of their bodies per se. The problematical nature of these codes arises, not from causing sexual violence or rape, but rather from the meanings they put into circulation within society and which are not confined to that which is conventionally designated as 'pornography' (1987: 321).

'Mags for the lads'

Coward's argument that there is a pornographic genre of representation prevalent throughout media of communication (including in advertising and fashion magazines) is an important one. There are indications that this style is becoming more widespread, perhaps even *the* dominant way of representing women within popular media culture, thereby making the space for alternative representations ever smaller (Smart 1989). One example of the expansion of the pornographic genre is men's magazines such as *Loaded* and *FHM*. These and similar publications are men's nearest equivalent to women's magazines as a genre, and emerged in Britain in the mid-1990s. Their content centres around the concerns and interests of 'New Laddism', a form of masculinity where pre-feminist traditional 'macho' interests of 'booze' (especially beer), 'babes/birds' (sexually attractive women), 'bad language' and sport (especially football) are resurrected and exaggerated in a self-conscious, ironic and (allegedly) humorous way (Raven 1994). Hence, *Loaded* is subtitled as a magazine for 'men who should know better'. Although not pornographic magazines in the conventional sense, these publications arguably utilise a pornographic regime of representation and depict women in a heavily sexualised manner (Hattenstone 1995; Landesman 1997). The 'high nipple count' within these magazines has led some companies and manufacturers to consider withdrawing their advertisements, but the magazines themselves continue to be very successful, with rising circulation figures and several million readers each month (Chaudhary 1997).

Arguably, the success of the new men's magazines (see Table 7.2), with their distinctive formula, and the spate of like-minded television programmes (including *Fantasy Football*, *They Think It's All Over* and *Men Behaving Badly*) are reflections of tension, confusion and ambivalence surrounding contemporary masculinity. Feminism has made unreconstructed traditional masculinity and its sexist treatment of women politically, socially and culturally unacceptable, but the 'New Man' lacks security as the alternative model of masculinity, and may be too 'effeminate' a replacement (Nixon 1996; see also Chapter 4). 'New Laddism' and the representations of it within popular media culture – sexist but in an ironic, self-conscious 'should know better' way – must be viewed in this context.

The growing popularity of the new men's magazines suggests that increasing numbers of men (particularly those aged between 15 and 34 who make up the majority of their readers – Chaudhary 1997) find their formula of 'booze, birds and football' meaningful. No doubt research is under way that will show that this meaning is as variable, complex and contradictory as is the meaning girls and women gain from 'their' magazines. Whilst recent approaches in media and cultural analysis give due respect to the audience as active and reflective towards the media they consume, Abercrombie cautions against regarding the audience as 'all-powerful' (1996: 203–4).

Genres of popular media culture (including the soap operas, girls and women's magazines, pornography and the new men's magazines discussed in this chapter) are 'genres' because they adhere to particular conventions or codes of representation, including representations of femininity. Through their conventions or codes, certain dominant meanings are promoted, which restricts the extent to which and the ways in which the audience can formulate their own meanings. For Morley, it is necessary simultaneously to acknowledge the active, reflexive audience and the forces of constraint which restrict their interpretations of texts. Included here are the dominant 'preferred reading' promoted within texts, the wider macro economic, political and ideological contexts acting on the construction of texts, and the micro contexts of everyday household settings and personal relationships within which texts are consumed (Morley 1996. See also Moores 1993).

Some evidence discussed in this chapter shows that, particularly in the 1980s and 1990s, popular media representations of femininity have changed and some alternative representations have had exposure. For example, Skeggs (1994) and McRobbie (1996) have argued that girls' and women's

Table 7.2 Average circulation size of men's lifestyle magazines[a], July–December 1997

Publication	Average circulation per issue	1996–97 % change (+/−)
FHM	644,110	+76.3
Loaded	441,567	+36.7
Maxim	249,096	+65.8
Men's Health	225,126	+41.6
Sky Magazine	186,961	+13.5
Total	1,746,860	

Source: Audit Bureau of Circulation (1997)

Note
a ABC category 'Men's Lifestyle' magazines, published monthly.

magazines like *Cosmopolitan* and *Marie Claire* have enabled feminist ideas to be more widely articulated in society. Yet, as other evidence in this chapter shows, stereotypical representations of femininity, positioning women either within domesticity or as objects of the masculine sexual gaze, continue. Moreover, as writers like McRobbie (1997) and Marshment (1997) argue, forms of popular media culture are often exclusionary in their representations of femininity, failing to address multiplicities of femininity arising from ethnicity, sexuality and ablebodiedness, for example (although see Barker 1998 on British Asian girls and soap opera). Representations of femininity in popular media culture have changed to a degree, but narrow and constricting images, especially around domesticity and sexual identities, continue to prevail. Even allowing for active, resistive audiences, this tendency means that popular culture media are a highly significant, if not wholly effective, brake on the pace of change in gender relations.

Chapter 8

Gendered justice: crimes and punishments

The publication each year of the official crime statistics invariably leads to much public debate, as concern is voiced over the 'rising crime rate' and the 'spiralling level of lawlessness' in contemporary society. Rarely mentioned in the debates is the fact that such statistics, in measuring crime and the legal processing of those who commit it, are primarily concerned with the activities of men. For example, in 1996 in England and Wales, 80 per cent of known offenders were men (Home Office 1997a). Those individuals whose job it is to detect, prosecute, defend, judge or imprison offenders are also predominantly men. The police force is 86 per cent male, whilst over 70 per cent of solicitors and barristers and over 90 per cent of the judiciary are men (EOC 1997f). Similarly the prison service is over 80 per cent male, with 91 per cent of those in the Prison Governor grade being men (Home Office 1992). Whether the focus is on offenders and their punishment or on professionals employed within the criminal justice system, crime has a very masculine profile. This chapter begins with a detailed examination of what statistical data show about men and women as criminal offenders. I also consider a number of explanations as to why gender differences are so marked, including the argument that the official crime statistics reflect the more lenient treatment of women within the criminal justice system. The second section of the chapter considers an area where women have featured extensively in public debates on crime; that is, as victims of men's violence. Here, my main focus is on the criminal justice system's response to women as victims of domestic violence and of rape.

Women behaving badly

Official statistical data on crime shows that only 20 per cent of known offenders (that is, those convicted by the courts or formally cautioned by the police) are women (Home Office 1997a). In 1995, just 4 per cent of those held in prisons were women (Home Office 1997b). Of all women born in 1953, 8 per cent had a conviction for a standard list offence by the time they were aged 40, compared to 34 per cent of men (Home Office 1997a).

One element of the public debate about crime, referred to earlier, is the extent to which crime statistics such as these are an accurate measure of criminal activity. The consensus is that they are not. The Home Office itself emphasises the limitations of its annual *Criminal Statistics* (see also Reiner 1996). Essentially, the figures cited above are based on police, court and prison statistics. As such, they can only tell us that more men than women are found guilty or are cautioned, and more men than women get sent to prison as a punishment. Strictly speaking, such statistics do not show that women are less likely than men to engage in criminal activity. It may be that, rather than women committing fewer crimes than men, they are more successful at avoiding detection, conviction and imprisonment. In other words, it may be that women and men are involved in crime to the same extent, but men are much less likely to 'get away with it' than women.

The idea that women are just as criminal as men, but their crimes are 'unknown' or 'hidden' and so do not appear in official statistics, was proposed by Pollak (1961). He argued that women's behaviour is less criminalised than men's, that women are more deceitful and cunning and so are more skilled at concealing their crimes than men, and that victims of women criminals are less likely to report them to the police. These features, for Pollak, mean that women offenders appear in criminal statistics to a much lesser extent than men. Pollak's interpretation of women's criminality proved influential for a time, largely 'because he lacked competitors and the topic interested no one else' (Heidensohn 1996: 121). Subsequently, Pollak's methodology and theorising have been subject to severe criticism (see Heidensohn 1996; Morris 1987) and his arguments are no longer taken seriously.

That is not to say that social scientists regard official statistics as an unproblematic source of data on gender differences in criminal behaviour. Indeed, other survey evidence has been used to help establish whether the different rate of criminal behaviour by women and men suggested by official crime statistics is 'real' rather than 'artificial'. In victim surveys (like the British Crime Survey) a nationally representative sample of people is asked about their experiences of crime, irrespective of whether these crimes were reported to the police or not. In self-report studies, a sample of people are asked to identify any offences they themselves have knowingly committed. Both types of surveys therefore provide evidence on the 'dark figure' of unrecorded crime, that is, crimes which are neither detected by nor reported to the police, for which the offender is neither cautioned, found guilty nor imprisoned and which, therefore, do not appear in the official crime statistics. If women are more successful than men at breaking the law and then 'getting away' with it, these surveys should reveal women's 'hidden' criminality. As sources of data on gender differences in criminal activity, victims surveys and self-report studies are not without their own shortcomings. Nevertheless, both sources show that men do engage in more criminal behaviour than women, although the disparity is not as marked as is suggested by official crime statistics. In the light of the available evidence, therefore, social scientists accept that criminal statistics do reflect the extent to which women really are far less likely to commit crimes compared to men.

As shown in Table 8.1, there are also differences in the types of offences committed by men and women. Whilst 'theft and handling stolen goods' is the single biggest category of offence for both women and men, it is much more important for women, accounting for 63 per cent of all those found guilty or cautioned in 1996 (38 per cent of male offenders). The only other indictable offence where more women than men were found guilty or cautioned was 'fraud and forgery' (7 per cent compared to 4 per cent).

Morris (1987) argues that it is not necessary to employ a single or special theory to explain why there are comparatively few women criminals, or to explain why women commit some offences more than others. She proposes that the social processes which lead to gender differences in criminal behaviour are the very same processes which lead to gender differences in say, paid work, resulting in (for example) men's overrepresentation in the criminal justice professions. One of these social processes is the way women and men have different *opportunities* to commit crime, linked to constraints such as girls' and women's greater confinement to the home compared to boys' and men's. Moreover, ideas about masculinity and femininity involve contrasting valuations of behaviour, for example, toughness and vulnerability, risk and danger. Arguably, as a consequence, boys and men are encouraged to engage in risky, dangerous activities whilst girls and women are encouraged to avoid them. The stronger association of masculinity with deviancy, delinquency and crime which arises out of gendered opportunities and constraints, and the content of ideas about risk and danger within masculinity and femininity, means that, unlike men, when women do commit crimes, they are likely to be viewed as neither statistically nor socially 'normal'. Consequently, although women and men are, in theory, equal before the criminal law, ideas about women as criminals may mean that, in practice, women offenders get treated differently to men offenders when their law-breaking behaviour leads them into contact with the criminal justice system.

Criminal women: getting off lightly?

At first reading, official criminal statistics do appear to show that men and women offenders are treated differently within the criminal justice system, specifically, that women are shown a greater leniency than men. For example, a higher proportion of women offenders are formally cautioned by the police compared to men. In 1996, the cautioning rate for indictable offences (persons cautioned as a percentage of those found guilty or cautioned) was 56 per cent for women and 36 per cent for men (Home Office 1997a). There are also gender differences in the sentences received by women and men offenders when found guilty by the courts. As shown in Table 8.2, women

Table 8.1 Offenders found guilty at all courts or cautioned, by type of offence and sex, 1996, England And Wales

Indictable offences	All	% Males	Females
Violence against the person	11	11	9
Sexual offences	1	2	0
Burglary	9	10	2
Robbery	1	1	1
Theft and handling stolen goods	42	38	63
Fraud and forgery	5	4	7
Criminal damage	3	3	1
Drug offences	17	18	10
Other (excluding motoring offences)	10	10	6
Motoring offences	2	2	1
	100	100	100

Source: Adapted from Table 5.10, Home Office (1997a)
Note: Figures may not total 100 due to rounding up

offenders are more likely to receive a discharge or a sentence of a community service order, but are less likely to receive a fine or immediate imprisonment than men offenders (Home Office 1997a). Moreover, the average length of sentences given to women offenders by the courts tends to be shorter than those for men offenders. In 1995, women found guilty of theft or handling stolen goods, or violence or fraud and forgery, received average sentences of 9 months, 18 months and 10 months respectively. In comparison, average sentences for men found guilty of the same group offences were 12 months, 23 months and 14 months. The only offences for which women and men received equal or near equal length average sentences were drug offences and criminal damage (Home Office 1997c).

What explanations have been put forward to account for the apparently more lenient treatment of women offenders compared to men? The higher proportion of women offenders who receive a caution may be a reflection of women's lower overall rate of offending (Morris 1987; Hedderman and Hough 1994). In other words, women offenders are less likely to have had a previous caution or conviction, compared to men. Between 1987 and 1990, for example, 40 per cent of women offenders were reconvicted within two years of the date of their conviction, compared with 56 per cent of men (Home Office 1995). The greater use of cautions for women offenders may also reflect the extent to which women commit less serious offences than men (Home Office 1992). As Morris explains, categories of offences such as 'violence against the person' or 'fraud and forgery' are 'legal labels

Table 8.2 Sentences received for indictable offences, 1995–96, England and Wales

Sentence	All aged 20 and over[1]		First-time offenders[2] aged 21 and over	
	Women	Men	Women	Men
	%		%	
Fine	25	33	52	45
Discharge	28	–	24	18
Community service order	31	25	19	19
Immediate custody	12	26	5	14

Source: Home Office (1997a)

Notes
1 Figures refer to 1996.
2 Figures refer to 1995.

[which] conceal a wide variety of activities' (1987: 28). Consequently, it is difficult to tell from the crime statistics whether or not there are gender differences in the seriousness of offences. Morris reviews a range of research evidence which suggests that women's offences are of a less serious nature than men's, even when grouped under the same 'legal label'. Thus, studies of shoplifting suggest that women steal both fewer items and items of a lesser value than men, whilst studies of fraud and forgery show that the monetary value of women's offences tend to be lower. Morris also notes that violence committed by women often differs from that committed by men. Women's violence is more likely to result from domestic or 'romantic' disputes and the victims of women's violence are more likely to be family members (1987: 28–9).

Given that the police have some powers of discretion in the interpretation of the law (for example, whether or not to caution or charge an offender), women's lower rate of offending and the tendency for any crimes they commit to be more 'trivial' in nature may, in combination, influence the greater use of cautions by the police. Morris (1987) identifies a third factor which may explain why women offenders are more likely to receive a caution than men. She cites a number of studies which point to the importance of the attitude and demeanour of an offender as an influence upon discretionary decisions made by the police. If an offender is co-operative, contrite and respectful in their interactions with the police, under some circumstances, this may encourage a police officer to issue a caution rather than charge them with an offence. The importance of demeanour and attitude is relevant for both women and men. However, 'it is plausible that, because of differential socialisation processes, women are more likely than men to demonstrate the behaviour which the police take as a sign of lack of 'troublesomeness' . . . ' (1987: 80). Having reviewed the evidence, Morris concludes that there is little support for the argument that women are treated leniently by the police *because* they are women. Instead, she suggests, important factors are the offender's criminal history, the nature of their offence and their attitude and demeanour in their interactions with the police.

Factors which are important in understanding why women offenders have a higher cautioning rate than men also feature in explanations of gender differences in sentencing patterns. Women are less likely to have been previously cautioned by the police or convicted by the courts, and women tend to commit more 'trivial' offences than men. Both of these features of women's criminal behaviour make it less likely that women offenders either choose or are committed for, a trial by jury at a Crown Court (Home Office 1992). In 1992, only 14 per cent of women aged 17 and over who were proceeded against for an indictable offence went to a Crown Court for trial, compared with 24 per cent of men (Hedderman and Hough 1994). The significance of this lies in the fact that, in comparable cases, offenders sentenced at a Crown Court are three times more likely to get a custodial sentence than those at Magistrates' Courts. Sentences issued by Crown Courts also tend to be longer than those issued by Magistrates' Courts (Hedderman and Hough 1994).

Differences in sentences received by women and men *first-time* offenders (see Table 8.2) suggests, however, that gender differentiation in offending rate and seriousness of crimes are not the only factors affecting sentencing patterns. Analysis of the Offenders' Index (a sample of 21,000 offenders convicted of a serious offence in 1991) shows that women first offenders were half as likely to be given a sentence of immediate custody than men (4 per cent compared to 8 per cent). Moreover, women with more than one previous conviction were also less likely to receive a custodial sentence than equivalent men (Hedderman and Hough 1994).

Case studies of very serious crimes further suggest that men and women offenders are treated differently. Wilczynski (1997) analysed case files involving child-killing or attempted child-killing by parents. Her findings were that, first, women were less likely than men to be prosecuted. Second, if prosecuted, women were more likely to use 'psychiatric' pleas in mitigation, whereas men tended to use 'normal' pleas. Third, women were more likely to receive psychiatric or non-custodial sentences, whereas men tended to receive prison sentences. In the light of these findings, Wilczynski concluded that, at all stages of the legal process, the criminal justice system responds very differently to women and men who kill their children. The more lenient treatment of women, including their sentencing, she argued, is in accordance with the view that women involved in such offences are 'mad and abnormal', whereas men are seen primarily as 'bad and normal' (Wilczynski 1997).

Hedderman and Hough (1994) focus on the example of domestic

homicide to show that women offenders have a lesser chance of receiving a custodial sentence than men. An analysis of cases dealt with between 1984 and 1992 showed that 23 per cent of women indicted for homicide were acquitted of all charges, compared to 4 per cent of men. Of those found guilty, 80 per cent of women and 61 per cent of men were found guilty of the lesser charge of manslaughter. Less than 50 per cent of the women convicted of manslaughter were given a prison sentence, compared to around 66 per cent of the men. In short, case studies of child-killing by parents and of domestic homicide indicate that women accused of these serious, non-trivial offences get treated in an apparently more lenient way than men.

A major study of sentencing patterns between women and men analysed a sample of offenders convicted of shoplifting, violence or drug offences in 1991, totalling 13,000 cases. (Hedderman and Dowds 1997; Dowds and Hedderman 1997). The study uncovered major differences in the use of non-custodial sentences for women and men. Women offenders were more likely than men offenders to be discharged, even when their circumstances appeared 'entirely comparable'. The authors of the study argued that differences in patterns of non-custodial sentencing centred around the sentencer's reluctance to impose fines on women offenders. This reluctance to fine women means that many receive a discharge and thus the result is greater leniency of treatment. However, Hedderman and Dowds note that the reluctance to fine women means that some women are treated more harshly, in that they are given a more severe non-custodial penalty (such as probation). This more severe treatment is problematic for the criminal justice system because it is more 'resource demanding' than imposing a fine. For women offenders who receive such a sentence, moreover, it represents a 'missed level' on the sentencing hierarchy. Consequently, any subsequent conviction may receive an even harsher sentence, such as imprisonment.

Analyses of differences in the use of custodial sentences for men and women offenders showed patterns that were more difficult to identify and interpret. For example, for a first-time violent offence, it was found that men and women stood an equal chance of going to prison. However, among repeat violent offenders, women were less likely to receive a custodial sentence than men found guilty of similar crimes. Amongst repeat drug offenders, women and men were equally likely to be sent to prison. However, amongst first-time drug offenders, women were significantly less likely to receive a prison sentence (Hedderman and Dowds 1997). The authors concluded that, while sentencers do not routinely reject the idea of imposing prison sentences on women, women do not stand an equal chance of custody overall (Dowds and Hedderman 1997).

A second study, linked to that by Hedderman and Dowds, explored magistrates' accounts of their sentencing decisions in an effort to understand why, for example, there is an apparent reluctance to fine women and a concern to avoid imprisoning them. Gelsthorpe and Loucks (1997) interviewed 200 magistrates about what they thought were the main influences on their sentencing decisions. At the outset, many magistrates said they found it hard to compare their decision-making rationales for women and men offenders, simply because they dealt with women offenders far less frequently. In their courts, the offenders magistrates routinely see are men and, moreover, men aged under 30. Furthermore, of the relatively few women magistrates have before them in their courts, most are there for shoplifting offences, whilst the range of offences committed by the men they sentence is much wider.

Gelsthorpe and Loucks found that magistrates tended to distinguish between offenders whom they perceived to be 'troubled' and those they regarded as 'troublesome', a categorisation which influenced their sentencing decisions. A number of factors in combination led magistrates to identify an offender as 'troubled' or 'troublesome'. The most important was the nature of the offence. However, other more subjective factors also came into play, including interpretations of the offender's personal and domestic circumstances, the way other individuals portrayed the offence and the offender in the courtroom, and the offender's appearance, behaviour and demeanour in court. Magistrates were found more often to locate women offenders in the 'troubled' category, arising out of their greater likelihood of being first-time offenders, their more 'trivial' offences and their more 'respectful' behaviour in court. In evaluations of the offender's behaviour during their court appearance, magistrates' perceptions of their appearance and 'body language' had an important, if unacknowledged, influence on their sentencing decisions. Men's body language was often perceived as conveying less respect for the court, as was the body language of ethnic minority offenders. In contrast, women, and by extension, white women, were generally seen to be 'deferential'. Magistrates also tended to attribute different motives for women's offending behaviour. For example, in shoplifting cases, it was found that magistrates often believed women stole for 'survival' reasons, including to feed and clothe their children.

Due to magistrates' perceptions of the relative infrequency of women's offending behaviour, their inexperience, their deference, their family responsibilities and the effects of these on their motivation for committing crimes, women were more often seen as not really 'criminals' but instead, as 'troubled'. Fines were therefore avoided because financial penalties would increase the 'trouble' women offenders found themselves in, and prison sentences were avoided due to effects on women offenders' children. Discharges or sentences of probation were favoured, in line with the belief that women offenders are 'troubled' and in need of positive assistance, rather than 'troublesome' and in need of negative punishment. Gelsthorpe and Loucks note that their findings support those of earlier studies of sentencing practices, which showed that magistrates considered family circumstances and responsibilities to be much more relevant when judging women offenders than with men offenders (Eaton 1986; Farrington and Morris 1983. See also Worrall 1990).

A range of evidence therefore suggests that gendered stereotypes held by criminal justice professionals influences the treatment of women and men offenders, with the result that women are often treated more leniently than men. As Morris points out, however, such findings raise the question as to the extent to which any lenient treatment of women within the criminal justice system is dependent upon conformity to 'traditional' or 'conventional' femininity. In other words, in the context of a criminal justice system dominated by professionals who are white, middle class and masculine, leniency may be reserved primarily for 'passive, unaggressive, remorseful, white, middle-class women' (1987: 82). Some women offenders may, consequently, be perceived as 'double deviants': first, as an individual who has committed a criminal offence; and second, as a woman who has transgressed against stereotypical feminine roles, behaviour or demeanour (Carlen 1995). The criminalising of women prostitutes, rather than their male clients, may be viewed as an example of this. Generally, however, as implied by Hedderman and Hough (1994), more research on disparities in treatment between different groups of women offenders is required. Moreover, whilst evidence suggests that some women offenders may be advantaged by the 'typifications of femininity' (Carlen and Worrall 1987) drawn upon by police, magistrates and others working within the criminal justice system, the fact that this system was developed for, and continues to primarily deal with, *male* offenders may disadvantage women in other ways (Hedderman and Hough 1994). For example, women in prison are a tiny minority, representing just 4 per cent of the total prison population in 1995 (Home Office 1997b). As argued by Heidensohn (1996), this means that there are very few women's prisons, and they are 'scattered haphazardly'. Therefore prisoners held in them may be many miles from their homes and families. Moreover, with such small numbers, there is not the same degree of specialisation of treatment or segregation of offenders found within the men's prison system. For these reasons, women prisoners may experience their sentence as a punishment of considerable severity.

Women as victims of crime: fear and reality

Heidensohn (1996: 19) comments that crime is so extensively gendered as to be 'peripheral' to women's lives, whilst deviancy and crime is a more integral part of masculine cultures and subcultures. This is an over simplification, not least because many women experience deviant, delinquent or criminal behaviour 'second hand', via being close relatives or partners of offending men. Moreover, describing women's relationship to crime as 'peripheral' underplays the significance of women as victims of crime (which, as we have seen, is predominantly committed by men) and their fear of crime.

Fearful women

Surveys show that women are consistently more fearful of crime than men. The 1998 British Crime Survey (Mirrlees-Black *et al.* 1998) found that more women than men worry about all types of crime, with the exception of 'theft from cars' (see Table 8.3). In the 1996 British Crime Survey, a much higher proportion of women than men reported that they felt, or would feel, unsafe walking alone in their locality after dark (47 per cent compared to 15 per cent). More women (11 per cent) than men (5 per cent) said they never went out after dark and of these more women (31 per cent) than men (15 per cent) gave crime-related reasons for their nocturnal confinement. Further evidence that women's greater anxiety about crime impacts upon their freedom of movement is indicated by gender differences in precautions taken to avoid crime when outside the home. Over half of women respondents said they always or usually avoided suspicious groups of people when they were out, compared to around a quarter of men. Going out accompanied by another person as a safety strategy also showed marked differences by gender, with 44 per cent of women saying they 'always or usually' made sure they went out with someone else compared to only 5 per cent of men. Younger women (aged 16–29) and older women (aged 60 and above) were even more likely to employ accompanied outings as a strategy of personal safety (Mirrlees-Black, Mayhew and Percy 1996).

In the 1998 British Crime Survey (Mirrlees-Black *et al.* 1998), as in earlier surveys, rape was the crime which more women were 'very worried' about than any other. Some groups of women, moreover, reported higher levels of fear of rape than others. Younger women (aged 16–29) were more worried about rape (39 per cent were very worried), than women aged 30–59 (31 per cent) and women aged 60 and over (25 per cent). Ethnic minority women also reported higher levels of fear of rape: 31 per cent of white women said they were worried about rape, compared to 43 per cent of black, 51 per cent of Indian and 49 per cent of Pakistani/Bangladeshi women (ONS 1998a).

Table 8.3 Gender differences in fear of crime, 1997

| | \% 'Very worried' about . . . | | | | | |
	Burglary	Mugging	Rape	Physical attack	Theft of cars	Theft from cars
Women	23	24	31	27	23	16
Men	15	10	6	8	20	18

Source: Adapted from Mirrlees-Black and Allen 1998, Table 2

Survey evidence clearly shows that women report higher levels of fear of crime than men, and that this fear more extensively impacts upon their feelings of safety, their fear of strangers and their overall freedom of movement. Goodey's (1995) research with children aged 11–16 showed that the gendered fear of crime is established in childhood. Girls were found to express greater fear when outside and greater fear of 'people' (but especially of men) than boys. Fear of crime is not shown to be the condition of the *majority* of women and nor do the majority of women routinely avoid going out after dark and especially on their own. Moreover, the survey evidence shows that gender differences in fear of crime are not always that dissimilar. As argued by Gilchrist and her colleagues (1998), these are findings which should caution us against stereotyping *all* women as fearful and *all* men as fearless of crime. Nevertheless, patterns of fear of crime and related behavioural strategies to minimise perceived risk do show consistent differences by gender. Moreover, a *substantial* minority of women say that they are fairly or very worried about crime in general. Amongst some groups of women, the majority report that they are fearful of crime. For all groups of women, the crime of rape is of particular concern, but especially for young women and ethnic minority women. Moreover, a *substantial* minority of women do say that they do routinely employ strategies of personal safety, which impact upon their freedom of movement, relative to men's. Not all women are fearful of crime, but a substantial minority are and this has real consequences for women's everyday lives.

Women's fear of crime has been noted to be far in excess of their actual risks of victimisation, at least in terms of violent crime. The 1998 British Crime survey found that women were less likely than men to be victims of violent crime (3.6 per cent compared to 6.1 per cent), with young men aged 16–24 living in inner city areas being the most at risk (Mirrlees-Black *et al.* 1998). Here, 'violent crime' includes domestic violence, mugging and 'other' contact violence but not sexual violence. Morris (1987) argues that victim surveys like the British Crime Survey under-record sexual violence, and that if incidences of sexual assault and rape were included more effectively in crime surveys then women's rate of victimisation would be much higher than men's. (The weakness of the British Crime Survey in measuring sexual offences is noted by the Home Office itself – see Mirrlees-Black *et al.* 1998: 5; Percy and Mayhew 1997).

The apparent disparity between women's fear of crime and their 'real' risks of being a victim of crime has generated considerable debate. Some authors have suggested that women's fear of crime is 'irrational', whilst others, more sympathetically, regard women's fear as understandable in the context of their socialisation which makes them feel physically less able to defend themselves, less secure and confident in public spaces and more fearful for the safety of others, especially children (see Gilchrist *et al.* 1998; Walklate 1995, for review). A further argument is that, far from women's fear of crime being unfounded and irrational, it is a reflection of their routine, everyday experiences of men's intimidating, often sexualised and sometimes violent behaviour, not all of which is conventionally categorised or penalised as 'criminal' (Walklate 1995: 69). In Stanko's words, 'Rather than informing us about officially recorded levels of victimisation and fear of crime, women's fear of crime may alert us to the unrecorded instances of threatening and violent behaviour by males' (1987: 129).

Evidence for women's everyday experiences of men's sexual violence which do not get reported to the police is provided by Kelly and Radford (1996). Interviews with women uncovered a range of experiences of men's sexually abusive behaviour, often from strangers in public places. This behaviour ranged from sexually abusive comments to threats, to unwanted physical contact and even attempted and actual sexual assault. These experiences invoked feelings of intense fear, sickness, intimidation and/or anger in those who were subjected to them. Yet, Kelly and Radford found that, often, the significance of the experience was minimised by the women through their use of the phrase 'but nothing actually happened' or 'nothing really happened'. Kelly and Radford argue that the use of this phrase in the face of the obvious distress such experiences of abuse had caused illustrates the extent to which women are encouraged to downplay the violence they routinely experience from men. As used by women, 'nothing really happened' actually means 'it could have been much worse', in that more violence or a full rape could have occurred, but it didn't. For Kelly and Radford, women's fear of crime reflects their knowledge and personal experiences of a complex range of abusive behaviour women encounter from men, only some of which is criminalised and very little of which gets reported to the police.

Minimising the significance of men's abusive, threatening and violent behaviour may be a common practice amongst women themselves, in the way suggested by Kelly and Radford (1996). It can also be said to be a common response of the criminal justice system when women *do* report their experiences of domestic violence or rape. Getting formal recognition from the criminal justice system that 'something did happen' can often prove a very difficult and extremely distressing experience in itself.

Domestic violence

The term 'domestic violence' is a contentious one, for it obscures the fact that the vast majority of such incidents involve men physically assaulting their women partners. For this reason Morris (1987), for example, prefers the less gender-neutral term 'wife abuse'. Others (for example, Maynard and Winn 1997; Walklate 1995), whilst noting its unwarranted gender-neutrality, continue to use the term largely because of its widespread currency. The extent of domestic violence is unknown. Violence between persons who are known to each other is even less likely to be reported to the police than violence involving strangers. Moreover, there is no specific offence of 'domestic violence' as such. In the unlikely event that a man is reported for physically assaulting his partner and subsequently gets charged and convicted, his offence would be 'actual bodily harm', or 'grievous body harm' or some such similar within the group offence 'violence against the person'.

Some aspects of domestic violence are suggested by the criminal statistics. For the period 1990–94, police records show that women victims of violence were more likely than men victims to have been attacked inside either their home or the home of their attacker (48 per cent compared with 18 per cent – Home Office 1997c). Domestic violence can sometimes culminate in homicide. Of women homicide victims in 1996, 44 per cent were killed by their current or former partner, whereas only 6 per cent of men victims were similarly killed (Home Office 1997c). In general, however, crime statistics based on police and court records massively under-record and obscure the extent of domestic violence.

In the light of the inadequacies of the criminal statistics on domestic violence, the British Crime Survey (although it does not measure it especially well either) represents an important source of data about domestic violence. In 1997, 835,000 incidents of domestic violence were reported, 582,000 (or 70 per cent) of them with women as victims (Mirrlees-Black et al. 1998). The 1996 Survey showed that aggressors were most often the woman victim's current partner (60 per cent of cases) or ex-partner (21 per cent). In two-thirds of cases, the violence took the form of punching and/or kicking. Around 3 per cent of domestic violence victims required hospital treatment, but nearly two-thirds received some medical attention overall. Of all the violent incidents against women uncovered by the British Crime Survey 1996, half were domestic violence (Mirrlees-Black et al. 1996). An analysis of the 1992 Survey calculated that 11 per cent of women who had ever lived with a male partner had experienced domestic violence at some point in their lives (Mirrlees-Black 1994).

Whilst eighteenth-century law gave husbands the right to beat their wives (as long as the violence used was not excessive and the stick was no thicker than a man's thumb – the original 'rule of the thumb'), twentieth-century law has improved the formal legal rights of women in violent situations, via, for example, the Domestic Violence and Matrimonial Proceedings Act, 1976 and the Domestic Violence Proceedings and Magistrates Courts Act, 1980. The activities of the feminist movement, particularly from the 1960s onwards proved crucial in problematising domestic violence and in the development of welfare responses in the form of refuges (see Dobash and Dobash 1992). However, as recently as the 1980s, the response of the police to domestic violence can best be described as 'dismissive'. In 1983, the Commissioner of the Metropolitan Police in London placed 'domestic disputes' in the same category as lost property and stray animals. He suggested that these were all examples of non-crime work which, if handed over to other agencies to deal with, would free-up the police for 'real crime work' (quoted in Morris 1987: 184–5). In this view, domestic 'disputes' were a private matter, between a husband and his wife. Neither party would benefit from or require the intervention of the police. Their involvement would amount to an intrusion into the sanctity of marriage and the privacy of family life. Feminist campaigners, and writers like Barratt and McIntosh (1982), argued that it was exactly this ideology which privileged masculine definitions over feminine ones and which allowed violence to go largely uncovered and uncriminalised 'behind closed doors'. In 1990, however, a shift in official policy was signalled in a Home Office circular. This recommended that the police adopt a more 'interventionist' approach to domestic violence. The police were encouraged to: record and investigate domestic violence cases in the same way as other assault cases; arrest assailants where an offence had been committed; offer protection and support to victims. In particular, police forces were advised to establish dedicated units to deal with cases of domestic violence, and to liaise with the relevant statutory and voluntary agencies in order to facilitate a co-ordinated response.

As Radford (1987) suggests, legislation and policy shifts may acknowledge domestic violence both as violence and as crime, but this is of little use if the legislation is not enforced and the policy is not put into practice. Research by Grace (1995) examined how far the 1990 recommendations on intervening in domestic violence cases were reflected in police policy and practice. In a telephone survey of all police forces in England and Wales, Grace found that all but three had produced a policy document on domestic violence. Just over half of the police forces had a specialist unit with some responsibility for domestic violence. However, only five had specialist units dedicated solely to domestic violence. Moreover, in a detailed study of five police forces, Grace found that over half of the constables and sergeants said they had not received any new guidelines on domestic violence. Grace also found that there was little systematic recording or monitoring of domestic violence cases. In the one force where there was systematic recording (the West Midlands police), the arrest rate in domestic violence cases was low, between 12 and 14 per cent, leading to a charge rate of 81 per cent.

Grace also studied the role and effectiveness of the dedicated Domestic Violence Officers. She found that they were 'somewhat marginalized' and had little to do with their uniformed colleagues. Most of the Domestic Violence Officers Grace interviewed were women and of low rank. Victims of domestic violence in the survey spoke very highly of the Domestic Violence Officers who had helped them, but there was significant criticism of the uniformed officers' attitudes and behaviour. Moreover, the victims

Grace spoke to were 'infuriated' by the way the courts dealt with domestic violence and many felt their case had not been taken seriously. In the light of her findings, Grace concluded that the new Home Office policy on domestic violence has not yet been fully put into practice. Similar findings were reported by Wright (1995). Her case study of a police division in Nottinghamshire suggests that the discretionary powers police have in recording and proceeding with cases of domestic violence mean that official policy changes in and of themselves are of little use. She found that victims' reports of domestic violence were often not recorded as such because the police did not adjudge them to be 'serious' or 'violent' enough to include them on the domestic violence register. Her recommendation is that police officers need to be re-educated, so that they recognise domestic violence for the crime that it is (Wright 1995: 425).

Earlier in this chapter, gendered assumptions were shown to influence the treatment of women offenders. Studies of the way the police and the courts handle cases of domestic violence are further revealing of the presence of gendered assumptions, but here it is men who are treated leniently as a result. Notions of the sanctity of marriage, the privacy of the family, men as heads of households and so on mean that violent masculine behaviour is privileged and women's experiences of that violence are downgraded to a 'dispute'. A further gendered assumption that works against women's interests, reflecting their lack of power relative to men's, is the idea that a woman victim of men's violence is somehow herself at fault. Edwards (1987: 141) argues that, whether in cases of sexual harassment, domestic violence or rape, the woman victim is 'frequently monitored for the extent to which she provoked her own demise'. In cases of domestic violence, this often means that the woman victim herself is blamed – for arousing anger in her aggressor, or in cases of repeated violence, for not leaving him (see Morris 1987, Walklate 1995). Gendered assumptions about women's culpability for men's violence against them also characterise the handling of rape cases.

Rape

The criminal statistics for England and Wales show that 6,700 rapes were reported to the police in 1997, of which 95 per cent had a woman victim (Povey, Prime and Taylor 1998). The number of rapes reported to the police has risen by about 10 per cent each year since 1986, when a Home Office circular laid out new recommendations for police practices in the recording of rape cases (Home Office 1997a). The official crime statistics on rape are widely recognised to be the tip of an iceberg. In other words, many more rapes occur, but do not get reported to the police. In a survey of 1,500 students at Cambridge University, 1 in 9 had been raped, but only 1 in 50 had reported their attempted rape or rape to the police. A survey of 2,000 women at Oxford Brookes University found that only 6 per cent of those who had been raped had reported it to the police. Their reasons for not reporting it centred around an expectation of an unsympathetic response from the police and a lack of faith in the judicial system (cited in Lees 1996: 101).

As with domestic violence, under pressure from feminist campaigners, there have been significant alterations in the extent to which and the ways in which the criminal justice system intervenes in sexual violence by men against women. For example, the Sexual Offences (Amendment) Act, 1976 included provisions to limit references in trials to a woman's past sexual history and character and provided complainants with anonymity in press reports. In 1986, new sentencing guidelines were issued and it was recommended that rape cases should be heard only by senior members of the judiciary. Also in 1986, a Home Office circular advised a change in police recording practices, so that only 'false' complaints of rape (rather than unsubstantiated or withdrawn complaints) should be 'no crimed' and thereby be excluded from the official figures. A further Home Office circular called for better training for police officers and specialist facilities for the medical examination and interviewing of victims. In 1991, following a decision by the Law Lords, rape within marriage became a criminal act (see Lees 1996; Walklate 1995 for more details of policy developments).

As Lees (1996) suggests, the steady rise in the number of rapes reported probably reflects a belief amongst the general public that the criminal justice system is now more favourable to rape complainants than it was in the past, as a result of the legislational and policy changes of recent decades. However, Temkin (1997) studied women rape victims whose cases were reported to the police after the policy changes to improve their handling of rape victims had been implemented. Temkin found that although the majority of the women in her sample were mainly or wholly positive about their treatment by the police, a sizeable minority (43 per cent) were not. This finding led Temkin to conclude that 'old' police attitudes and practices are still prevalent, which cause rape victims trauma over and above that which they have already suffered.

Despite evidence of change in the response of the criminal justice system to women victims of men's sexual violence, writers such as Morris (1987), Walklate (1995) and especially, Lees (1996, 1997) maintain that whilst 'the law ostensibly constrains male violence against women . . . in substance [it] allows such violence to continue' (Lees 1997: 2). Of particular recent concern is the disparity between the rise in reported rapes and the decline in the rate of convictions of those accused of rape. Lees' research, for example, focuses on the ways in which reports of rape and other sexual violence are 'progressively decriminalised by the judicial system' (1996: 99).

Lees (1996) identifies a process of attrition, which explains how rape cases are lost or dropped inbetween the victim's initial reporting of rape and the conviction stage. This attrition process means that fewer than 1 in 10 reports of rape results in a conviction. In 1996, although there were 6,000 rapes recorded by the police, there were only 600 offenders convicted of rape (Home Office 1997a). For Lees, there are four key points in the attrition process. The first two points of attrition occur at the initial reporting stage. Here, despite the Home Office guidelines, Lees found that reported rapes were recorded as 'no crimes' due to the victim withdrawing her complaint, a lack of corroborative evidence or the perceived unreliability of the complainant. Around 38 per cent of the cases in Lees' study were 'no crimed', a much higher rate than for other reported crimes. A Home Office study also found that police officers' practices of 'no criming' often contravened official policy (Harris 1998 cited in Travis 1998). At this stage, Lees also found evidence of police 'downgrading' reported rapes or other sexual offences to less serious crimes, including indecent assault and actual or grievous bodily harm.

The third main point of attrition occurs when the lawyers of the Crown Prosecution Service decide whether or not a case should go to court. The main criterion here is whether there is a 'realistic prospect' of conviction. Another study suggests that some rape cases fail even to be referred by the police to the Crown Prosecution Service in the first place. Harris found that two-thirds of the 309 cases of reported rape in her sample were not referred to the Crown Prosecution Service. According to Harris's study, one reason for the low (and falling) rates of conviction in rape cases, is the rise in 'date rapes' being reported to the police (Harris 1998 cited in Travis 1998). 'Date rapes' are those where the assailant is the current or former partner or close friend of the victim. In such cases, consent to sexual intercourse is more likely to be assumed to have been mutually negotiated. As Morris (1987) notes, in rape cases a 'yes' to sex on a previous occasion is often assumed to be a 'yes to all' on subsequent occasions. (This is the main reason why 'rape within marriage' was legally impossible until 1991). Lees (1996) argues that the law encompasses a masculine view of women's availability for and acquiescence to sexual use by men. Rapes by known persons, especially if a former lover, thus become even more difficult to prove than rape by strangers. Rape cases are least likely to reach court if there is no evidence of violence or injury and if there is a degree of consensual contact between the alleged rapist and the woman victim (Harris 1998 cited in Travis 1998). This latter factor is significant, not least because 46 per cent of rapes recorded by the police between 1990 and 1994 were alleged to have been committed by either the victim's spouse or lover (15 per cent) or other acquaintance (31 per cent) (Home Office 1997c).

The fourth point of attrition occurs in court, during the rape trial itself. It is at this stage, more than any other, that the woman complainant is frequently 'monitored for the extent to which she provoked her own demise' (Edwards 1987: 161). Lees (1997) argues that several key factors affect the outcome of rape trials. The court procedures and legal rules themselves are argued to weight the trial in favour of the defendant. For example, the legal definition of rape is penetration of the vagina by the penis without a woman's consent (note that the Criminal Justice and Public Order Act, 1994 widened the definition to include male rape, that is, penetration of the anus). Other studies have established the importance of the consent issue, particularly in terms of the way defence lawyers may, with the judge's discretion, attack a complainant's sexual reputation and character in efforts to undermine her claim that intercourse was non-consensual or indeed that it took place at all (Temkin 1998). Lees (1997) claims, on the basis of her research, that the narrow legal definition of rape minimises the significance of a victim's strategies of survival ('if she has no injuries, she must have consented') or her state of mind afterwards (where distressed behaviour is not regarded as relevant or corroborative evidence that an assault took place).

Evidence on the process of attrition and the far from transformed attitude of the police towards women rape victims suggest the extent to which the criminal justice system operates with stereotypical notions of normal masculine heterosexuality, which is privileged over women's sexuality (see also Chapter 5). In rape trials, this may mean that women victims are held to be somehow responsible for their own experience. For example, through 'leading' the man on to a point where his 'sexual urge' for intercourse 'had to be satisfied', or for dressing 'provocatively' or for going to his hotel room at 2 a.m. or accepting a lift in his car, or for not knowing that her body *really* wanted intercourse, rather than any other form of sexual contact or even no sexual contact at all (Smart 1989; Temkin 1998; Walklate 1995).

Brereton (1997), however, questions whether complainants in rape trials are subjected to forms of questioning or use of evidence that would be unacceptable in other trials. Brereton compared the conduct of rape trials with assault trials. Some differences between the two types of trials were identified, particularly in relation to the questioning of a woman's sexual history in rape trials and the more lengthy amount of time complainants in rape trials spent in the witness box. However, Brereton claims to have found substantial similarities between rape trials and assault trials. Complainants in both sorts of trials were likely to be subjected to attacks on their characters and credibility and to have any apparent inconsistencies in their evidence vigorously scrutinised by defence lawyers. Brereton concludes that such features are the result of broader factors which govern the conduct of a whole range of trials, including the laws of evidence, judicial concepts of relevance, lawyers' practices of cross-examination and interpretation of evidence and the constraints imposed by the adversarial nature of courtroom processes. According to Brereton, rape trial researchers have tended not to compare rape trials with other trials and therefore have underestimated, or even ignored the role of these factors. In his view, as a consequence, too much attention has focused on how to improve rape trials in particular, rather than on the shortcomings of the criminal trial process in general. Brereton's work draws some useful parallels between rape trials and other trials. However, his research did uncover some significant differences between the conduct of rape trials and assault trials. Moreover, he tends to underestimate the extent to which feminist analyses have criticised in a fundamental way the workings of the criminal justice system in debates about the need for a feminist jurisprudence.

Feminist jurisprudence?

Theoretically, women and men are treated equally under the law, but in practice the law is interpreted and applied in a social context where gender differences are manifest and which are supported by well developed and deeply ingrained ideologies about masculinity and femininity. As shown in this chapter, whilst gendered assumptions about femininity may advantage some women offenders, who may be treated leniently as a result, assumptions about normal masculinity and heterosexuality act to disadvantage women who are beaten, sexually assaulted or raped by violent men. As Radford, Kelly and Hester (1996) note, differences in women's positions in relation to the power structures of 'race' and class also influence the response of the criminal justice system to women as both offenders and victims of crime.

One response to the recognition that there is a congruence between the criminal justice system and (white, middle-class) masculine culture (Smart 1989) is the development of an alternative, feminist jurisprudence. In this viewpoint, rather than merely changing individual laws, what is required is a fundamental change in the values, concepts and established procedures which underpin the criminal justice system in its present formulation (see Walklate 1995 for review). Dworkin and Mackinnon's attempt to reformulate the legal understanding of the harm pornography causes, away from a concern with morality and toward a concern with its effects on women's civil rights as gendered citizens (see Chapter 7) can be seen as an example of feminist jurisprudence (Smart 1995).

As Walklate (1995) notes, different authors have contrasting views on the need to develop a criminal justice system which would better represent women's interests. Smart (1995) is sceptical, on the grounds that, first, it fails to challenge the legitimacy of the power of the law to regulate and organise peoples' lives and, second, that it is unlikely that a 'feminist' jurisprudence would adequately represent the interests of the diverse category of 'women'. Smart argues that the law needs to be recognised as a process which works in a variety of complex and contradictory ways, sometimes serving women, sometimes exploiting them. The way forward is to understand the criminal justice system as a 'technology of gender', in that it actively *produces* fixed gender identities amongst those who come into contact with it, rather than as something which simply applies law to *previously* gendered subjects. Rather than developing a feminist jurisprudence, Smart suggests 'deconstructing' the ways the criminal justice system is 'gendered in its visions and practices'. The issue then becomes one of challenging and resisting the dominant constructions of femininity the criminal justice system actively produces and reproduces (1995: 191, 223).

Smart proposes that the criminal justice system itself is one of the social systems that are productive of gender difference. For women who 'behave badly' and engage in lawbreaking, this often means the criminal justice system offers them the opportunity 'to neutralise' (Worrall 1990) their criminality, through representing their selves as 'troubled' rather than 'troublesome' or 'mad' rather then 'bad'. Yet, for women who experience men's violence, the criminal justice system often 'neutralises' that violence through recourse to the idea that 'it is in the nature of women's bodies to invite trouble' from men (Smart 1995: 225). Whether as criminals or as victims of crime, therefore, gendered typifications (interacting with those of class, ethnicity and sexuality) continue to shape the treatment of women within the criminal justice system.

Although Smart is sceptical of the possibility and desirability of feminist jurisprudence, others argue for a general strategy of the feminisation of masculine-dominated institutions as a means of improving women's status throughout society. Increased women's representation, it is argued, will transform masculinised organisational and institutional values and practices. As I show in the next chapter, this perspective is particularly evident in discussions of women's participation in formal politics.

Chapter 9

Making a difference? Politics and participation

In the light of evidence on the widespread and enduring inequalities between women and men presented throughout this book, in this chapter I consider the involvement of women in political activity as a key means of improving women's status and position in society. The first part of the chapter focuses on the presence of women in formal politics, especially in parliament and in government. I examine the argument that, the more women in positions of power in these key institutions, the better women's issues and concerns are represented and the greater likelihood there is of attaining gender equality throughout society. In the second part of the chapter, I develop the idea that women's participation in formal politics is a necessary but not sufficient strategy to achieve gender equality, through a focus on feminism as a social movement: its achievements, status and influence at the closing of the twentieth century.

Formal politics: from the suffragists to 'Blair's Babes'

For the 'first wave' British feminist movement, of the late nineteenth and early twentieth century, the struggle for suffrage (for the right to vote) was a primary concern. In 1918, most men and some women won the right to vote. Women were eligible as long as they were over the age of 30, were local government ratepayers, wives of local ratepayers or university graduates. Bryson (1994) calculates that these qualifications restricted the vote to about half the population of adult women. Also in 1918, all women aged over 21 became eligible to stand for election to political office. In that year, the first woman was elected as a Member of Parliament: Countess Markiewicz, an Irish Nationalist who never took up her seat. Following a by-election in 1919, Lady Nancy Astor, a Conservative who won in the Plymouth constituency, became the first woman Member of Parliament to sit in the House of Commons. However, as Alberti (1989) notes, the suffragist movement's initial reaction to Lady Astor's achievement was muted and cautious. Prior to running for the Plymouth seat, which was previously held by her husband, Lady Astor had apparently shown no personal interest in politics and she was not a noted campaigner for women's right to vote. Nevertheless, important links between Lady Astor and the National Union of Women's Suffrage Societies (the main suffrage organisation) were quickly established. Lady Astor acknowledged the significance of her achievement, saying that 'I feel it is a great responsibility to be the first woman to sit in Parliament, and I know that I shall need all the help that other women can give me'. By 1923, Lady Astor was praised in a pro-suffrage women's publication as 'doing all the work which we had dreamed that our first woman in parliament could do' (quoted in Alberti: 1989: 97).

It was not until 1928 that women were granted the vote on the same terms as men. In 1929, another 'first' was achieved when Margaret Bondfield, a Labour Member of Parliament, became a Cabinet Minister. The number of women Members of Parliament rose gradually over time. Between 1918 and 1924, there were never more than 8 women MPs and between 1929 to 1955, there were never more than 24. In 1964, there were 29 women MPs but by 1979, this had fallen to 19 (see Puwar 1997). In the 1970s, two other important 'firsts' occurred, both achieved by Margaret Thatcher, a Conservative MP. In 1975 she became the first woman leader of a political party and in 1979, she became the first woman Prime Minister. However, and unlike Nancy Astor, Margaret Thatcher repeatedly denied the gender significance of her achievements (Pilcher 1995).

In the 1987 General Election, significantly more women were elected as MPs than ever before (41 compared to the previous highest number of 29 in 1964). However, this still meant that women were just 6.3 per cent of Members of Parliament. The 1992 election saw 60 women elected as Members of Parliament. The most significant increase, doubling the number of women in the House of Commons, came in the 1997 General Election. Women won 120 of the 659 seats in the House of Commons, numbering 18 per cent of MPs. Two black women MPs were elected. Historically, and despite the example of the Conservative Lady Astor, women MPs have been more likely to belong to the Labour Party than any other party, and this tendency was also apparent in the 1997 election. Of the 120 women MPs elected, 101 of them represented the Labour Party (EOC 1997f). In addition to women's representation in the House of Commons doubling, their representation in government positions also massively increased. Between 1918 and 1997, there were only 8 women Cabinet Ministers, in total (Puwar 1997). The 1997 Labour Government's first Cabinet almost doubled that in one go, with five women Cabinet Ministers. Moreover, their responsibilities included areas never previously held by women (Puwar 1997), namely, President of the Board of Trade (Margaret Beckett), Leader of the House of Commons (Ann Taylor) and Secretary of State for Northern Ireland (Mo Mowlam).

What difference does it make?

In the decades between the opening and closing of the twentieth century, it is clear that fundamental change has occurred in women's involvement in formal politics. From completely lacking the vote prior to 1918, to becoming Prime Minister in 1979, from holding one parliamentary seat in 1919 to holding 120 seats in 1997, women have greatly improved their representation at the highest level of the democratic process. Why, though, are these changes in women's presence in the formal political sphere held to be of significance? Why is it that efforts continue to be made, by campaigns like the 300 Group (which aims to have half of the House of Commons seats held by women) and Emily's List, to increase women's representation in parliament still further?

Norris (1996) suggests that a general argument for bringing more women into parliament is to do with sustaining the claim that it is a fully democratic institution. In other words, the legitimacy and authority of parliament is undermined if it fails to reflect the diversity of the people whose interests it purports to represent. Symbolically, therefore, since women make up half the population, the Houses of Parliament should reflect this in their gender profile. However, there are more complex arguments for increasing women's representation in formal political processes. These centre around a belief that women in the general public have particular interests and concerns which are best represented by women politicians.

The idea that women's perspectives are more effectively conveyed when women, rather than men, are in positions of power and influence has been encountered earlier in this book. For example, when discussing images of women's bodies in popular media culture (Chapter 7), one solution to masculine-dominated 'misrepresentations' was argued to be an increase in the involvement of women as producers of sexually explicit material, so that it becomes more 'women-centred'. Similarly, one aspect of the development of a feminist jurisprudence (Chapter 8) is to increase the involvement of women as professionals in the presently masculine-dominated criminal justice system and thereby make the legal process more sensitive to women's needs, both as criminals and as victims of men's violence. The recurrent demand for increasing women's presence amongst decision makers is based on an understanding 'sometimes publicly argued, sometimes simply assumed' that women have interests which are most effectively represented by women (Lovenduski 1996: 1).

Norris (1996) identifies the reasoning behind the idea that women as a social group have distinctively different interests and perspectives compared to men as a social group. This understanding, she suggests, is based on the recognition that there are structural differences in women's and men's positions in society, which is in turn reflected in the distinctive perspectives women have compared to men. As a consequence, therefore, women's perspectives have to be as adequately represented in the political process as men's already are, and the best way to ensure that this is achieved is through more women politicians (see also Phillips 1991).

'Women', though, are a diverse grouping: it is unsatisfactory to assume that a few women MPs will be able to speak for the interests of all women (Lovenduski 1996; Norris 1996; Phillips 1991). Nevertheless, there is an assumption within 'the equal participation leads to equal representation' viewpoint that the more women politicians, the better reflected will be the diverse range of women's interests and concerns. The argument is that 'bringing more women in' will make a difference in two main ways. First, more women in the political process would help ensure that issues of particular interest to women, either for biological reasons (cervical cancer screening, for example) or for social reasons (childcare provision), are higher on the political agenda and that women's perspectives on other political issues, like economics or education, are fully taken into account (Lovenduski 1997). Second, more women in the political process would help transform the style in which political decision making gets done, away from the competitive, aggressive 'yah boo' point-scoring, to a more effective, professional, 'kinder, gentler' politics (Norris 1996).

As both Lovenduski (1996) and Norris (1996) note, arguments that bringing women into positions of political power will 'make a difference' are often made without much recourse to evidence. Do women in the electorate have distinct perspectives and concerns compared to men? Do women politicians themselves have women's political interests and issues as especial concerns, and are they distinctive in their style of politics? What evidence is there that a large numerical presence of women in parliament makes a difference, both to the political culture and to improving gender equality in society as a whole?

Women voters' perspectives and expectations

Lovenduski (1997) reviews evidence which does suggest that women voters place greater priority on issues of particular concern to them than do men, and that women perceive general political issues in a different way to men. For example, whilst both women and men voters are likely to agree that economic issues are of great importance politically, evidence suggests that, for women, economic issues like low pay, pensions and part-time work are of key importance whilst for men unemployment is a major concern (see also the *British Social Attitudes* series of surveys). There is also some evidence that women expect women politicians actively to promote their interests as women, in other words, to use their political power to help other women (Pilcher 1995).

Women politicians: distinctively different?

Norris (1996) uses data from the 1992 British Candidate Study (a major survey of politicians and members of political parties, which included MPs) which shows that women politicians do have different attitudes and political styles than men politicians. 'Women tended to give stronger support for issues of women's rights, they express greater concern about social policy issues and they give a higher priority to constituency casework' (Norris 1996: 101). Similarly, Lovenduski (1997) reports findings from the 1997 Representation Study, which surveyed 1,000 politicians, who were either candidates for election or Members of Parliament. This study shows that 'women politicians are consistently more likely to take a pro-woman line than men' (Lovenduski 1997: 211), for example, on policies of positive discrimination (or affirmative action) and better childcare provision, where the purpose is to increase the proportion of women in parliament. Moreover, the survey found that women politicians are more likely than men to be 'pro-choice' on abortion, to favour equal opportunity policies and to agree that women should have access to a variety of social roles (1997: 211).

In 1997, the doubling of the number of women MPs and the near doubling of the number of women ever to hold a Cabinet post did represent a significant advancement in terms of women's penetration of formal, institutionalised political power. Less impressive, however, is the fact that women were still only 18 per cent of MPs, a figure which places Britain twentieth in the world in terms of the proportion of women in national legislatures (Lovenduski 1997). The reasons why so few women become Members of Parliament are the very same reasons why women are rarely found in any prestigious, well-paid and powerful positions. Lovenduski (1996) argues that, to run for parliament, an individual must have financial security, public networks, social status, policy experience, technical and social skills and time available to devote to political activism. Women's greater household and caring responsibilities (see Chapter 4), combined with their concentration in low-status, low-paying occupations means that fewer women than men have the resources to facilitate a high-level political career. Lovenduski emphasises the importance of the type of employment that feeds into a parliamentary career. Those who have 'brokerage jobs', such as barristers, trade union officials, journalists, lecturers and political researchers, work in areas which are complementary to politics. This enables ready translation of skills gained in employment to the political context. As shown in Chapter 3, these are the very professions where men historically and currently (albeit to a lesser extent) outnumber women, an imbalance which, in turn has been an outcome of long-term gender inequalities in education (see Chapter 2).

Having successfully overcome the obstacles to gaining political office, women MPs may face particular difficulties while they are there. Puwar

(1997) interviewed women members of the 1992–97 Parliament. Many believed that they were discriminated against by some men MPs, who were described as exclusionary in their practices and sexist in their attitudes. Moreover, criticism was also directed at the organisation and procedures of the House of Commons, in that these reflected the historical position of MPs as 'gentlemen', rather than individuals with domestic responsibilities. For example, the House often continues to sit late into the night, and whilst there is a rifle range there are no crèche facilities (Puwar 1997: 4–5).

Evidence suggests that women MPs also face difficulties in the 'management' of their femininity, through the 'technologies of femininity' they employ (see also Chapter 6). In attaining political power, women politicians have 'transgressed' traditional gender roles (Puwar 1997: 4), because in Britain, as elsewhere, public, political power has been 'consistently defined as undoubtedly masculine' (Franklin, Lury and Stacey 1991: 32). As noted earlier, this means that women politicians are expected, and themselves may seek, to advance the interests of other women, through actively promoting and prioritising women's issues. Similarly, they may also be expected, and may themselves seek, to transform the way in which masculine-dominated politics gets done. Yet, the danger in this is that women politicians who emphasise women's interests and 'women's ways' may be marginalised and seen not to be 'proper' politicians, concerned with 'real political issues' and who enjoy and excel at the 'rough and tumble' of 'real politics'.

Raven (1997) is especially critical of the way the new intake of women MPs was described in the press as a 'civilising' influence on the House of Commons. Women MPs , it was suggested, would make it less aggressive and competitive, and more soft and co-operative, while the bright and colourful clothes worn by women members makes the whole place 'easier on the eye'. Raven notes that women politicians themselves have sometimes engaged in this portrayal of their influence (for examples, see Longrigg 1997). For Raven, such stereotypical depictions are damaging, because they act to place women politicians above politics and make them somehow not 'proper' politicians at all. 'Seldom discussed as individuals, they are identified by this retrograde essentialist version of gender which claims that all women are nice' (Raven 1997: 7).

Further evidence on media portrayals of women politicians is provided by Sreberny-Mohammadi and Ross (1996). They interviewed a sample of both Conservative and Labour women MPs on their perceptions of media coverage they received. Most said that their 'outward appearance' was the focus of considerably more media attention than that given to their men colleagues. Their age, looks, and fashion sense was nearly always noted in any newspaper report, and references were frequently made to their domestic and family circumstances. Many of the women MPs interviewed in the study were said to be 'infuriated' by their portrayal in the press, especially because of the implied links between such factors as their appearance or their family circumstances and their ability to do their job. The authors of the study concluded that 'a woman politician is always described as such, her gender is always the primary descriptor' (1996: 109). Evidence on the way the media represents women politicians suggests that women politicians are all too often 'casually commodified' in stereotypically feminine ways with more interest shown in their 'neatly crossed legs' than in their 'sharply tuned minds' (Sreberny-Mohammadi and Ross 1996: 114). In other words, media portrayals may concentrate on a woman MP's femininity rather than her political skills and attributes and thereby damage perceptions about her as professional politician (see also Ross and Sreberny-Mohammadi 1997; Norris 1995). Yet, other evidence suggests that being a woman with political power may damage perceptions others hold about her *femininity*. Interviews with women on their responses to Margaret Thatcher, for example, showed that the juxtaposition of her femininity and her holding office as a powerful Prime Minister was a problematical issue, leading some to describe her as 'more like a man, really' (Pilcher 1995).

Taken together, evidence suggests that women politicians are distinctly different. They are a numerical minority, in a masculine-dominated institution, whose attitudes and political practices often differ from their men colleagues and who face a range of difficulties in negotiating the relationship between their gender and their political office.

Transforming political culture and improving gender equality?

At the time of writing, it is too soon to say with any conviction whether the increased number of women politicians, and the number of women politicians of Cabinet rank, will contribute to a shift in political culture whereby women's concerns and perspectives become more centrally represented, and whether the style in which politics 'gets done' will be transformed. For the time being, the evidence for change is somewhat unclear and contradictory.

On the positive side, there is evidence of an increased concern with women's issues and women's perspectives in recent decades. The various Conservative Governments from 1979 to 1997 did make efforts to place women's issues more centrally on the political agenda, although this was done with varying degrees of enthusiasm. Under Margaret Thatcher's premiership, there was a Ministerial Group on Women's Issues but, according to Lovenduski (1996), the Prime Minister herself failed to attend any of its meetings and other ministers only reluctantly engaged with it. Under John Major, a Cabinet Sub-committee on Women's Issues was set up, with 18 ministers as members, representing key government departments. Moreover, there was also a Ministry of Women, albeit submerged within the Department of Education and Employment (Lovenduski 1996). Under the Labour Government elected in 1997, there was a (part-time) Minister for Women, a Cabinet Sub-committee on Women's Issues, and a Women's Unit. This last initiative was a cluster of 35 civil servants, responsible for ensuring that all government departments listen to women and for monitoring the impact of policies on women. Headed by a woman since its inception, it has been credited with influencing the Government's childcare programme (see Chapter 4), the content of the *Fairness at Work* white paper and is engaged in developing a strategy for tackling men's violence against women (Ward 1998a; 1998b). Moreover, Lovenduski (1997) claims that within a few weeks of taking their parliamentary seats, the 101 Labour women MPs had already formed a network in order to work together on suitable issues. In summary, there is some evidence that the increased proportion of women MPs over the recent decades has been accompanied by a higher priority placed on women's issues and a greater concern to take account of women's perspectives.

However, on the negative side, the 1997 Labour Government attracted criticism for failing to meet its pre-election promise of a full-time Women's Minister of Cabinet rank. Moreover, the junior Minister for Women who backs the part-time Minister, is unpaid and the Women's Unit has no spending budget or legislative programme (Lovenduski 1997; Ward 1998a). Furthermore, the contingent of women Labour MPs attracted early criticism for failing to defend the interests of single mothers in terms of rights to welfare payments.

Evidence on media portrayals of women politicians, discussed earlier, also serves to caution against the assumption that the larger number of women MPs are set to make a difference. In reporting the political 'breakthrough for women' in the 1997 General Election, some sections of the media arguably trivialised the significance of that achievement. For example, it was widely reported that more women in parliament would lead to a requirement for additional toilet facilities and that the House of Commons barber was to be replaced by a unisex hairstylist. A further problematical aspect of the media coverage of the increased number of women MPs was the labelling of the Labour MPs as 'Blair's Babes'. Although the description may not have had the intention of doing so, it trivialised the achievements of the new intake of women politicians. Through grouping the 101 Labour women together and linking them to Blair, the label implied that these women 'belonged' to Blair in a way that the 317 male Labour MPs did not. Moreover, the term 'babes' is a slang term for women who are sexually attractive to men, and thus the image of women politicians it conveys is a heavily sexualised one.

In summary, there are several positive signs of change for women's relationship with formal politics. There are many more women MPs and more women Cabinet Ministers than ever before, and they have apparently developed informal links between themselves. The Labour Government has shown a greater engagement with women, via the Women's Unit and its childcare strategy, for example. However, there are negative signs too, in that the government failed fully to deliver its promise to prioritise women's issues and perspectives. The media representation of women politicians continues to be highly problematical, acting to trivialise and stereotype women with political power.

A 'critical mass'?

Some theorists would argue that such problems persist because, within British politics, the representation of women has only very recently reached the level of a 'critical mass'. As Puwar (1997) explains, the idea of a critical mass developed in the Scandinavian context, where women have had relatively high representation in parliament for longer. In Sweden, for example, over 40 per cent of the parliamentary body is female, whilst in Norway, women held 35 per cent of parliamentary seats in 1989 (Puwar 1997; Bystydzienski 1992). The argument is that, once women's representation in traditionally masculine-dominated institutions reaches a critical mass (calculated at around 15 per cent), then the presence of women begins to affect the policy and practice of those institutions. In her case study of Norway, Bystydzienski (1992: 22) argues that, 'since the influx of larger numbers of women into public politics, women's issues, interests, values and perspectives have become incorporated into political discourse and policy-making'. In the British context, as Lovenduski concludes, 'whether more women in parliament will make a difference, only time will tell' (1997: 211).

Norris (1996), having reviewed cross-national research on whether a critical mass of women politicians serves to transform political culture, says that the evidence is 'inconclusive'. Some studies have stressed women's distinctive contribution, whilst others have emphasised the similarities between men and women politicians. A further set of research evidence suggests that gender differences in politics are influenced by the broader institutional context, especially the existence of links between women politicians and extra-parliamentary women's organisations. The example of Margaret Thatcher is relevant here. Margaret Thatcher has been described as an anti-feminist politician, because of the lack of significance she attributed to gender, her policies which did not favour the interests of women and her unequivocally negative opinions on feminism (Pilcher 1995). Britain's first (and to date, only) woman Prime Minister is, therefore, a reminder that it is not merely sufficient for women to gain positions of public political power in order for gender equality policies to be enacted. For, without a pro-feminist consciousness, women politicians (of whatever political hue) are unlikely to advocate policies to improve women's status and positions within society. Bystydzienski (1992) in her study of Norway and Carroll (1992) in her study of the United States both emphasise the importance of the initial development and long-term maintenance of links between women politicians and women's organisations. In other words, women in political power have to be reminded and encouraged to use their position to represent the interests of women, and here feminism as a social movement has a key role to play (Pilcher 1995).

Feminism: from margins to mainstream

The word 'feminism' is French in origin (Jaggar 1983) and dates from the 1890s when *féminisme* began to be used as synonym for the emancipation of women. However, concern for the rights of women had emerged much earlier, and Randall (1982) locates the French Revolution of 1789 as the arena where the first concerted demands for women's rights were made. In the case of Britain, though, it is not until the nineteenth century that we can really identify the existence of a feminist movement.

Drawing on the work of writers like Banks (1981) and Coote and Campbell (1987), I have argued elsewhere that the history of the British feminist movement can be divided into five more or less distinct phases (Pilcher 1993). First, the nineteenth century, when the central concern was 'equality of rights' including employment, legal rights over property and custody of children, and the right to vote. In the second phase, during the early decades of the twentieth century, the struggle for the vote emerged as the predominant concern. The struggle for suffrage bestowed unity on 'the women's movement' (as it was then called, see Alberti 1989; Dyhouse 1989), a unity which dissipated in the years after the vote had been achieved. This third period, of the inter-war years (1919–38), was characterised by ideological and institutional divisions within the movement, which increasingly came to be referred to as 'feminism' (Alberti 1989; Banks 1981). The 'new feminists' (as they were then called) concentrated on issues such as family allowances (or 'endowment'), birth control and protective legislation. Priorities such as these were not favoured by equal rights feminists, whose fundamental emphasis was a reorientation of women away from the domestic sphere (Alberti 1989).

As the title of Spender's (1982) book proclaims, there has always been a women's movement this century, yet activity was muted following the divergence of the two feminisms in the 1920s and 1930s. This quiet period continued up until the 1970s, when the 'second wave' of feminism swept over society. The 'ideological catalysts' (Randall 1982) of this fourth phase of the women's movement were undoubtedly the American liberation movements (that is, the black liberation movement, the student protest movement and the women's movement). Moreover, there was a vibrant culture of left-wing politics in Britain, as evidenced by the British student movements and the increased militancy of working-class women. One example here is the 1968 Ford strike, where women workers demanded equal pay (Banks 1981). The late 1960s also saw the rise of women's groups and in 1970, the first national conference of the Women's Liberation Movement was held at Ruskin College, Oxford. The conference, amongst other things, defined the most immediate problems facing women as an oppressed group and four demands were formulated. The demands, which were to become the focus for demonstrating and campaigning, were: equal pay, equal education, 24-hour nurseries, and free contraception and abortion (Wandor 1972).

Other notable aspects of the 'second wave' movement were: the campaign against the 1970 Miss World contest, which gave rise to the 'bra burning' myth; marches in London and Liverpool, with the four demands prominently displayed on banners; the addition of three further demands: an end to discrimination against lesbians and the right of all women to define their own sexuality; freedom from violence and sexual coercion; an end to all the laws, assumptions and institutions that perpetuate male dominance and men's aggression towards women (Segal 1987). Although the vocabulary of this period was primarily one of 'liberation', 'oppression' and of women uniting together as a 'sisterhood' (Randall 1982), there was continuity with earlier phases via concerns over 'equal rights'. The 'second wave' also saw the setting up of national organisations such as the Women's Aid Federation (to help women victims of domestic violence), the National Abortion Campaign, Rape Crisis Centres (Coote and Campbell 1982) and the rise of the women's peace movement centred around the Greenham Common nuclear missile base in Berkshire (Lovenduski and Randall 1993). It is important to note, though, that during the 1960s and 1970s, women organising together was not called 'feminism'. This was a position adopted by or ascribed to particular groups, for example, the radical or revolutionary feminists within the Women's Liberation Movement (Delmar 1986).

The fifth historical phase of feminism had parallels with the third phase, in that following a period of strength, unity and a high public profile, the movement became characterised by divisions, especially between the radical and revolutionary feminists and others of more 'liberal' views. Writing in 1987, Segal notes that it has been 'many years since we could talk meaningfully of any single entity called "the women's movement"' and points to the last national conference in 1978 and the decline of locally based networks that were a characteristic feature of the movement at its height. There has been some funding for women's groups of various kinds from local councils, but these are isolated and do not form part of a national or regional network (Segal 1987: 56–7). Since the fragmentation of the Women's Liberation Movement, there has been a gradual replacement of the term 'women's liberation' by the term 'feminism'. This change in vocabulary has been argued to represent a move from a position of common revolutionary struggle to a more restricted, realistic and less revolutionary orientation (Wier and Wilson 1984: 79).

The characteristics of the fifth stage of the feminist movement are elaborated by Lovenduski and Randall (1993), in their study of developments since the late 1970s. Lovenduski and Randall argue that the period between the late 1970s and the early 1990s was one of both losses and gains for the feminist movement.

On the one hand, there has been a decline from the 'high tide' of feminist activism of the 1970s. Moreover, there has been internal conflict, between radical feminists and other feminists, between black feminists and white feminists, and there has been fragmentation via the weakening of nationally co-ordinated activities. However, these features were neither universal nor uniform across Britain. For example, feminist activity was particularly vibrant in Scotland for the period covered by Lovenduski and Randall's study. Throughout Britain, activism fluctuated around individual issues, for example, Women Against Pit Closures and Greenham Common in the early to mid-1980s, shifting to campaigns around pornography by the early 1990s (see Chapter 7) along with campaigns on reproductive issues in the context of the Human Fertilisation and Embryology Act (see Chapter 6).

On the other hand, 'the decline and deradicalisation of the British Women's movement since the end of the 1970s was accompanied by and in many ways was a consequence of, its greater involvement with state agencies and the growing presence of feminists in mainstream institutions' (Lovenduski and Randall 1993: 15). In other words, Lovenduski and Randall argue that the 'high tide' of feminism has left behind a solid core of committed feminists who have established themselves in a range of mainstream political organisations and who have 'a good foothold' in central state institutions. With varying degrees of success, women's presence has made itself felt in the political parties (especially the Labour Party), the trade unions, in local government, in the higher levels of the civil service, in education at all levels, and, to a more limited extent, in the judiciary (Lovenduski and Randall 1993: Chapter 5). Some data on women's representation in these institutions and organisations is shown in Box 9.1 (see also Chapters 3 and 8). This process of institutionalisation has been accompanied by a 'diffusion' of feminist values into the mainstream of political and public life. According to Lovenduski and Randall, survey evidence on popular attitudes toward gender issues (for example, the *British Social Attitudes* series) show a marked degree of change. 'Ideas and attitudes about women's rights and entitlements that seemed radical at the beginning of the 1970s are widely accepted today' (1993: 351).

In Lovenduski and Randall's analysis, the losses of the feminist movement (mainly its decline and fragmentation) are directly connected to its gains (institutionalisation and diffusion), a process which, they conclude, is both inevitable and desirable. The feminist movement has changed but, they argue, it is 'still very much alive' (1993: 2). However, they express unease about the decline of feminism as an activist, organised, nationally coherent movement. Like Bystydzienski (1992) and Carroll (1992), they argue that 'feminists *inside* a system are more likely to be effective and motivated if there is a strong, autonomous feminist movement outside the system' (original emphasis, Lovenduski and Randall 1993: 13).

Box 9.1 Proportion of women in trade unions, local government and public bodies

Women in trade unions

In 1996, Labour Force Survey figures show that 45 per cent of employee members of trade unions were women. However, their representation on executive councils, as full-time union officials and as delegates to the Trade Union Congress is much lower. In 1995, there were only four women General Secretaries of Unions affiliated to the TUC. Of the 48 seats on the TUC General Council, only 16 were held by women.

Women in local government and the European Parliament

In 1993, around one quarter of local government councillors were women. In 1998, of 87 British Members of the European Parliament, 17 were women.

Women in public appointments

In 1996, women were 31 per cent of all appointees to public bodies, the boards of nationalised industries and public corporations.

Sources: Central Office of Information (1996), EOC (1997f), Trade Union Congress (1998), European Parliament (1998).

Responses to feminism

Any review of the status and influence of feminism in contemporary Britain must consider the ways in which women themselves respond to it. Despite the importance of feminism, historically and currently, there is, however, surprisingly little evidence on how it is interpreted and understood amongst its main constituency, women.

It is known that feminism and feminists have long faced hostility from certain quarters of society. In Britain, for example, Mary Wollstonecraft was described as a 'hyena in petticoats' in 1792 (Neustatter 1990), whilst the suffragists were depicted as ugly, unfeminine spinsters by newspapers of the Edwardian period. Activists of the 'second wave' of the women's movement in the 1970s were similarly depicted as 'unattractive man-haters' (Holdsworth 1988: 185–6, 198). The practice of equating feminism with lesbianism has been used since the turn of the century to scare women away from feminism, and to dismiss and compartmentalise women who are feminists (Tuttle 1986; see also Rowland 1984). Furthermore, the abbreviations 'women's lib' and 'women's libbers', and the term 'bra burners', have been interpreted as 'demeaning' and as 'trivialising' the women's movement and its activists (Tuttle 1986: 361). In contemporary Britain, the phrase 'I'm not a feminist but ...' is widely recognised as a standard way for women to distance themselves from feminism, whilst simultaneously agreeing with aspects of its agenda. The apparent negativity with which feminism is perceived in contemporary Britain is further indicated by newspaper surveys. For example, in 1991 the *Guardian* found that most respondents believed feminism was frowned upon (7 March, 1991).

Some academic studies have examined women's responses to feminism. Oakley (1974) found that her sample of housewives held predominantly negative attitudes toward the women's liberation movement, whilst Griffin (1989) found that young women displayed attitudes that could be recognised as feminist, yet tended to avoid identifying themselves *as* feminists. One study compared responses to and understandings of feminism held by women of different age cohorts (Pilcher 1993, 1998). Younger women (especially those aged 17–29) were found to be more knowledgeable of and positive towards feminism than older women (particularly those who were aged over 60). Moreover, younger women were also much more likely to describe themselves as 'feminists' than older women. However, the younger women were not wholly positive about feminism and viewed it with some ambiguity. In particular, the youngest cohort of women showed a sensitivity to stereotypical depictions of feminists as lacking in femininity and as obsessive, and to the 'extreme' versions of feminism. The young women agreed with feminist arguments on equality between women and men in the distribution of household work, and in the worlds of education and paid work. However, they did not tend to share a feminist perspective on the objectification of women's bodies in publications such as 'Page Three' of the *Sun* newspaper. Significantly, when discussing gender issues, the youngest cohort often used individualist vocabularies (stressing the rights of individuals), rather than feminist vocabularies, where gender is more of a central concern. Whilst ideologies of individualism and feminism can both be viewed as progressive, the tendency for younger women to employ the former rather than the latter means that the collective oppression of women on the basis of their gender loses prominence, along with recognition of the role played by structural disadvantages and systematic sexist practices (Pilcher 1998).

Taken together, the research evidence suggests that women's responses to feminism are often ambivalent, even amongst young women who, arguably, have benefited the most from the social changes feminism has helped to bring about. Furthermore, survey data suggest that only a small minority of women (2 per cent in 1993) belong to women's groups or feminist organisations (CSO 1995). In the analyses of one author, the ambivalence with which contemporary feminism is regarded is a sign that feminism needs to reorientate itself. Walter (1998) suggests that certain aspects of feminist politics encourage younger women, influenced by the 'Wonderbra' culture of contemporary femininity, to distance themselves from feminism. Instead of politicising what women wear on and do with their bodies, and criticising women for making themselves sexually attractive to men, Walter argues that the 'new feminism' should be primarily concerned with the continuing political and economic inequalities between women and men. Walter has, however, been heavily criticised by other feminists, not least for misrepresenting the concerns of 'old' feminism by ignoring the fact that it has always been centrally concerned with structural inequalities of power and resources (see, for example, Phillips 1998; Walter and Cottam 1998).

It is a matter of debate whether or not there is a need for a 'new feminism' to ensure that contemporary young women find it an appealing and relevant social movement. Yet, Walter's book and the controversy it generated arguably reflects real concerns as to the remit of feminism at the close of the twentieth century and, in the light of its concrete successes from which younger women especially benefit, how best to ensure that it continues to be seen as both necessary and relevant to women's lives.

Towards a 'new world' of gender relations?

In this chapter, I have examined changes in women's representation in formal politics in Britain, from the early decades of the twentieth century to its close. In 1997, women represented 18 per cent of MPs. This is a proportion some analysts have identified as a 'critical mass', enabling women politicians to make a difference to political culture and to gender equality throughout society. In the pursuit of gender equality, writers like Lovenduski and Randall (1993) argue that close links are necessary between women politicians 'inside the system' and women's organisations 'outside the system'. As noted earlier, such links have been established since Lady Astor was the first elected woman MP to take her seat, in 1919. The creation and maintenance of networks between women politicians and women's organisations may benefit both parties, through supporting women politicians who are negotiating their way through a masculine-dominated institution, and through ensuring that these women use their power effectively to improve the status and position of women elsewhere in society. For, as evidence presented throughout this book shows, there are a range of enduring and persisting inequalities between women and men in society. Despite some changes and real improvements for many women, gender remains a primary social division in Britain at the end of the twentieth century. If further progress is to be made in the next century, this will require not only a greater number of women politicians at the heart of formal structures of power, supported by a strong and autonomous feminist movement outside the system, but also an increased awareness of how gender 'gets done' by 'ordinary' individuals in their everyday life. To paraphrase Connell (1995: 86), we are all engaged in constructing gender and so have some degree of influence in creating a 'new world' of gender relations, albeit constrained by our particular social circumstances which limit both what can be attempted and what can be achieved.

Bibliography

Abbott, P. and Sapsford, R. (1987) *Women and Social Class*, London: Tavistock.

Abbott, P. and Wallace, C. (1992) *The Family and the New Right*, London: Pluto.

Abbott, P. and Wallace, C. (1996) *An Introduction to Sociology: Feminist Perspectives*, second edition, London: Routledge.

Abercrombie, N. (1996) *Television and Society*, Cambridge: Polity.

Abortion Law Reform Association (no date) *Campaign for Choice*, London: Abortion Law Reform Association.

Abraham, J. (1995) *Divide and School: Gender and Class Dynamics in Comprehensive Education*, London: Falmer Press.

Alberti, J. (1989) *Beyond Suffrage: Feminists in War and Peace 1914–1928*, London: Macmillan.

Alexander, S. (1976) 'Women's Work in Nineteenth Century London', in Oakley, A. and Mitchell, J. (eds), *The Rights and Wrongs of Women*, Harmondsworth: Penguin.

Allen, R. (1995) (ed.) *To Be Continued . . . , Soap Operas around the World*, London: Routledge.

Anthias, F. and Yuval-Davies, N. (1992) *Racialised Boundaries*, London: Routledge.

Anwar, M. (1998) *Between Two Cultures: Continuity and Change in the Lives of Young Asians*, London: Routledge.

Arber, S. and Ginn, J. (1991) *Gender and Later Life*, London: Sage.

Arber, S. and Ginn, J. (1995) 'Gender Differences in the Relationship between Paid Employment and Informal Care', *Work, Employment and Society*, 9 (3): 445–71.

Arditti, R., Klein Duelli, R. and Minden, S. (eds) (1989) *Test-tube Women*, second edition, London: Pandora Press.

Armitage, B. and Babb, P. (1996) 'Population Review: (4) Trends in Fertility', *Population Trends*, 84: 7–13.

Audit Bureau of Circulation (1997) *Circulation Review (Consumer Press)*, Serial 132, Berkhamstead: Audit Bureau of Circulation Ltd.

Babb, P. and Bethune, A. (1995) 'Trends in Births Outside Marriage', *Population Trends*, 81: 17–22.

Baker, D. and Jones, D. (1992) 'Opportunity And Performance: A Sociological Explanation for Gender Differences in Academic Mathematics', in Wrigley, J. (ed.), *Education and Gender Equality*, London: Falmer.

Banks, O. (1981) *Faces of Feminism: A Study of Feminism as a Social Movement*, Oxford: Martin Robertson.

Barker, C. (1998) ' "Cindy's a Slut": Moral Identities and Moral Responsibilities in The "Soap Talk" of British Asian Girls', *Sociology*, 32(1): 65–81.

Barrett, M. (1988) *Women's Oppression Today*, London: Verso.

Barrett, M. and McIntosh, M. (1982) *The Anti-Social Family*, London: Verso.

Barron, R. and Norris, G. (1976) 'Sexual Divisions and the Dual Labour Market', in Barker, D. and Allen, S. (eds) *Dependence and Exploitation in Work and Marriage*, London: Longman.

Basit, T. (1997) ' "I Want More Freedom, but not too Much": British Muslim Girls and the Dynamism of Family Values', *Gender And Education*, 9 (4): 425–39.

Baxter, J. and Western, M. (1998) 'Satisfaction with Housework: Examining the Paradox', *Sociology*, 32(1): 101–20.

Beck, U. (1992) *Risk Society*, London: Sage.

Beechey, V. and Perkins, T. (1987) *A Matter of Hours: Women, Part-time Work and the Labour Market*, Cambridge: Polity.

Berrington, A. (1994) 'Marriage and Family Formation among the White and Ethnic Minority Populations in Britain', *Ethnic and Racial Studies*, 17(3): 517–44.

Best, L. (1993) ' "Dragons, Dinner Ladies And Ferrets": Sex Roles In Children's Books', *Sociology Review*, 2(3): 6–8.

Bhavnani, R. (1994) *Black Women and the Labour Market: A Research Review*, Research Series, Manchester: Equal Opportunities Commission.

Bhopal, K. (1997) *Gender, 'Race' and Patriarchy*, Aldershot: Ashgate.

Bott, E. (1971) *Family and Social Network: Roles, Norms and External Relationships in Ordinary Urban Families*, second edition (original 1957), London: Tavistock.

Bottero, W. (1998) 'Clinging to the Wreckage? Gender and the Legacy of Class', *Sociology*, 32(3): 469–90.

Boulton, M. (1983) *On Being a Mother: A Study of Women with Pre-school Children*, London: Tavistock.

Bradshaw, J., Clegg, S. and Trayhum, D. (1995) 'An Investigation into Gender Bias in Educational Software Used in English Primary Schools', *Gender And Education*, 7(2): 167–74.

Brah, A. and Shaw, S. (1992) *Working Choices: South Asian Young Muslim Women and the Labour Market*, Research Paper No. 91, London: Department of Employment.

Brannen, J. and Moss, P. (1991) *Managing Mothers: Dual Earner Households after Maternity Leave*, London: Unwin Hyman.

Brannen, J., Meszavos, G., Moss, P. and Poland, G. (1994), *Employment and Family Life: A Review of Research in the UK (1980–1994)*, Research Series No. 41, Sheffield: Employment Department.

Braverman, H. (1974) *Labour and Monopoly Capital*, New York: Monthly Review Press.

Braybon, G. and Summerfield, P. (1987) *Out of the Cage: Women's Experiences in Two World Wars*, London: Pandora.

Brereton, D. (1997) 'How Different Are Rape Trials?', *British Journal of Criminology*, 37(2): 242–61.

Brown, M. (1994) *Soap Opera and Women's Talk: The Pleasure of Resistance*, London: Sage.

Brownmiller, S. (1975) *Against Our Will: Men, Women and Rape*, London: Secker and Warburg.

Bruegel, I. (1979) 'Women as a Reserve Army of Labour', *Feminist Review*, 3: 12–23.

Brunsdon, C. (1995) 'The Role of Soap Opera in the Development of Feminist Television Scholarship', in Allen, R. (ed.), *To Be Continued. . . . Soap Operas around the World*, London: Routledge.

Bryson V. (1994) *Women in British Politics*, Huddersfield Pamphlets in History and Politics, Huddersfield: Department of Humanities, University of Huddersfield.

Buckingham, L. and Finch, J. (1998) 'Breakthrough for Poorest Parents', Budget Supplement, *Guardian*, 18 March.

Burchell, B., Dale, A. and Joshi, H. (1997) 'Part-time Work among British Women', in Blossfield, H. and Hakim, C. (eds) *Between Equalisation and Marginalisation: Women Working Part-time in Europe and the United States of America*, Oxford: Oxford University Press.

Butler, J. (1990) *Gender Trouble,* London: Routledge.

Butler, J. and Scott, J. (eds) (1992) *Feminists Theorise the Political*, New York: Routledge.

Bystydzienski J. (1992) 'Influence of Women's Culture on Public Politics in Norway', in Bystydzienski, J. (ed.) *Women Transforming Politics*, Bloomington: Indiana University Press.

Cairns, J. and Inglis, B. (1989) 'A Content Analysis of Ten Popular History Textbooks for Primary Schools', *Educational Review*, 41 (3): 221–6.

Cameron, D. and Frazer, E. (1992) 'On the Question of Pornography and Sexual Violence: Moving beyond Cause and Effect', in Itzin, C. (ed.) *Pornography*, Oxford: Oxford University Press.

Carlen, P. (1995) 'Women, Crime, Feminism and Realism', in Naffine, N. (ed.), *Gender, Crime and Feminism*, Aldershot: Dartmouth.

Carlen, P. and Worrall, A. (1987) 'Introduction', in Carlen, P. and Worrall, A. (eds), *Gender, Crime and Justice*, Milton Keynes: Open University Press.

Carroll, S. (1992) 'Women State Legislators, Women's Organisations and the Representation of Women's Culture in the United States', in Bystydzienski, J. (ed.), *Women Transforming Politics*, Bloomington: Indiana University Press.

Carvel, J. (1998) 'Girls suffering "unhealthy obsession" with slimming', *Guardian*, 17 March.

Central Office of Information (1996) *Women in Britain*, Aspects of Britain series, second edition, London: HMSO.

Central Statistical Office (1995) *Social Focus on Women*, London: The Stationery Office.

Charles, N. (1993) *Gender Divisions and Social Change*, Hemel Hempstead: Harvester Wheatsheaf.

Charles, N. and Kerr, M. (1986), 'Food for Feminist Thought', *The Sociological Review*, 34: 537–72.

Chaudhary, V. (1997), 'Backlash against lads' Mags', *Guardian*, 28 August.

Chaudhary, V. (1998). 'Pre-school for All this Year', *Guardian*, 28 March.

Chazan, Y. (1995) 'IVF Age Limit Left to Centres', *Guardian*, 14 April.

Clarricoates, K. (1987a) 'Dinosaurs In The Classroom – The "Hidden" Curriculum In Primary Schools', in Arnot, M. and Weiner, G. (eds), *Gender and the Politics of Schooling*, London: Hutchinson/Open University Press.

Clarricoates, K. (1987b) 'Child Culture at School: A Clash between Gendered Worlds', in Pollard, A. (ed.), *Children and Their Primary Schools,* London: Falmer.

Cockburn, C. (1987) *Two Track Training: Sex Inequalities and the YTS*, London: Macmillan.

Connell, R. W. (1987) *Gender and Power*, Cambridge: Polity Press.

Connell, R.W. (1995) *Masculinities*, Cambridge: Polity Press.

Connolly, P. (1995) *Racisms, Gendered Identities Aand Young Children: An Ethnographic Study of a Multi-ethnic, Inner-city Primary School*, unpublished Ph.D., University of Leicester.

Connolly, P. (1998) *Racism, Gender Identities and Young Children*, London: Routledge.

Coote, A. and Campbell, B. (1987) *Sweet Freedom: The Struggle for Women's Liberation*, second edition, Oxford: Basil Blackwell.

Coppock, V., Haydon, D. and Richter, I. (1995) *The Illusions of 'Post-feminism'*, London: Taylor and Francis.

Corea, G. *et al.* (1987) *Man Made Women*, Bloomington: Indiana University Press.

Corti, L., Laurie, H. and Dex, S. (1994) *Caring and Employment*, Research Series No. 39, Sheffield: Department of Employment.

Cowan, R. Schwartz (1989) *More Work for Mother: The Ironies of Household Technology from the Open Hearth to the Microwave*, London: Free Association Books.

Coward, R. (1987) 'Sexual Violence and Sexuality', in Feminist Review (ed.), *Sexuality: A Reader*, London: Virago.

Cowgill, J. (1994) 'Beveridge, Women and the Welfare State', *Critical Social Policy*, 41: 53–78.

Craig, J. (1997) 'Population Review: (9) Summary of Issues', *Population Trends*, 88: 5–12.

Crompton, R. (1996) 'Paid Employment and the Changing Systems of Gender Relations: A Cross-national Comparison', *Sociology*, 30(3): 427–45.

Crompton, R. (1997) *Women and Work in Modern Britain*, Oxford: Oxford University Press.

Crompton, R. and Sanderson, K. (1990) *Gendered Jobs and Social Change*, London: Unwin Hyman.

Crowe, C. (1990) 'Whose Mind over Matter? Women, In Vitro Fertilisation and the Development of Scientific Knowledge', in McNeil, M., Varcoe, I. and Yearley, S. (eds), *The New Reproductive Technologies*, London: Macmillan.

Darling, J. and Glendinning, A. (1996) *Gender Matters in Schools*, London: Cassell.

David, M., Weiner, G. and Arnot, M. (1997) 'Strategic Feminist Research on Gender Equality and Schooling in Britain in the 1990s', in Marshall, C. (ed.), *Feminist Critical Policy Analysis*, London: Falmer.

Davis, K. (1995) *Reshaping the Female Body: The Dilemma of Cosmetic Surgery*, London: Routledge.

Davis, K. (1997a) 'Embody-ing Theory: Beyond Modernist and Postmodernist Readings of the Body', in Davis, K. (ed.), *Embodied Practices: Feminist Perspectives on the Body*, London: Sage.

Davis, K. (1997b) 'My Body is My Art': Cosmetic Surgery as Feminist Utopia?', in

Davis, K. (ed.), *Embodied Practices: Feminist Perspectives on the Body*, London: Sage.

Delamont, S. (1990) *Sex Roles And The School*, second edition, London: Routledge.

Delmar, R. (1986) 'What is Feminism?', in Mitchell, J. and Oakley, A. (eds), *What is Feminism?* Oxford: Basil Blackwell.

Delphy, C. (1984) *Close to Home: A Materialist Analysis of Women's Oppression*, London: Hutchinson.

Delphy, C. (1993) 'New Reproductive Technologies', in Jackson, S. (ed.), *Women's Studies: A Reader*, Hemel Hempstead: Harvester Wheatsheaf.

Delphy, C. and Leonard, D. (1992) *Familiar Exploitation*, Cambridge: Polity.

Dennis, N., Henriques, F. and Slaughter, C. (1969) *Coal is our Life: An Analysis of a Yorkshire Mining Community*, second edition, London: Tavistock (first published 1956).

Department For Education (1993) 'Women In Post-Compulsory Education', *Statistical Bulletin*, 26/93, London: Government Statistical Service.

Dobash, R. and Dobash, R. (1992) *Women, Violence and Social Change*, London: Routledge.

Dolan, B. (1994) 'Why Women? Gender Issues and Eating Disorders: Introduction', in Dolan, B. and Gitzinger, I. (eds), *Why Women? Gender Issues and Eating Disorders*, London: Athlone.

Dowds, L. and Hedderman, C. (1997) 'The Sentencing of Men and Women', in Hedderman, C. and Gelsthorpe, L. (eds), *Understanding the Sentencing of Women*, Home Office Research Study, 170, London: Home Office.

Duncombe, J. and Marsden, D. (1993) 'Love and Intimacy: The Gender Division of Emotion and "Emotion Work"', *Sociology*, 27(2): 221–41.

Dunne, G. (1997) *Lesbian Lifestyles: Women's Work and the Politics of Sexuality*, London: Macmillan.

Dworkin, A. (1981) *Pornography*, London: The Women's Press.

Dyer, C. (1997) 'Belgians Will Treat UK Widow', *Guardian*, 7 November.

Dyhouse, C. (1989) *Feminism and the Family in England 1880–1939*, Oxford: Basil Blackwell.

Eaton, M. (1986) *Justice for Women?*, Milton Keynes: Open University Press.

Edgell, S. (1980) *Middle Class Couples: A Study of Segregation, Domination and Inequality in Marriage*, London: George Allen and Unwin.

Edwards, R., Gordan, D. and Reich, M. (1975) *Labour Market Segmentation*, Lexington, Mass: Lexington Books.

Edwards, S. (1987) '"Provoking Her Own Demise": From Common Assault to Homicide', in Hanmer, J. and Maynard, M. (eds), *Women, Violence and Social Control*, London: Macmillan.

Elliot, B. J. (1991) 'Demographic Trends in Domestic Life 1945–87', in Clark, D. (ed.), *Marriage, Domestic Life and Social Change*, London: Routledge.

Elliot, F. Robertson (1996) *Gender, Family and Society*, London: Macmillan.

Elliott, L. (1997) '£739bn – The Hidden Earning Power in Your Home that Gets Swept under the Carpet', *Guardian*, 7 October.

Equal Opportunities Commission (1996a) *Educational Reforms and Gender Equality in Schools: Summary of Research Findings*, Manchester: Equal Opportunities Commission.

Equal Opportunities Commission (1996b) *Pay,* Briefings on Women and Men in Britain, Manchester: Equal Opportunities Commission.

Equal Opportunities Commission (1997a) *Education And Vocational Training in England And Wales,* Briefings on Women And Men in Britain, Manchester: Equal Opportunities Commission.

Equal Opportunities Commission (1997b) *The Labour Market,* Briefings on Women and Men in Britain, Manchester: Equal Opportunities Commission.

Equal Opportunities Commission (1997c) *Management and the Professions,* Briefings on Women and Men In Britain, Manchester: Equal Opportunities Commission.

Equal Opportunities Commission (1997d) *Work and Parenting,* Briefings on Women and Men in Britain, Manchester: Equal Opportunities Commission.

Equal Opportunities Commission (1997e) *Income and Personal Finance,* Briefings on Women and Men in Britain, Manchester: Equal Opportunities Commission.

Equal Opportunities Commission (1997f) *Facts about Women and Men in Great Britain 1997,* Manchester: Equal Opportunities Commission.

Equal Opportunities Commission And Office for Standards In Education (1996) *The Gender Divide,* London: HMSO.

European Parliament (1998) <http://www.europarl.eu.int/>.

Evans, J. (1995) *Feminist Theory Today,* London: Sage.

Fagan, C. and O'Reilly, J. (1998) 'Conceptualising Part-time Work', in O'Reilly, J. and Fagan, C. (eds), *Part-time Prospects: An International Comparison of Part-time Work in Europe, North America and the Pacific Rim,* London: Routledge.

Farrington, D. and Morris, A. (1983) 'Sex, Sentencing and Reconvictions', *British Journal of Criminology,* 23(3): 229–48.

Felstead, A. and Jewson, N. (1996) *Homeworkers in Britain,* London: HMSO.

Felstead, A., Goodwin, J. and Green, F. (1995) *Measuring up to the National Training Targets: Women's Attainment of Vocational Qualifications,* Leicester: Centre For Labour Market Studies, University of Leicester.

Ferguson, M. (1983) *Forever Feminine: Women's Magazines and the Cult of Femininity,* Aldershot: Gower.

Ferri, E. (1993) (ed.) *Life at 33: The Fifth Follow-up of the National Child Development Study,* London: National Children's Bureau.

Ferri, E. and Smith, K. (1996) *Parenting in the 1990s,* London: Family Policy Studies Centre.

Filakti, H. (1997) 'Trends in Abortion 1990–1995', *Population Trends,* 87: 11–19.

Finlayson, L., Ford, R. and Marsh, A. (1996) 'Paying More for Childcare', *Labour Market Trends,* 104(7): 295–302.

Firestone, S. (1971) *The Dialectic of Sex,* London: Jonathan Cape.

Ford, R. (1998) *Childcare in the Balance,* London: Policy Studies Institute.

Forna, A. (1992) 'Pornography and Racism: Sexualising Oppression and Inciting Hatred', in Itzin, C. (ed.), *Pornography,* Oxford: Oxford University Press.

Franklin, S., Lury, C. and Stacey, J. (1991) 'Introduction 2: Feminism, Marxism and Thatcherism', in Franklin, S., Lury, C. and Stacey, J. (eds), *Off-Centre: Feminism and Cultural Studies,* London: Harper Collins.

Fraser, N. and Nicholson, L. (1989) 'Social Criticism without Philosophy: An Encounter between Feminism and Postmodernism', in Ross, A. (ed.), *Universal Abandon: The Politics of Postmodernism,* Edinburgh: Edinburgh University Press.

Frazer, E. (1987) 'Teenage Girls Reading *Jackie*', *Media, Culture and Society,* 9(4): 407–25.

Gavron, H. (1983) *The Captive Wife: Conflicts of Housebound Mothers*, second edition (originally published 1966, Harmondsworth: Penguin), London: RKP.

Gelsthorpe, L. and Loucks, N. (1997) 'Magistrates' explanations of sentencing decisions', in Hedderman, C. and Gelsthorpe, L. (eds), *Understanding the Sentencing of Women*, Home Office Research Study 170, London: Home Office.

Geraghty, C. (1991) *Women and Soap Opera*, Cambridge: Polity Press.

Germov, J. and Williams, L. (1996) 'The Sexual Division of Dieting: Women's Voices', *Sociological Review*, 44(4): 630–47.

Gershuny, J. (1997a) *The Changing Nature of Work*. Paper presented at The British Association Conference, Leeds, 8 September.

Gershuny, J. (1997b) *The Changing Nature of Work*, Press Release, ESRC Research Centre on Micro-social Change, University of Essex.

Gershuny, J., Godwin, M. and Jones, S. (1994) 'The Domestic Labour Revolution: A Process of Lagged Adaptation', in Anderson, M., Bechhofer, F. and Gershuny, J. (eds), *The Social and Political Economy of the Household*, Oxford: Oxford University Press.

Gibson, P. Church and Gibson, R. (eds) (1993) *Dirty Looks: Women, Pornography and Power*, London: British Film Institute.

Giddens, A. (1991) *Modernity and Self-identity*, Cambridge: Polity Press.

Gilchrist, E., Bannister, J., Ditton, J. and Farrall, S. (1998) 'Women and the "fear of crime": Challenging the Accepted Stereotype', *British Journal of Criminology*, 38(2): 283–98.

Gillborn, D. and Gipps, C. (1996) *Recent Research on the Achievements of Ethnic Minority Pupils*, OFSTED Reviews of Research, London: HMSO.

Gittins, D. (1993) *The Family in Question*, second edition, London: Macmillan.

Goldberg, S. (1979) *Male Dominance: The Inevitability of Patriarchy*, London: Abacus Sphere.

Goodey, J. (1995) 'Fear of Crime: Children and Gendered socialisation', in Dobash, R. Emerson, Dobash, R. and Noaks, L. (eds), *Gender and Crime*, Cardiff: University of Wales Press.

Gorman, T. and Whitehead, M. (1989) *The Amarant Book of Hormone Replacement Therapy*, London: Pan.

Gottfried, H. (1998) 'Beyond Patriarchy? Theorising Gender and Class', *Sociology*, 32(3): 451–68.

Government Statistical Service (1998) *Civil Service Statistics 1997*, London: HMSO.

Grace, S. (1995) *Policing Domestic Violence in the 1990s*, Home Office Research Study 139, London: HMSO.

Graham, H. (1993) *Hardship and Health in Women's Lives*, Hemel Hempstead: Harvester Wheatsheaf.

Gray, A. (1992) *Video Playtime: The Gendering of a Leisure Technology*, London: Routledge.

Gray, J. (1992) *Men Are from Mars, Women Are from Venus: A Practical Guide for Improving Communications and Getting What You Want in Your Relationship*, New York: Harper Collins.

Green, F. (1993) 'The Determinants of Training of Male and Female Employees in Britain', *Oxford Bulletin of Economics and Statistics*, 55(1): 103–22.

Greer, G. (1991) *The Change: Women, Ageing and the Menopause*, London: Hamish Hamilton.

Gregson, N. and Lowe, M. (1994a) *Servicing the Middle Classes: Waged Domestic Labour in Britain in the 1980s and 1990s*, London: Routledge.

Gregson, N. and Lowe, M. (1994b) 'Waged Domestic Labour and the Renegotiation of the Domestic Division of Labour Within Dual Career Households', *Sociology*, 28(1): 55–78.

Griffin, C. (1989) ' "I'm not a Feminist but . . .": Feminism, Consciousness and Identity', in Skevington, S. and Baker, D. (eds), *The Social Identity of Women*, London: Sage.

Grogan, S. (1998) *Men, Women and Body Image*, London: Routledge.

Grogan, S, and Wainwright, N. (1996) 'Growing Up in the Culture of Slenderness', *Women's Studies International Forum*, 19(6): 665–73.

Hakim, C. (1979) *Occupational Segregation*, Department of Employment, Research Paper No 9. London: Department of Employment.

Hakim, C. (1991) 'Grateful Slaves and Self-made Women: Fact and Fantasy in Women's Work Orientations', *European Sociological Review*, 7: 101–21.

Hakim, C. (1995) 'Five Feminist Myths about Women's Employment', *British Journal of Sociology*, 46: 429–55.

Hakim, C. (1996) *Key Issues in Women's Work*, London: Athlone Press.

Hanmer, J. (1987) 'Transforming Consciousness: Women and the New Reproductive Technologies', in Corea, G. *et al.*, *Man-made Women*, Bloomington: Indiana University Press.

Hanmer, J. (1993) 'Women and Reproduction', in Richardson, D. and Robinson, V. (eds), *Introducing Women's Studies*, London: Macmillan.

Haraway, D. (1991) *Simians, Cyborgs and Women: The Reinvention of Nature*, London: Free Association.

Harding, S. (1986) *The Science Question in Feminism*, Milton Keynes: Open University Press.

Hartmann, H. (1979) 'Capitalism, Patriarchy and Job Segregation by Sex', in Eisenstein, Z. (ed.), *Capitalist Patriarchy and the Case for Socialist Feminism*, London: Monthly Press.

Haskey, J. (1995) 'Trends in Marriage and Cohabitation', *Population Trends*, 80: 5–15.

Haskey, J. (1996) 'Population Review: (6) Families and Households in Great Britain', *Population Trends*, 85: 7–24.

Haskey, J. (1998) 'One Parent Families and Their Dependent Children', *Population Trends*, 91: 5–14.

Hattenstone, S. (1995) 'Sex and the Single Man's Mag', *Guardian*, 10 April.

Hawkes, G. (1996) *A Sociology of Sex and Sexuality*, Buckingham: Open University Press.

Hedderman, C. and Dowds, L. (1997) *The Sentencing of Women*, Research Findings No. 58, Home Office Research and Statistical Directorate, London: Home Office.

Hedderman, C. and Hough, M. (1994) *Does the Criminal Justice System Treat Men and Women Differently?*, Research Findings No. 10, Home Office Research and Statistics Department, London: Home Office.

Heidensohn, F. (1996) *Women and Crime*, second edition, London: Macmillan.

Hepworth, M. (1987) 'The Mid-life Phase', in Cohen, G. (ed.), *Social Change and the Life Course*, London: Tavistock.

Hermes, J. (1995) *Reading Women's Magazines*, Cambridge: Polity Press.

Hey, V. (1997) *The Company She Keeps: An Ethnography of Girls' Friendships*, Buckingham: Open University Press.

Hill, A., Oliver, S. and Rogers, P. (1992) 'Eating in the Adult World: The Rise of Dieting in Childhood and Adolescence', *British Journal of Clinical Psychology*, 31: 95–105.

Hill, D., Cole, M. and Williams, C. (1997) 'Equality and Primary Teacher Education', in Cole, M., Hill, D. and Shan, S. (eds), *Promoting Equality In Primary Schools*, London: Cassell.

Holdsworth, A. (1988) *Out of the Dolls House: The Story of Women in the Twentieth Century*, London: BBC Books.

Holland, J., Ramazanoglu, C., Sharpe, S. and Thomson, R. (1996) 'Reputations: Journeying into Gendered Power Relations', in Weeks, J. and Holland, J. (eds), *Sexual Cultures*, London: Macmillan.

Home Office (1992) *Gender and the Criminal Justice System*, London: Home Office.

Home Office (1995) *Information on the Criminal Justice System in England and Wales, Research and Statistics Department*, Croydon: Home Office.

Home Office (1997a) *Criminal Statistics, England and Wales 1996*, London: Governmental Statistical Service.

Home Office (1997b) *Prison Statistics, England and Wales 1996*, London: Government Statistical Service.

Home Office (1997c) *Aspects of Crime: Gender*, Crime and Criminal Justice Unit, Research and Statistical Directorate, London: Home Office.

hooks, b. (1984) *Feminist Theory: From Margin to Center*, Boston, Mass.: Southend Press.

Houghton-James, H. (1995) *Sexual Harassment*, Cavendish: London.

Howitt, D. and Cumberbatch, G. (1990) *Pornography: Impacts and Influences*, London: Home Office Research and Planning Unit.

Human Fertilisation and Embryology Authority (1996) *Fifth Annual Report*, London: HFEA.

Hunt, A. (1988) 'Women and Paid Work: Issues of Equality. An Overview', in Hunt, A. (ed.), *Women and Paid Work*, London: Macmillan.

Hunter, M. and O'Dea, I. (1997) 'Menopause: Bodily Changes and Multiple Meanings', in Ussher, J. (ed.), *Body Talk*, London: Routledge.

Itzin, C. (1992a) (ed.) *Pornography*, Oxford: Oxford University Press.

Itzin, C. (1992b) 'Introduction: Fact, Fiction and Faction', in Itzin, C. (ed.), *Pornography*, Oxford: Oxford University Press.

Itzin, C. (1992c), 'Pornography and the Social Construction of Sexual Inequality', in Itzin, C. (ed.), *Pornography*, Oxford: Oxford University Press.

Itzin, C. (1992d) 'Legislating against Pornography without Censorship', in Itzin, C. (ed.), *Pornography*, Oxford: Oxford University Press.

Jackson, E. (1995) 'The Problem with Pornography: A Critical Survey of the Current Debate', *Feminist Legal Studies*, 3(1): 49–70.

Jackson, S. (1993) 'Even Sociologists Fall in Love: An Exploration in the Sociology of Emotions', *Sociology*, 27(2): 201–20.

Jackson, S. (1997) 'Women, Marriage and Family Relationships', in Robinson, V. and Richardson, D. (eds), *Introducing Women's Studies*, second edition, London: Macmillan.

Jackson, S. and Scott, S. (1996) 'Sexual Skirmishes and Feminist Factions', in Jackson, S. and Scott, S. (eds), *Feminism and Sexuality: A Reader*, Edinburgh: Edinburgh University Press.

Jaggar A. M. (1983) *Feminist Politics and Human Nature*, Brighton: Harvester Press.

James, A. and Prout, A. (1997) *Constructing and Reconstructing Childhood*, second edition, London: Falmer.

Kappeler, S. (1986) *The Pornography of Representation*, Cambridge: Polity Press.

Kelly, L. and Radford, J. (1996) '"Nothing Really Happened": The Invalidation of Women's Experiences of Sexual Violence', in Hester, M., Kelly, L. and Radford, J. (eds), *Women, Violence and Male Power*, Buckingham: Open University Press.

Kenton, L. (1995) 'Pause for Thought', *Guardian*, 7 September.

Kiernan, K. (1992) 'Men and Women at Work and at Home', in Jowell, R., Brook, L., Prior, G. and Taylor, B. (eds), *British Social Attitudes. The 9th Report*, Aldershot: Dartmouth.

Kilborn, R. (1992) *Television Soaps*, London: Batsford.

King, A. (1993) 'Mystery and Imagination: The Case of Pornography Effects Studies', in Assiter, A. and Carol, A. (eds), *Bad Girls and Dirty Pictures*, London: Pluto.

Klein Duelli, R. (1987) 'What's "New" about the "New" Reproductive Technologies?', in Corea, G. *et al.*, *Man-Made Women*, Bloomington: Indiana University Press.

Klein, R. and Dumble, L. (1994) 'Disempowering Mid-life Women: The Science and Politics of Hormone Replacement Therapy', *Women's Studies International Forum*, 17(4): 327–43.

Komesaroff, P., Rothfield, P. and Daly, J. (1997) 'Mapping Menopause', in Komesaroff, P., Rothfield, P. and Daly, J. (eds), *Reinterpreting Menopause*, New York: Routledge.

Landesman, C. (1997) 'Boyzone', *Guardian*, 1 December.

Lees, S. (1986) *Losing Out: Sexuality and Adolescent Girls*, London: Hutchinson.

Lees, S. (1989) 'Learning to Love: Sexual Reputation, Morality and the Social Control of Girls', in Cain, M. (ed.), *Growing Up Good*, London: Sage.

Lees, S. (1996) 'Unreasonable Doubt: The Outcomes of Rape Trials', in Hester, M., Kelly, L., and Radford, J. (eds), *Women, Violence and Male Power*, Buckingham: Open University Press.

Lees, S. (1997) *Ruling Passions: Sexual Violence, Reputation and the Law*, Buckingham: OUP.

Lloyd, B. and Duveen, G. (1992) *Gender Identities and Education*, Hemel Hempstead: Harvester Wheatsheaf.

Lobban, G. (1974) 'Presentation of Sex Roles in British Reading Schemes', *Forum*, 16(2): 57–60.

Longrigg C. (1997) 'Winning Women Overturn Male Culture of Commons', *Guardian*, 3 May.

Lovenduski, J. (1996) 'Sex, Gender and British Politics', *Parliamentary Affairs*, 49(1): 1–16.

Lovenduski, J. (1997) 'Gender Politics: A Breakthrough for Women?', in Norris, P. and Gavin, N. (eds), *Britain Votes 1997*, Oxford: Oxford University Press.

Lovenduski, J. and Randall, V. (1993) *Contemporary Feminist Politics*, Oxford: Oxford University Press.

Lummis, T. (1982) 'The Historical Dimension of Fatherhood: A Case Study 1890–1914', in McKee, L. and O'Brien, M. (eds), *The Father Figure*, London: Tavistock.

Lupton, D. (1996a) 'Constructing the Menopausal Body: The Discourses on Hormone Replacement Therapy', *Body and Society*, 2(1): 91–7.

Lupton, D. (1996b) *Food, the Body and the Self*, London: Sage.

Mac An Ghaill, M. (1994) *The Making of Men*, Buckingham: Open University Press.

Mackinnon, C. (1992) 'Pornography, Civil Rights and Speech', in Itzin, C. (ed.), *Pornography*, Oxford: Oxford University Press.

McRae, S. (1991) 'Occupational Change over Childbirth: Evidence from a National Survey', *Sociology*, 25(4): 589–605.

McRae, S. (1993) *Cohabiting Mothers: Changing Marriage and Motherhood*, London: Policy Studies Institute.

McRobbie, A. (1996) '*More!* New Sexualities in Girls' and Women's Magazines', in Curran, J., Morley, D. and Walkerdine, V. (eds), *Cultural Studies and Communications*, London: Arnold.

McRobbie, A. (1997) 'The Es and the Anti-Es: New Questions for Feminism and Cultural Studies', in Ferguson, M. and Golding, P. (eds), *Cultural Studies in Question*, London: Sage.

MacSween, M. (1993) *Anorexic Bodies*, London: Routledge.

Main, B. (1988) 'The Lifetime Attachment of Women to the Labour Market', in Hunt, A. (ed.), *Women and Paid Work*, London: Macmillan.

Mansfield, P. and Collard, J. (1988) *The Beginning of the Rest of Your Life? A Portrait of Newly-Wed Marriage*, London: Macmillan.

Marsh, A. and McKay, S. (1993) 'Families, Work and the Use of Childcare', *Employment Gazette*, 101(8): 361–70.

Marshall, B. (1994) *Engendering Modernity*, Cambridge: Polity Press.

Marshment, M. (1997) 'The Picture is Political: Representation of Women in Contemporary Popular Culture', in Robinson, V. and Richardson, D. (eds), *Introducing Women's Studies*, second edition, London: Macmillan.

Martin, J. and Roberts, C. (1984) *Women and Employment: A Lifetime Perspective*, London: HMSO.

Mason, J. (1987) 'A Bed of Roses? Women, Marriage and Inequality in Later Life', in Allatt, P. , Keil, T., Bryman, A. and Bytheway, B. (eds), *Women and the Life Cycle*, London: Macmillan.

Matthews, J. (1984) *Good and Mad Women: The Historical Construction of Femininity in Twentieth Century Australia*, Sydney: George Allen and Unwin.

Maynard, M. (1990) 'The Reshaping of Sociology? Trends in the Study of Gender', *Sociology*, 24(2): 269–90.

Maynard, M. (1995) 'Beyond the "Big three": The Development of Feminist Theory into the 1990s', *Women's History Review*, 4(3): 259–81.

Maynard, M. and Winn, J. (1997) 'Women, Violence and Male Power', in Robinson, V. and Richardson, D. (eds), *Introducing Women's Studies*, second edition, London: Macmillan.

Measor, L. and Sikes, P. (1992) *Gender and Schools*, London: Cassell.

Mihill, C. (1995) 'Backing for Fertility Treatment for Women past Menopause', *Guardian*, 2 June.

Mihill, C. (1997) 'New Man Still Shunning Equal Share of Chores', *Guardian*, 8 September.

Mirrlees-Black, C. (1994) 'Estimating the Extent of Domestic Violence: Findings from the 1992 British Crime Survey', *Home Office Research Bulletin*, No. 37, London: Home Office Research and Statistics Directorate.

Mirrlees-Black, C. and Allen, J. (1998) *Concern about Crime: Findings from the 1998 British Crime Survey*, Research, Development and Statistics Research Findings No. 83, London: Home Office.

Mirrlees-Black, C., Budd, T., Partridge, S. and Mayhew, P. (1998) *The 1998 British Crime Survey, England and Wales*, Home Office Statistical Bulletin 21/98, Research, Development and Statistics Directorate, London: Government Statistical Service.

Mirrlees-Black, C., Mayhew, P. and Percy, A., (1996) *The 1996 British Crime Survey, England and Wales*, Home Office Statistical Bulletin 19/96, London: Government Statistical Service.

Mirza, H. (1992) *Young, Female and Black*, London: Routledge.

Mirza, H. (ed.) (1997) *Black British Feminism: A Reader*, London: Routledge.

Modood, T., Berthoud, R., Lakey, J., Nazroo, J., Smith, P. , Virdee, S. and Beishon, S. (1997) *Ethnic Minorities in Britain*, London: Policy Studies Institute.

Mogey, J. M. (1956) *Family and Neighbourhood: Two Studies in Oxford*, Oxford: Oxford University Press.

Moores, S. (1993) *Interpreting Audiences: The Ethnography of Media Consumption*, London: Sage.

Morgan, D. (1992) *Discovering Men*, London: Routledge.

Morley, D. (1986) *Family Television*, London: Comedia.

Morley, D. (1996) 'Populism, Revisionism and the "New" Audience Research', in Curran, J., Morley, D. and Walkerdine, V. (eds), *Cultural Studies and Communications*, London: Arnold.

Morris, A. (1987) *Women, Crime and Criminal Justice*, Oxford: Basil Blackwell.

Morris, L. (1985a) 'Renegotiation of the Domestic Division of Labour in the Context of Male Redundancy', in Newby, H., Bujra, J., Littlewood, P. , Rees, G. and Rees, T. L. (eds), *Restructuring Capital: Recession and Reorganisation in Industrial Society*, London: Macmillan, 221–43.

Morris, L. (1985b) 'Local Social Networks and Domestic Organisation: A Study of Redundant Steel Workers and Their Wives', *Sociological Review*, 33(2): 327–42.

Morris, L. (1990) *The Workings of the Household*, Cambridge: Polity Press.

Murgatroyd, L. and Neuburger, H. (1997) 'A Household Satellite Account for the UK', *Economic Trends*, No. 527, October, 63–71.

Neustatter, A. (1990) *Hyenas In Petticoats: A Look at Twenty Years of Feminism*, Harmondsworth: Penguin.

Nicholson, L. (ed.) (1990) *Feminism/Postmodernism*, London: Routledge.

Nixon, S. (1996) *Hard Looks: Masculinities, Spectatorship and Contemporary Consumption*, London: UCL Press.

Norris, P. (1995) (ed.) *Women, the Media and Politics*, Oxford: Oxford University Press.

Norris, P. (1996) 'Women Politicians: Transforming Westminster?', *Parliamentary Affairs*, 49(1): 89–102.

Oakley, A. (1974) *The Sociology of Housework*, London: Martin Robertson.

Oakley, A. (1998) 'Science, Gender and Women's Liberation: An Argument Against Postmodernism', *Women's Studies International Forum*, 21(2): 133–46.

Office For National Statistics (1997a) *Living in Britain: Results from the 1995 General Household Survey*, London: The Stationery Office.

Office For National Statistics (1997b) *Abortion Statistics 1995*, London: The Stationery Office.

Office For National Statistics (1998a) *Social Trends 28*, London: Government Statistical Service.

Office For National Statistics (1998b) *Living in Britain: Results from the 1996 General Household Survey*, London: The Stationery Office.

Office Of Population Census and Surveys (1991) *Standard Occupational Classification*, Vol. 3, London: HMSO.

Owen, D. (1994) *Ethnic Minority Women and the Labour Market: Analysis of the 1991 Census*, Research Series, Manchester: Equal Opportunities Commission.

Paechter, C. (1998) *Educating the Other: Gender, Power and Schooling*, London: Falmer.

Pahl, R. (1984) *Divisions of Labour*, Oxford: Basil Blackwell.

Parker, G. and Lawton, D. (1994) *Different Types of Care, Different Types of Carer: Evidence from the General Household Survey*, London: HMSO.

Parry, O. (1990) ' "We Don't Contravene the Sex Discrimination Act" – Female Students at Journalism School', *Gender and Education*, 2(1): 3–16.

Peace, H. (1993) *The Pretended Family: A Study of the Division of Domestic Labour in Lesbian Families*, Discussion Papers in Sociology No. S93/3, Leicester: University of Leicester, Department of Sociology.

Percy, A. and Mayhew, P. (1997) 'Estimating Sexual Victimisation in a National Crime survey: A New Approach', *Studies on Crime and Crime Prevention*, 6(2): 125–50.

Philips, D. and Haywood, I. (1998) *Brave New Causes: Women in British Postwar Fictions*, London: Leicester University Press.

Phillips, A. (1991) *Engendering Democracy*, Cambridge: Polity Press.

Phillips, A. (1998) 'Been There, Done That', *Guardian*, 20 January.

Phizacklea, A. (1990) *Unpacking the Fashion Industry*, London: Routledge.

Phoenix, A., Woollet, A. and Lloyd, E. (1991) *Motherhood: Meanings, Practices and Ideologies*, London: Sage.

Piachaud, D. (1984) *Round About Fifty Hours a Week*, London: Child Poverty Action Group.

Pilcher, J. (1993) ' "I'm not a feminist, but . . .": Understanding Feminism', *Sociology Review*, 3(2): 2–6.

Pilcher, J. (1994) 'Who Should Do the Dishes? Three Generations of Welsh Women Talking about Men and Housework', in Aaron, J., Rees, T., Betts, S. and Vincentelli, M. (eds), *Our Sisters' Land: The Changing Identities of Women in Wales*, Cardiff: University of Wales Press.

Pilcher, J. (1995) 'The Gender Significance of Women in Power: British Women talking about Margaret Thatcher', *European Journal of Women's Studies*, 2(4): 493–508.

Pilcher, J. (1998a) 'Gender Matters? Three Cohorts of Women Talking About Role Reversal', *Sociological Research On-line*, 3 (1): <http: //www.socresonline.org.uk/socresonline/3/1/10.html>.

Pilcher, J. (1998b) *Women of Their Time: Generation, Gender Issues and Feminism*, Aldershot: Ashgate.

Pollak, O. (1961) *The Criminality of Women*, New York: A.S. Barnes.

Pollert, A. (1996) 'Gender and Class Revisited; or, The Poverty of Patriarchy', *Sociology*, 30(4): 639–59.

Population Trends (1996) 'In Brief – Childlessness', 85: 1–2.

Povey, D., Prime, J. and Taylor, P. (1998) *Notifiable Offences, England and Wales 1997*, Home Office Statistical Bulletin 7/98, Research, Development and Statistics Directorate, London: Government Statistical Service.

Prout, A. and James, A. (1990) 'A New Paradigm For The Sociology Of Childhood?', in James, A. and Prout, A. (eds), *Constructing and Reconstructing Childhood*, London: Falmer Press.

Purdy, L. (1996) 'What Can Progress in Reproduction Mean for Women?', *The Journal of Medicine and Philosophy*, 21: 499–514.

Puwar, N. (1997) 'Gender and Political Elites: Women in the House of Commons', *Sociology Review*, 7(2): 2–6.

Radford, J., Kelly, L. and Hester, M. (1996) 'Introduction', in Hester, M., Kelly, L. and Radford, J. (eds), *Women, Violence and Male Power*, Buckingham: Open University Press.

Radford, L. (1987) 'Legalising Woman Abuse', in Hanmer, J. and Maynard, M. (eds), *Women, Violence and Social Control*, London: Macmillan.

Randall, V. (1982) *Women and Politics*, London: Macmillan.

Raven, C. (1994) 'Away the Lads (Again)', *Guardian*, 10 October.

Raven, C. (1997) 'Skirting the Issues', *Guardian*, 1 July.

Rees, T. (1992) *Women And The Labour Market*, London: Routledge.

Rees, T. (1994) 'Women and Paid Work In Wales', in Aaron, J., Rees, T., Betts, S. and Vincentelli, M. (eds), *Our Sisters' Land*, Cardiff: University of Wales Press.

Reiner, R. (1996) 'The Case of the Missing Crimes', in Levitas, R. and Guy, W. (eds), *Interpreting Official Statistics*, London: Routledge.

Ribbens, J. (1994) *Mothers and their Children*, London: Sage.

Rich, A. (1980) 'Compulsory Heterosexuality and Lesbian Existence', *Signs*, 5 (4): 631–60.

Richardson, D. (1993) 'Sexuality and Male Dominance', in Richardson, D. and Robinson, V. (eds), *Introducing Women's Studies*, London: Macmillan.

Richardson, D. (1993) *Women, Motherhood and Childrearing*, London: Macmillan.

Richardson, R. (1986) 'The Hidden Messages of Schoolbooks', *Journal of Moral Education*, 15(1): 26–42.

Riddell, S. (1989) 'Pupils, Resistance and Gender Codes: A Study of Classroom Encounters', *Gender And Education*, 1(2): 183–97.

Riddell, S. (1992) *Gender and the Politics of the Curriculum*, London: Routledge.

Roberts, E. A. (1984) *A Woman's Place: An Oral History of Working Class Women 1890–1940*, Oxford: Blackwell.

Roberts, H. (1981) 'Male Hegemony in Family Planning', in Roberts, H. (ed.), *Women, Health and Reproduction*, London: Routledge.

Rodgerson, G. and Wilson, E. (eds), (1991) *Pornography and Feminism*, London: Lawrence and Wishart.

Ross, K. and Sreberny-Mohammadi, A. (1997) 'Playing House – Gender, Politics and the News Media in Britain', *Media, Culture and Society*, 19(1): 101–09.

Rosser, C. and Harris, C. (1965) *The Family and Social Change: A Study of Family and Kinship in a South Wales Town*, London: Routledge and Kegan Paul.

Rowland R. (ed.) (1984) *Women Who Do and Women Who Don't Join the Women's Movement*, London: RKP.

Rubery, J., Horrell, S., and Burchell, B. (1994) 'Part-time Work and Gender Inequality in the Labour Market', in MacEwen Scott, A. (ed.), *Gender Segregation and Social Change*, Oxford: Oxford University Press.

Rubin, G. (1993) 'Misguided, Dangerous and Wrong: An Analysis of Anti-Pornography Politics', in Assiter, A. and Carol, A. (eds), *Bad Girls and Dirty Pictures*, London: Pluto.

Russell, D. (ed.) (1993) *Making Violence Sexy: Feminist Views on Pornography*, Buckingham: Open University Press.

Salisbury, J. (1996) *Educational Reforms and Gender Equality in Welsh Schools*, (bilingual), Cardiff: Equal Opportunities Commission.

Sawicki, J. (1993) 'Disciplining Mothers: Feminism and the New Reproductive Technologies', in Jackson, S. (ed.), *Women's Studies: A Reader*, Hemel Hempstead: Harvester Wheatsheaf.

Scott, J., Alwin, D. and Brown, M. (1996) 'Generational Changes in Gender Role Attitudes', *Sociology*, 30(3): 471–92.

Segal, L. (1987) *Is the Future Female? Troubled Thoughts on Contemporary Feminism*, London: Virago.

Segal, L. (1993) 'Does Pornography Cause Violence?', in Gibson, P. , Church, P. and Gibson, R. (eds), *Dirty Looks: Women, Pornography and Power*, London: British Film Institute.

Sharpe, S. (1994), *Just Like a Girl?*, second edition, Harmondsworth: Penguin.

Shilling, C. (1993) *The Body and Social Theory*, London: Sage.

Siltanen, J. (1994a) 'Domestic Responsibilities and the Structuring of Employment', in Crompton, R. and Mann, M. (eds), *Gender and Stratification*, Cambridge: Polity Press.

Siltanen, J. (1994b) *Locating Gender: Occupational Segregation, Wages and Domestic Responsibilities*, London: UCL Press.

Skeggs, B. (1994), 'Review of McCracken, E., *Decoding Women's Magazines*', *Journal of Gender Studies*, 3(2): 225–6.

Sly, F. (1996) 'Women in the Labour Market: Results from the Spring 1995 Labour Force Survey', *Labour Market Trends*, 103(3): 91–113.

Sly, F., Thair, T. and Risdon, A. (1998), 'Women in the Labour Market: Results from the Spring 1997 Labour Force Survey', *Labour Market Trends*, 106(3): 97–119.

Smart, C. (1989) *Feminism and the Power of the Law*, London: Routledge.

Smart, C. (1995) *Law, Crime and Sexuality*, London: Sage.

Smith, A. (1992) 'Resisting the Erasure of Lesbian Sexuality', in Plummer, K. (ed.), *Modern Homosexualities*, London: Routledge.

Smith, M., Fagan, C. and Rubery, J. (1998) 'Where and Why is Part-time Work Growing in Europe?', in O'Reilly, J. and Fagan, C. (eds), *Part-time Prospects*, London: Routledge.

Snell, A. (1986) 'Equal Pay and Sex Discrimination', in *Feminist Review* (eds), *Waged Work: A Reader*, London: Virago.

Sontag, S. (1979) 'The Double Standard of Ageing', in Carver, V. and Liddiard, P. (eds), *An Ageing Population*, New York: Holmes and Meier.

Spender, D. (1982) *There Has Always Been a Women's Movement this Century*, London: Pandora.

Sreberny-Mohammadi, A. and Ross, K. (1996) 'Women MPs and the Media: Representing the Body Politic', *Parliamentary Affairs*, 49(1): 101–15.

Stacey, J. (1997) 'Feminist Theory: Capital F, Capital T', in Robinson, V. and Richardson, D. (eds), *Introducing Women's Studies*, second edition, London: Macmillan.

Stanko, E. (1987) 'Typical Violence, Normal Precaution: Men: Women and Interpersonal Violence in England, Wales and the USA', in Hanmer, J. and Maynard, M. (eds), *Women, Violence and Social Control*, London: Macmillan.

Stanworth, M. (1983) *Gender And Schooling*, London: Hutchinson.

Stanworth, M. (1987) 'Reproductive Technologies and the Deconstruction of Motherhood', in Stanworth, M. (ed.), *Reproductive Technologies,* Cambridge: Polity Press.

Stationery Office Agencies (1998) *Labour Market Trends*, 106(1).

Strinati, D. (1995) *An Introduction to Theories of Popular Culture*, London: Routledge.

Tannen, D. (1991) *You Just Don't Understand: Women and Men in Conversation*, London: Virago.

Temkin, J. (1997) 'Plus ça change: Reporting Rape in the 1990s', *British Journal of Criminology*, 37 (4): 507–528.

Temkin, J. (1998) 'Rape in Court', *Guardian*, 27 October.

Thomas, R. (1997) 'Wife and Mother Beyond Price', *Guardian*, 19 May.

Thompson, P. (1975) *The Edwardians: The Remaking of British Society*, London: Weidenfeld and Nicholson.

Thomson, K. (1995) 'Working Mothers: Choice or Circumstances?', in Jowell, R., Curtice, J., Park, A. and Brook, L. (eds), *British Social Attitudes: The 12th Report*, Aldershot: Dartmouth.

Trade Union Congress (1998) <http: //www.tuc.org.uk/>.

Travis, A. (1998) 'Alarm over "Date Rapes"', *Guardian*, 16 June.

Turner, E., Riddell, S. and Brown, S. (1995*) Gender Equality In Scottish Schools: The Impact of Recent Educational Reforms*, Glasgow: Equal Opportunities Commission.

Tuttle, L. (1986) *Encyclopaedia of Feminism*, Harlow, Essex: Longman.

Wagg, S. (1998) 'Punching Your Weight: Conversations with Jo Brand', in Wagg, S. (ed.), *Because I Tell a Joke or Two: Comedy, Politics and Social Difference*, London: Routledge.

Wajcman, J. (1991) *Feminism Confronts Technology*, Cambridge: Polity Press.

Walby, S. (1990) *Theorising Patriarchy*, Oxford: Blackwell.

Walby, S. (1994) 'Post-postmodernism? Theorising Gender', in *The Polity Reader in Social Theory*, Cambridge: Polity Press.

Walby, S. (1997) *Gender Transformations*, London: Routledge.

Walker, G. and Shaw, J. (1994) 'The Media Influence on Eating Disorders', in Dolan, B. and Gitzinger, I. (eds), *Why Women? Gender Issues and Eating Disorders,* London: Athlone.

Walkerdine, V. (1990) *Schoolgirl Fictions*, London: Verso.

Walkerdine, V. (1998) *Counting Girls Out: Girls and Mathematics*, second edition, London: Falmer.

Walklate, S. (1995) *Gender and Crime*, London: Prentice Hall/Harvester Wheatsheaf.

Walter, N. (1998) *The New Feminism*, London: Little Brown.

Walter, N. and Cottam, H. (1998) 'Is Maggie Thatcher a Heroine of the New Feminism?', *Guardian*, 17 January.

Wandor, M. (1972) *The Body Politic: Women's Liberation in Britain*, London: Stage 1.

Ward, L. (1998a) 'Meet the New Girl', *Guardian*, 1 June.

Ward, L. (1998b) 'Sisters In High Places', *Guardian*, 22 September.

Warde, A. and Hetherington, K. (1993) 'A Changing Domestic Division of Labour? Issues of Measurement and Interpretation', *Work, Employment and Society*, 7(1): 23–45.

Wardle, J., Bindra, R., Fairclough, B. and Westcome, A. (1993) 'Culture and Body Image: Body Perception and Weight Concern in Young Asian and Caucasian British Women', *Journal of Community and Applied Social Psychology*, 3: 173–81.

Weeks, J. (1986) *Sexuality*, London: Tavistock.

Weiner, G., Arnot, M. and David, M. (1997) 'Is the Future Female? Female Success, Male Disadvantage and Changing Gender Patterns in Education', in Halsey, A., Lauder, H., Brown, P. and Wells, A. (eds), *Education, Culture, Economy and Society*, Oxford: Oxford University Press.

Wellings, K., Field, J., Johnson, A. and Wadsworth, J. (1994) *Sexual Behaviour in Britain*, London: Penguin.

Werner, B. (1987) 'Fertility Statistics from Birth Registrations in England and Wales 1837–1987', *Population Trends*, 48: 4–10.

West, C. (1989) 'Review of *Gender and Power* by R.W. Connell', *American Journal of Sociology*, 94: 1487–9.

Wheelock, J. (1990) *Husbands at Home*, London: Routledge.

Whelehan, I. (1995) *Modern Feminist Thought*, Edinburgh: Edinburgh University Press.

Wier, A. and Wilson, E. (1984) 'The British Women's Movement', *New Left Review*, 148: pp 74–103.

Wilczynski, A. (1997) 'Mad or Bad? Child-killers, Gender and the Courts', *British Journal of Criminology*, 37(3): 419–36.

Wilson, E. (1977) *Women and the Welfare State*, London: Tavistock.

Wilson, E. (1983) 'Feminism and Social Policy', in Loney, M., Boswell, D., and Clarke, J. (eds), *Social Policy and Social Welfare*, Milton Keynes: Open University Press.

Winckler, V. (1987) 'Women and Work in Contemporary Wales', *Contemporary Wales*, 1: 53–71.

Winship, J. (1992) 'The Impossibility of *Best*: Enterprise meets Domesticity in the Practical Women's Magazines of the 1980s', in Strinati, D. and Wagg, S. (eds), *Come on Down? Popular Media Culture in the Post-War Decades*, London: Routledge.

Witherspoon, S. (1985) 'Sex Roles and Gender Issues', in Jowell, R. and Witherspoon, S. (eds), *British Social Attitudes*, Aldershot: Gower.

Witherspoon, S. and Prior, G. (1991) 'Working Mothers: Free to Choose?', in Jowell, R., Brook, L. and Taylor, B. (eds), *British Social Attitudes: The 8th Report*, Aldershot: Dartmouth.

Worrall, A. (1990) *Offending Women: Female Lawbreakers and the Criminal Justice System*, London: Routledge.

Wright, S. (1995) 'The Role of the Police in Combating Domestic Violence', in Dobash, R. Emerson, Dobash, R. and Noaks, L. (eds), *Gender and Crime*, Cardiff University of Wales Press.

Young, M. and Willmott, P. (1975) *The Symmetrical Family*, Harmondsworth: Penguin (first published 1973).

Zweig, F. (1952) *Women's Life and Labour*, London: Victor Gollancz.

Index